Crosscultural Transgressions

Research Models in Translation Studies II
Historical and Ideological Issues

Edited by

Theo Hermans

St. Jerome Publishing
Manchester, UK & Northampton MA

Published by

St. Jerome Publishing
2 Maple Road West, Brooklands
Manchester, M23 9HH, United Kingdom
Tel +44 161 973 9856
Fax +44 161 905 3498
stjerome@compuserve.com
http://www.stjerome.co.uk

ISBN 1-900650-47-9 (pbk)

Printed and bound in Great Britain by
T. J. International Ltd., Cornwall, UK

Cover design by
Steve Fieldhouse, Oldham, UK (+44 161 620 2263)

Typeset by
Delta Typesetters, Cairo, Egypt
Email: delttyp@starnet.com.eg

British Library Cataloguing in Publication Data
A catalogue record of this book is available from the British Library

Library of Congress Cataloging-in-Publication Data
Crosscultural transgressions : research models in Translation Studies II: historical and ideological issues / edited by Theo Hermans.
    p. cm.
Includes bibliographical references and index.
  ISBN 1-900650-47-9 (pbk. : alk. paper)
  1. Translating and interpreting--Research--Methodology. I. Hermans, Theo.
P306.5 .C76 2002
418'.02'072 – dc21
                                2001006630

Contents

Preface

Poor Holmes! Intrigued by what others overlooked, he gathered his evidence into a speculative but coherent whole, a bold and lucid vision which he set down in crisp, disciplined paragraphs. The construction had everything going for it. An object of inquiry had presented itself, a critical mass of hungry investigators was itching to take it on, all that was needed was a sense of purpose and a sound methodology. That was what the vision fleshed out. In 1972 Holmes wrote it up, in an elegant essay that has come to be seen as one of the founding documents of the emergent discipline of translation studies. 'The Name and Nature of Translation Studies' outlined a branch of the human sciences that would combine observation and explanation, description and prediction, fieldwork and theory. The discipline would systematically quarry, catalogue, document and explicate the phenomena of translation.

Perhaps the discipline lacked discipline. Maybe it proved too rich for its own good. Or the climate changed. At any rate, while the study of translation received a momentous boost from Holmes' pioneering blueprint, it did not develop along the measured lines of accumulation and progression he foresaw. The explosive growth of interest in translation in recent decades has brought in its wake a proliferation of types and areas of research. Translation studies today look more varied and volatile than Holmes can ever have imagined. Even the discipline's name is now less assured than it once seemed, as at one end the field embraces travel, sign language and intercultural pragmatics while on the other 'translation' has come to encompass all forms of crosscultural and intracultural negotiation.

Like its companion volume (*Intercultural Faultlines. Research Models in Translation Studies I: Textual and Cognitive Aspects*, edited by Maeve Olohan), the present collection charts old and new territory. It deals with research in translation, its nature, aims, range, procedures, contexts and modalities. The focus is more specifically on historical and ideological issues, from epistemological questions of historiography to the politics of language – often in combination. The aim is to offer a sampling of approaches and case studies that, together, reflect innovative directions in and raise pertinent questions about current translation research.

The volume falls into roughly two parts. The first part (chapters 1-7) is primarily concerned with elaborating and updating the methodological toolbox of translation description and history. In part two (chapters 8-12) issues of ideology are more in the foreground. There is no sharp dividing line separating the two halves. Both parts tackle not just the question how to do research on translation, but some of the underlying issues as well: why certain questions are asked, who asks them, with what aim, in which language, and why that matters.

What all the contributions have in common is a strong self-reflexive element. The heart-searching and self-examination have as their object both the speculations about methodology and the more politicized scrutiny of the institutional positioning of research and scholarship, but they extend to the epistemology of representation – which here includes the representations produced by translators and by those who write on translation.

All the essays are also mindful of their desire to capture the unphotographable: assumptions and motivations, relations and agency, the social and intellectual forces which elude direct observation and must be inferred. Much attention is paid to this process of triangulation and its conditioning, to the reporting of findings and interpretations, and to the constructed nature of the ensuing edifice. They know, too, the limitations of research models and frameworks. Paradigms have their blind spots, and conceal as much as they reveal.

Maria Tymoczko's linking of micro-level and macro-level investigation serves as a reminder not only of the perennial problem of marrying texts with contexts – so simple in theory, so hard in practice – but also of the expanding purview of translation research, for which the micro is becoming miniaturized and the macro a matter of geopolitics. In rehearsing the ground rules of scholarly research, Tymoczko throws dictionary definitions of 'hypothesis' and 'theory' at the reader, stresses such things as clarity of focus and replicability of procedure, and recalls that research is conducted within certain paradigms. But she goes much further. She acknowledges the social positioning of researchers and the institutional constraints within which translation research is conducted. In this respect she takes note of those other eminently crosscultural disciplines, anthropology and ethnography, and the crisis of representation as experienced there in recent decades – a key event also referred to in Michaela Wolf's contribution (chapter 12).

That crisis – how to offer a representation of a cultural practice without doing violence to it – has led to ironic modes of academic writing. The irony stems from the awareness of transgression, from the knowledge that any representation is compromised and therefore problematic, but that we cannot do without representations. It is an irony that pervades not only ethnography but also such disciplines as historiography, sociology and critical linguistics. In a crosscultural field like translation studies, the material we work on consists of representations of texts in other codes, languages, scripts, traditions, thought-worlds; in turn, our studies offer representations of those representations. The appreciation of the problematic nature of representation feeds a self-reflexive stance, the translation scholar's critical double.

Edoardo Crisafulli's meta-level discussion, straddling theory and methodology, testifies to the continuing quest for a viable framework for historical research. Sceptical of hasty generalizations and the idea of detached observation dear to much descriptive work, Crisafulli aims at a reassessment of descriptive studies and argues for what he calls 'historical empiricism', which seeks to combine descriptivism and hermeneutics, the quantitative and the qualitative, the historical and the political, the empirical and the ideological. Such a form of eclecticism, he suggests, will be

able to do justice to the unique occurrence, the special case, that which is historically significant but does not fall into a pattern – the singular, the creative – not at
the expense of the transindividual but as a complement to it. Like Jeremy Munday
(chapter 5), Crisafulli is willing to see his proposals put to the test and ends up with
a actual checklist.

Şehnaz Tahir-Gürçağlar is similarly preoccupied with issues of methodology and historiography. Her investigation of translation norms as manifested in
twentieth-century Turkish renderings from European languages has led to a particular interest in the paratexts of translation. The essay brings Gérard Genette's
terminology to bear on the matter, but not after a critical disagreement in which
Tahir-Gürçağlar takes issue with Genette's characterization of translations as
paratexts and thus as subordinate – a view she regards as unnecessarily restrictive.

Tahir-Gürçağlar's study illustrates the potential that paratexts offer for research.
Their assertions and judgements, their covert and overt polemics, their very vo-
cabularies are indicative of the way the nature, function and boundaries of translation
are perceived, and thus allow the researcher to construct the underlying conceptions
of translation. At the same time, the paratexts shed light on the sociocultural world
in which the texts were produced.

Insofar as scholarly comments also live paratextually off original and translated
texts, Tahir-Gürçağlar pays heed to the implications of the descriptive terminology
used by the researcher. Genette distinguishes, for example, between authorial and
allographic prefaces; the former are written by the author of the book in question,
the other by a third party. As Tahir-Gürçağlar astutely notes, calling a translator's
preface 'allographic' disempowers that translator as the authorial voice of the translated text. The terms of our descriptions release more than just descriptions.

Elsie Chan's essay about the Chinese translator Yan Fu takes its cue from Even-
Zohar's polysystem theory, but builds equally on André Lefevere's work on
patronage, ideology and institutions. The aim however is not to confirm or disprove
the validity of a theoretical apparatus but to use elements of it to prise open the
social, political and cultural environment of Yan Fu's famous three terms describing the requirements of good translation. The essay focusses on agency, in the form
of the complex interplay between the translator's agenda and the social and cultural
forces around it. Where the range of meanings of Yan Fu's terms, their historical
echoes and their interrelations are at stake, Chan is mindful that writing about this
in English brings its own problems of translation and representation.

Jeremy Munday's article, which takes up Maria Tymoczko's emphasis on systematic and replicable studies, is entirely methodological. Munday operates close to
Gideon Toury's vision of descriptive studies as following a set of explicit analytical
procedures. In this respect he continues the tradition of Kitty van Leuven-Zwart,
combining a clearly defined linguistic model with more interpretive moves. Like
Van Leuven-Zwart, Munday derives his linguistic arsenal from Halliday's systemic-
functional grammar, but his tool is not restricted to narrative texts and it avoids both

the formal identification of units of comparison and the pigeon-holing of translation shifts that made Van Leuven-Zwart's model conceptually problematic as well
as cumbersome to apply. Another advance on Van Leuven-Zwart is Munday's flexible deployment of computer technology and corpus linguistics to take care of
number-crunching and suggest aspects that might repay closer examination. It also
goes beyond previous models in its attempt to tie description to explanation, drawing on political and sociocultural contexts to supply motivations and reasons for the
patterns observed. Not only is the model fully illustrated with an analysis of a text
by Gabriel García Márquez in three English translations, but Munday, like Crisafulli,
provides checklists to facilitate further applications and testing.

The sociocultural context which Munday incorporates into his model but does
not elaborate, receives detailed attention in **Jean-Marc Gouanvic**'s approach.
Gouanvic builds on Pierre Bourdieu's cultural sociology, indeed his *Sociologie de
la traduction* (1999) is the major example of a Bourdieu-inspired brand of translation studies to date. The essay in the present collection serves as an introduction to
Bourdieu's key concepts of habitus, field and trajectory, heuristic tools which are
here illustrated with a case study of two twentieth-century French translators of
American fiction. An unusual feature of Gouanvic's historical analyses is that they
are process-oriented or, more precisely, production-oriented. Their focus is on the
shaping of specific translations, texts which emerge with a certain form, at a certain
moment, in a certain context, as the outcome of singular trajectories. The question
of agency resurfaces here, as the concepts of habitus and trajectory connect the
individual translator's actions with the social forces that make up the field in which
he or she operates. For all their differences, Gouanvic has much in common with
Crisafulli in that both are in search of explanatory models to relate the individual to
the collective and the singular to the social and historical context.

For **Derek Boothman**, translation happens not just between different natural
languages but also intralingually between theoretical or conceptual frameworks,
that is, between paradigms. The case in point is Antonio Gramsci translating terms
and concepts from the idealist philosophy of his compatriot Benedetto Croce into
his own Marxist frame of thought. Even the terms denoting the two 'languages'
involved are fluid: Gramsci also speaks of translating from speculative into historicist or 'realist historicist' language. Interestingly, the process can be viewed in both
directions, as Gramsci equally regards Croce's philosophy as the 'retranslation' into
idealist terms of the 'realist historicism' of his own Marxist philosophy of praxis.

In patiently scrutinizing how Croce's concept of ethico-political history is as-
similated into Gramsci's notion of historical block, and how Croce's dialectic of
'distincts' is rendered applicable to Gramsci's discourse about levels of the superstructure, Boothman makes it clear that what we are witnessing is not a matter of
matching term for term and concept for concept, but a complex philosophical and
ideological negotiation whereby the other's terms and concepts are not just renamed
but inspected, reinterpreted, criticized, rearranged and relocated in a different

intellectual idiom and tradition. As Boothman is at pains to stress, terms are embedded in conceptual structures, which are themselves historical entities. Gramsci himself raises the issue of homology in this connection. While translation between homologous structures or systems may be possible, structures that are not homologous present serious problems of commensurability and hence translatability. On a different note Boothman reminds us that for Gramsci translation comprises an experiential side. Translating is a act of engagement. The hermeneutics of understanding requires more than a coldly intellectual routine, it calls for commitment, respect and, as Gramsci puts it, feeling.

Gramsci's labour of translation could stand as a prototype for the crosstemporal and interparadigmatic translation of the concepts and vocabulary of translation and translation studies. This becomes especially evident in **Saliha Paker**'s essay. At one level this is a study in historical semantics, preoccupied as it is with the meanings of various Ottoman terms denoting practices that seem to correspond to 'translation' and 'imitation'. But it goes beyond that. In its search for reasons why certain aspects of Ottoman cultural history have received such scant attention from scholars, the essay delves into the institutional and therefore the political and ideological determinants of modern Turkish scholarship and research. On an epistemological level it recognizes that the modern academic study of translation, as a product of the contemporary world and of certain intellectual traditions, necessarily operates with particular, culture-bound concepts of translation – which however do not automatically equip us to deal with the extent of past practices and their attendant metalanguages. Those practices may show family resemblances with latter-day concepts of translation, paraphrase, imitation, but they cannot be reduced to them, and they cluster differently in the contemporary metadiscourses.

On top of this comes the matter of the reporting language. Like the majority of contributors to the present volume, Paker is alive to the ironies of articulating in English the cultural tradition she feels part of. She has to translate the historical terms handed down by the primary material as well as the nuances and distinctions pertaining to those terms, and the vocabulary employed by modern Turkish scholarship to cover them. In what language is 'translation' to be understood, and what does it translate? The issue has a political as well as an epistemological face. Paker knows the need for 'frontloading' – the term is Tymoczko's, and Şebnem Susam-Sarajeva (chapter 12) will take it up: writing in English about Turkish imposes a need to provide basic background information in a manner and to a degree that does not apply to some of the more visible western cultures English-language scholarship regards as its 'normal' theatre of operations. The choice of a disciplinary vehicle reveals asymmetries of power between languages.

Paker's forays into the multilingual world of Ottoman culture also lead her to challenge the comfortable equation of one culture, one nation, one language – the ground for the binarism that used to dominate a translation studies given to thinking in discrete terms of sources here, targets there, and translations speeding from one to the other. Instead, she tries to get a grip on her material via the fuzzier concept of a hybrid intercultural contact zone where several languages and a variety of literary forms of different provenance and allegiance intermingle.

Like Saliha Paker's, **Martha Cheung**'s article is concerned with the forces acting on translation research as much as those acting on translation itself. Cheung extracts the political subtext from three central moments in the discipline's institutional history in China. Her tack is political in more respects than one. Apart from unpacking the ideological load of scholarly work, she flags up the immediate context – Hong Kong's return to Chinese sovereignty in 1997 – which makes it imperative for her to push politics to the top of her agenda.

This conscious self-positioning supports the interpretive effort. The three texts Cheung examines do not flaunt their political message, it has to be teased out by means of a focussed reading and pertinent contextualization. Once the angle has been set, she is able to discern agency in translation research, reading the apparently sedate work of scholars and philologists as ideologically charged interventions in the institutional and sociocultural formations from which it springs and to which it returns.

Gordon Brotherston's essay is an eye-opener of a different order. With reference to two specific pre-Cortesian examples Brotherston demonstrates the challenge which Native American scripts pose even the specialist interpreter. They defy linear reading. They are coded and relate to their world in ways utterly unfamiliar to most modern readers. They should make translation scholars sit up and think. How much can be taken for granted about forms of information storage and transmission, about modes of meaning generation? It may no longer be the case that most of what is said and written today about translation is based on a handful of Indo-European languages and alphabetic scripts, but the complexities of notation and expression manifested in these Native American texts alert us to dimensions well beyond the assumptions underpinning vast swathes of current translation research.

There are other lessons to be learnt. Deciphering visual texts and attempting to convey in, say, English, what they state in their own notation, would seem to be eminently a form of translation. If so, claims about so-called universals and laws of translation – the laws of explicitation, simplification, standardization – begin to look bewilderingly thin, and betray their over-reliance on a painfully restricted range of text types, time-frames and scripts. In this respect too Brotherston's article should prove salutory. The implications of an engagement with documents like these are, again, political as well as linguistic, cultural and philosophical. It is hard to remain blind to the reasons why so few documents of this nature survive and why so little is known about the traditions that produced them.

Michaela Wolf engages with the overlap between ethnography and translation in the context of postcolonial theory, deconstruction and cultural studies. Harking back to the 'writing culture' debate among anthropologists in the 1980s, she homes in on the representation of 'otherness' by both ethnographers and translators, and on the filters of language, discourse and power such representations bring into play. The theoretical frame in which Wolf considers these questions seeks to escape the dead weight of binary distinctions and work instead with more fluid, non-essentialist, dynamic categories: the 'self' is continually being constituted in a syncretic process of intertextuality and transformation, and culture is thought of as pluricentric and the outcome of constant negotiation – indeed of translation. In this context it is the itinerary travelled, the route towards the representation that gains prominence and becomes the site of reflection and interest, just as such provisional, unstable, fuzzy notions as the 'in-between' or Homi Bhabha's 'third space' become sites of enunciation. Studying translation in accordance with these models demands more than attention to issues of context and power. It places an onus on researchers to recognize the constructed nature of their own discursive representations, the location of their research, and the implications of their selection and handling of texts and topics.

Critical consciousness-raising of this type accompanies a great deal of contemporary scholarly research and reporting in the wake of gender and postcolonial studies. It also informs **Şebnem Susam-Sarajeva**'s article, which fixes on the politics of intellectual discourse in the global market place. The asymmetric power relations between the world's languages of scholarship privilege centres rather than peripheries. As in the economic sphere, peripheries supply raw materials – objects of intellectual curiosity – while the terms of the trade – academic standards, prestigious degrees, allegedly universal models – are decided in the centre. As Susam-Sarajeva shows, language is only one aspect of this imbalance. Theories, methodologies, paradigms tend to be exported from the centre, imported by the periphery; they enhance their range and validity by being tested out first in 'familiar' then in 'exotic' conditions. The postcolonial world however is one where the superiority of western models and modes of thought no longer goes unchallenged – even if, ironically, the challenge may need a language like English to secure international resonance.

A translation studies that was truly international and multilingual would resist the dominance of a single disciplinary language. It would thereby gain in depth and diversity, and thus in intellectual vigour. It would be a discipline committed not just to translation but to translating. It would translate itself, deliberately, passionately.

Theo Hermans

References

Holmes, James (1988) 'The Name and Nature of Translation Studies' [1972], in his *Translated! Papers on Literary Translation and Translation Studies*, Amsterdam: Rodopi, 67-80.

Olohan, Maeve (ed) (2000) *Intercultural Faultlines. Research Models in Translation Studies I: Textual and Cognitive Aspects*, Manchester: St Jerome.

Connecting the Two Infinite Orders
Research Methods in Translation Studies

MARIA TYMOCZKO

Abstract: *Using as an analogy the seventeenth-century crisis of knowledge spurred by the development of the telescope and the microscope, this paper argues that a similar crisis in knowledge itself has occurred with the intellectual developments of the twentieth century. Two new infinite orders have opened up: the virtually inexhaustible possibilities suggested by segmenting texts into smaller and smaller units, and the equally inexhaustible possibilities offered by the relationship of texts to layer upon layer of context. Translation studies reflect the new shift in the debate between those who assert the preeminence of linguistic approaches to translation and those who advocate primarily cultural studies approaches to translation. This article argues for research methods that combine both approaches, offering examples of how such research should proceed in translation studies.*

The history of optics and optical engineering is a long and complex one. To the ancients, vision and the principles of image formation were mysterious, with debate engaged about whether something moved from the object seen to the eye, or from the eye to the object seen.[1] By the early medieval period, pragmatics had advanced, and simple lenses were in use as magnifiers; some centuries later, by the fourteenth century, eyeglasses had been developed. From the use of simple lenses for magnification, however, it was more than a thousand years until the first compound microscope was invented in about 1590 by Zacharias Janssen, a young Dutch lad, together with his father, makers of spectacles. Though it gave only small magnification, their invention paved the way for all subsequent investigations depending on optics, from our understandings of the minute workings of both animate and inanimate matter to our knowledge of the cosmos.

In Middelburg in the year 1608, together with Hans Lippershey, Zacharias Janssen also made the first telescope. A year later, in 1609, Galileo learned of the invention, and himself constructed a telescope with threefold magnification, soon improving its magnification to the power of 32. Galileo was a mathematician who by then had already made great discoveries regarding the laws of motion; although he had become convinced of the Copernican model of the universe (namely that the planets revolve around the sun) early in his career, he had been deterred from avowal of the theory by lack of positive proof and by fear of ridicule. In 1609 Galileo turned his

---

[1] For additional background on the references to optics and to Galileo in this essay, see Drake (1980) and *Encyclopedia Britannica* (15th ed.) entries on 'Galileo', 'Medicine, History of', 'Optical Engineering', and 'Optics, Principles of'.

telescope to the skies to observe astronomical bodies, the first person to do so in part because he had devised a method of checking the curvature of the lenses he used, thus permitting sufficient accuracy of resolution for astronomical observation. By the end of 1609, he began announcing a major series of discoveries, including the mountains of the moon, the satellites of Jupiter, the phases of Venus, the rings of Saturn, and sunspots (which he showed were on the rotating sun), all of which validated the Copernican theory.

In 1610 Galileo discovered a means of adapting his telescope to the examination of minute objects, but he only became acquainted with the compound microscope in 1624 when he saw one in Rome. With characteristic ingenuity, he introduced several improvements in the construction of the microscope. He was the first to lay stress on the value of measurement in this science, replacing theory and guesswork with accuracy. In fact, Galileo's most far-reaching achievement was perhaps the re-establishment of mathematical rationalism against Aristotle's logico-verbal approach, insisting that the "Book of Nature is written in mathematical characters", thus laying the foundation of the modern experimental method.[2] This emphasis on measurement in all scientific observation effaced the distinction that had been drawn between methods appropriate to cosmic realms and the sublunary realm of humanity.

The telescope was used by Galileo to challenge dominant theories of the cosmic order, and this in turn undermined accepted theological doctrines. Ultimately Galileo was summoned to Rome, tried by the Inquisition, ordered to recant and forced to spend the last eight years of his life under house arrest. The Jesuits perceived the danger of his scientific methods and discoveries, insisting to the Pope that Galileo's doctrines could have worse consequences for the established system "than Luther and Calvin put together".[3] Thus, in the seventeenth century, the invention of the microscope and the telescope precipitated a crisis of knowledge that went far beyond optics. The domains of both science and religion were exploded as people attempted to integrate the realms opened by the new scientific tools into pre-existing structures of thought.

In some ways the extent of the crisis is not altogether surprising. In Indo-European languages knowledge has always been connected with sight and vision, with the same lexical roots giving rise to words in both domains. To see is to know. In the second half of the seventeenth century, Pascal wrote about the shattering implications of these new realms of vision, referring to them as "les deux infinis" ('the two infinities') in his *Pensées* in 1670, and arguing in 'Misère de l'homme sans Dieu' (1690) that without God, man could be at best miserable and lost between these two infinities of existence, knowledge and vision. Jonathan Swift's

---

[2] Cf. *Encyclopedia Britannica* 7.851; Drake 1980: 70.
[3] *Encyclopedia Britannica* 7.852.

Gulliver's Travels (1726) owes something to the optical discoveries of the seventeenth century, projecting man into both gigantic and minuscule realms, and in 1752 Voltaire played on the two infinities in his story *Micromégas*, with his gigantic hero from Sirius adventuring in smaller and smaller orders of magnitude, of which the smallest he can apprehend is that of our own. Despite such imaginative explorations of the issues during the Enlightenment, one sees traces of the religious crisis and anxiety precipitated by the two infinities well into the nineteenth century. The intellectual crisis caused by the developments in optics was, thus, long lasting, taking three centuries to resolve, and its solutions set the terms of our own scientific inquiry and contemporary religious frameworks.

I take my title from this cultural crisis caused by optics, which I have elaborated upon at some length here, because I believe that something very similar has happened in the last century or so in the realm of the humanities and the social sciences. The analogy with the earlier development of knowledge is appropriate for several reasons. First, of course, the revolution that has happened in our time has been modeled upon the earlier scientific revolution. Scientific attitudes and methods that can be traced to the late sixteenth and early seventeenth centuries, epitomized by Galileo's dictum about the Book of Nature being written in mathematical characters, have come to characterize the social sciences and increasingly the humanities as well, from linguistics and history to literary studies. The humanities and social sciences also live by metaphors from optics, metaphors like 'the universe of discourse' that is used to contextualize social interactions or the prefixes 'micro-' and 'macro-' used routinely by everyone from economists to those who analyze poetics.

More importantly, from the earlier revolution in knowledge we have learned to see – and hence to know – differently in all fields. To turn more narrowly to the subject at hand, with the explosion of knowledge in both linguistics and social theory, for example, it is no longer possible to approach any text in a simple or unproblematized manner, least of all translations which de facto link two languages and two cultures. In a sense two new infinite orders have opened up: the virtually inexhaustible possibilities suggested by segmenting texts into smaller and smaller linguistic units, and the equally inexhaustible possibilities suggested by the relationship of texts to layer upon layer of context, including the context of other texts. Moreover, as in the seventeenth-century crisis of knowledge, we have come to recognize that there are more than one equally valid ways to see and describe the same phenomena, depending on intellectual context.

An example from the natural sciences will illustrate my meaning here. The biological and chemical descriptions of the workings of an organism complement each other – becoming increasingly inseparable in fact – and are complemented in turn by taxonomy and naturalist descriptions. Thus in the realm of biology, we could have many different but equally valid descriptions of the entity *wolf*, including the following. There is *wolf* from the viewpoint of physiological description, looking at the animal as a biological system. There is *wolf* from the viewpoint of chemical and biochemical descriptions, giving a chemical breakdown of the composition of its body or a description of its physiological systems in terms of biochemical processes. There is *wolf* from the viewpoint of taxonomic descriptions, setting the animal in the context of other canines, carnivores, and so forth. And there is *wolf* as the naturalists or ecologists would describe the animal, setting it in the context of the environment it inhabits. In the same way we approach social and humanistic domains with the recognition that data can be viewed and described in valid ways from a variety of perspectives, with a variety of tools. Different fields or disciplines offer different ways of seeing, conceiving and knowing phenomena that are not competitive but mutually enlightening and reinforcing.

If we look at the domains opened up by turning a microscope on language, so to speak, we would have to include fields such as the following. There would be phonics and phonetics, with their insights about phonemes, allophones, and other aspects of phonology. New prospects have opened up in morphology and syntax, including the insights offered by transformational grammar about surface and deep structures of language. The field of semantics has burgeoned, developing indispensable concepts and tools, not the least of which pertain to semantic fields and sense relations in languages. Awareness and analysis of the varieties of language have deepened, sensitizing us to features not only of socioeconomic and geographic dialects, but linguistic registers and specialized languages as well. Greater understanding has developed of the maintenance and persistence of linguistic norms, as well as variation from and evolution of such norms. These various domains have in turn found expression in comparative linguistics, spurring inquiry about the ways that languages differ in these various respects. Obviously this is a very cursory and representative survey of the fields developed for the microscopic linguistic analysis of texts, and I'm sure that I've omitted some essential domain near and dear to the heart of every reader. They illustrate, however, how these microscopic analyses of language have opened up our understanding of the activity that is most paradigmatically human in ways that are not only more profound but also characterized by greater and greater degrees of delicacy.

When we turn to the macroscopic investigations of language and text – those that can be seen by turning a telescope on the larger and larger contexts of a text and of humanity, so to speak – the explosion of knowledge has been equally impressive. Increasingly the specifics of language can be seen in ever widening contexts including the following. Both semiotics and semiology have approached human language as a system of signs that can be located within other systems of signs and within larger contexts of communication and cognition as well. Sociolinguistics has explored functional aspects of language, including linguistic practices pertaining to gender and class. Study of the illocutionary force of utterances (or speech acts) and questions of modality have illuminated the relationship between language and still other social practices. The study of literacy practices and of orality and oral literature has shed light on many facets of the relationship between oral and written language, as well as oral and written cultures. Exploration of discourses has opened up the relationship of language to structures of knowledge and social organization, including hierarchies and power relations. Investigations pertaining to intertextuality have explored the relationship of texts to texts, showing how the context of textuality itself shapes both the production and reception of texts. And systems analyses have shown the relationship of text to multiple social contexts (including materialist conditions, economics, governments, ideologies, and so forth), unpacking the relationship of textual practices and textual systems to many other cultural and social contexts. Again this is only a cursory survey of a few of the new perspectives and tools that have developed in the last century and that are representative of the possibilities of macroscopic investigations of texts.

Important areas of inquiry have also emerged that combine both micro- and macro-perspectives and that are informed by both modes of analysis. Thus, for example, the understanding of language and texts has been affected by such domains as the field of language acquisition – a field with both microscopic and macroscopic dimensions – which has investigated the linguistic mechanics of language acquisition as well as the sociolinguistic aspects of the process. The radical shifts in ways that meaning is modelled is another such domain that combines both micro- and macro-approaches, from the Whorfian hypothesis that has led to an understanding of how a person's language community influences the very structures of perception, with the ensuing implication that meaning is language specific, to the philosophical revolution in the modeling of meaning as other than a Platonic relationship between word and object, in favor of theories of reference, truth value, language games, and so forth. And, of course, anthropology and folklore have drawn on both microscopic and macroscopic approaches to language and text, in turn influencing each other.

It should be noted here that there are differences as well as similarities between the two revolutions in knowledge that I am discussing. One difference is that the revolution of the last century has generated much less anxiety than the revolution that began in the seventeenth century. Largely because the second revolution built upon the earlier scientific revolution that had been in process for three hundred years, it has been experienced more as a birthright than a threat. Moreover, the earlier revolution in optics had essentially two tools – the microscope and telescope, one each for micro- and macro-investigations. It took centuries to develop extensions of these primary tools – the electron microscope and radio telescope, for example. But in this more recent revolution in humanistic knowledge and the social sciences, whole classes of tools have been developed for the investigation of the most minute and the largest phenomena, as the listings above indicate. In a very short time, multiple intellectual tools have been generated for viewing and understanding the humanities and social sciences, tools that sometimes even, paradoxically, seem to compete and overlap in their domains.

The seventeenth-century revolution in optics differs in yet another respect from the current situation. One conception of the old infinite orders can be seen in some treatments of the theme: the belief that at every order of magnitude, the same world organization would be replicated. So in a drop of water there might be a solar system or galaxy like that of our own, with the minute inhabitants of that galaxy facing the sorts of issues that we ourselves face. Conversely, our galaxy at times could be conceived of as being akin to a drop of water in a larger universe, where again the social arrangements were played out on a larger scale. By contrast, we have learned in the intervening time that there is generally no such replication as we change orders of magnitude. Instead phenomena seen from different orders of magnitude generate multiple descriptions and varying data; thus, the investigation of things from different perspectives is not only useful, but essential, with as a goal a unified field that can link these varied orders of magnitude and the descriptive materials they generate.

Clearly translation studies reflects this recent revolution in social and humanist knowledge. The proliferation of scholarship in translation studies can be correlated with the development of these various new fields and their approaches to language, texts and culture, and the extension of their insights to the processes and products of translation. Indeed, almost every development pertaining to language or text has some relevance to translation studies. Moreover, because translation studies involves not only theory but practice, it has been fertile ground for applications of both linguistic and contextual approaches to texts; not surprisingly, applied versions of most of the various proliferating perspectives on language, text and culture have appeared within translation studies. In turn, scholars inside and out of translation studies have come to realize that translation could offer important data that could be used to test emerging theoretical structures in many domains touched by this new revolution in knowledge. Such scholars and theoreticians range from W.V.O. Quine to Homi Bhabha.

This more recent revolution in knowledge, with its two new infinite orders, is also at the heart of the debate in translation studies about the validity of linguistic approaches versus cultural studies approaches to translation. Ironically we can say that those in translation studies who assert the exclusive validity of either approach are in the position of seventeenth-century scientists who might have asserted the exclusive validity of the perspective offered by either the microscope or the telescope, rejecting the discoveries opened by the other. The ridiculousness of such a posture is obvious at this juncture, yet many of our colleagues find it difficult to accept both infinite orders of our time and they persist in denying the validity and utility of one of them.

In the remainder of this essay, I would like to explore the rationale for research that connects the two infinite orders and to suggest some practical methods that will do so. If large translation effects investigated by cultural studies approaches to translation are the result of small word-by-word, sentence-by-sentence and text-by-text decisions by translators that can be analyzed with contemporary linguistic tools, then research methods in translation studies will generally benefit from connecting those two realms. Frequently it will be not only helpful but actually essential to identify and retrace linguistic specificities of textual construction, so that translation effects are understood as products of textual construction and production. Only if one believes that the data from another order of magnitude will replicate those data generated by the level one is working on, will a researcher reject other tools for viewing the subject matter and other perspectives, but research on texts in the last half century has shown that such replication is rarely the case.

In what follows I am basing my examples on research methods for descriptive studies of translations as products, rather than translation as process, but the principles I articulate here are transferable to other types of research in translation studies. I take descriptive studies as my domain because this has been the subject of my own research; hence it is what I know most about and can speak about with a measure of authority.

In conducting research on translation,[4] as is the case with other textual studies, it is a given that one cannot look at most texts exhaustively. The meaning of a text (whether oral or written in origin) as an organized artifact and as an object in a social context is in many, many respects overdetermined. Thus, any extended text offers too much information to the researcher to be distilled into a normal academic 'unit' – whether the unit is a class presentation, a conference paper, an article or a chapter of a book. The researcher therefore must select what is to be investigated and must focus the research, and the prime method of focus or selection is the research design, as is standard in research and scholarship in most fields. Although a researcher may at times replicate the research design of another study or use established research protocols for a particular purpose, normally each project will require a specific research design.[5]

---

[4] For the purposes of this paper, I am using Gideon Toury's very broad definition of *translation*: "a translation will be any target language text which is presented or regarded as such within the target system itself, on whatever grounds" (Toury 1982: 27; cf. Toury 1980: 14, 37, 43-45). Only such a broad definition can cover research in translation studies as a whole, which is the topic of this paper, and Toury's formulation of this definition (in part synthesizing the work of his predecessors) was one of the major breakthroughs that has led to the explosion of research in translation studies in the last two decades. As Pym (1998: ch. 4) has pointed out, however, in most cases a more narrow definition of translation will be incorporated into the research design, so as to restrict and define the field of study, a topic to be discussed further below. For another recent discussion of this question of definition, see Hermans (1999: ch.4).

[5] Here I would like to underscore the criticisms of Hermans (1999: ch. 5) about exhaustive and totalizing programmes of research that have been undertaken in translation studies. Such programmes may generate a great deal of information, but much of what is generated may be of little use in addressing questions relevant to specific texts and contexts. Mechanical and exhaustive methods of this sort are seldom productive in humanistic research, any more than they are in the natural and social sciences, and their results rarely justify the effort they require. As Pym (1998:

A normal feature of a research design is that the researcher must know what she wishes to find or what she expects to find – that is, the research must begin with and be based upon a hypothesis.[6] It is important to make the distinction between a *hypothesis*[7] and a *theory*.[8] A theory provides the paradigm (cf. Kuhn 1962) within which whole programmes of research proceed; within such a theory or paradigm, a hypothesis is a specific extension of knowledge that is to be tested. If a researcher is unaware of this distinction and oblivious of theory – focusing only on hypotheses – when constructing a research design, it does not mean that she has no theory. Rather it signifies that the research is being conducted within some dominant theoretical framework or controlling paradigm of which the researcher may not be fully conscious.[9]

In descriptive studies one usually wishes to answer questions such as the following. What relationship exists between two cultures at a certain point in time? Has that relationship changed over time and, if so, how has it changed? What is the position of translators in the source and/or receiving culture? What impact did a specific translation have on its receiving culture? What impact did the source and/or receiving cultural context have on the translation methods and product? How did the translation manipulate or shift the source and/or receiving culture, and how did the receiving and/or source culture manipulate the translation? What patterns of translation choices can one discern, or, to put it another way, what norms were adopted in the course of translation? How do those norms intersect with the cultural impact of the translation and with the cultural expectations within which the translation was produced?

Questions such as these provide the large structures within which the specific hypothesis of a case study is framed; the hypothesis in turn acts as a guide for where to start and what texts to focus on. We should observe that in translation studies, as

---

49-50) notes, one needs just enough information to confirm or deny the pertinent hypotheses governing one's research. Although programmatic schemes may provide good reminders of things a researcher should think about, they cannot substitute for the development of a specific research design pertinent to each given project.

[6] We could digress into a discussion of scientific method at this point, to justify this statement, but I am assuming that readers of this book understand that research is not a walk in the park during which one happens to notice random interesting views.

[7] Defined in the *American Heritage Dictionary* as "an assertion subject to verification or proof", including "a conjecture that accounts, within a theory or ideational framework, for a set of facts and that can be used as a basis for further investigation".

[8] Defined in the *American Heritage Dictionary* as "a system of assumptions, accepted principles, and rules of procedure devised to analyze, predict, or otherwise explain the nature or behavior of a specified set of phenomena". Those who suggest the need for a "concrete theory" specific to each research project fail to make the distinction between theory and hypothesis; see Hermans (1999: 71) for additional criticisms of the concept of a "concrete theory".

[9] Hermans (1999: 34) notes that no focused observation is possible without a theory to tell the observer what to look for and how to assess the significance of what is observed.

in textual studies in general, there is not usually a single hypothesis, but rather a cluster of hypotheses. Thus, in my investigations of the translation of early Irish heroic tales into English, I hypothesized that there would be some problem areas for the translator, in view of the highly politicized context of translation and the considerable differences between source and receiving cultures. In my initial hypothesis these problem areas included the type of heroism displayed, the sexual and scatological content of the texts, the distinctive form of Irish hero tale which mixes poetry and prose, the textual 'disarray' resulting from oral variants recorded in the written documents (as well as degradation caused by the complex textual history and age of the manuscripts), and the humour typical of early Irish literature. I was able to construct this complex hypothesis on the basis of my knowledge of early Irish literature and culture and also on the basis of my knowledge of the reception context, including the mores of the Victorianized, highly religious culture in Ireland at the turn of the twentieth century, in which an extremely hostile climate of colonization had undermined the very idea of Irish culture and in which colonial values had been introjected by the Irish themselves.

In answering such questions and in testing hypotheses, a researcher can approach the research from two directions: from the macroscopic direction, by looking at the big picture, by turning a telescope on the culture, so to speak; or from the microscopic direction, by looking at the particularities of the language of a translation through a microscope, as it were. Ultimately, however, in my view the best work shows a convergence – working toward the macroscopic from the direction of the microscopic, or vice versa, so that one's data from the macroscopic level are complemented and confirmed by data from the microscopic level.

Let us suppose that one begins from the direction of a macroscopic framework, asking some large and ideally important questions that might be typical of a cultural studies approach.[10] It is the hypothesis that will determine the research design, including where to begin and what working definition of translation to adopt.[11] Then in a descriptive study – assuming the hypothesis itself does not concern a particular

---

[10] I would second Pym's insistence (1998: ch. 2) that research should be done on questions of importance and that importance should be a guiding criterion for deciding on scholarly engagement altogether.

[11] Working definitions are adopted on the level of research design, whether one's research involves a large or small number of translations. Here Pym is right (1998: ch. 4) that working definitions are essential to delimit research, but wrong in attacking Toury's theoretical definition of translation, most clearly formulated in Toury's early work. The importance of Toury's initial definition of translation is theoretical: it delineates a position for accepting a broad range of translations in studies of translation, permitting any culture's definition of translation to be treated as equally valid. This definition operates on the level of theory; on the level of research hypothesis, however, any researcher may and usually even must limit the scope of inquiry for practical reasons. At the same time, it is incumbent on the researcher to make the limits of the inquiry explicit for the reader and recipient of the research.

translation – the first task is obviously to identify one or more relevant and revealing translations to investigate. The translations will be chosen because they set in high relief the cultural or ideological issues related to the cultural interface at hand. In turn, because it is impossible (and usually irrelevant) to study exhaustively the full text of one or more translations, the second task will be to pick perspicuous passages that will serve to test one's hypothesis or hypotheses.

Thus, to give examples from my own research and that of my students, in Mahasweta Sengupta's study of Tagore's translations of his own poetry, she focused on transformation of genre in the erotic devotional poem, because she reasoned that these poems would present multiple problems of cultural interface in India's colonial context in the early twentieth century.[12] In my own research, I tested my hypotheses by locating a passage in an Irish hero tale that contained heroic material, but that also was scatological and humorous, presenting generic problems as well in the form of a difficult but powerful poem.

Once such texts and passages are identified, the task is to look for linguistic anomalies and perturbations reflecting the cultural issues that are being investigated. This is the actual point at which one is gathering data, and one must devise ways to record the data systematically. In looking for textual evidence, one should have either a mental or formal checklist of the various linguistic levels to watch: phonology (as reflected in names or borrowed words, for example), lexis, semantics, morphology, grammar, syntax, idioms, metaphors, register, dialect, and so forth. One should also consider physical aspects of the translation as object at this stage, including the form of publication, publisher, series and publishing context, cost, binding, title, illustrations and typeface. In my experience, if the research design is well conceived and one has chosen productive passages from signficant translations, one generates an enormous amount of raw data relatively quickly. As an example, in about two or three weeks of analyzing translations in 1979, I generated enough rough data to map out the territory for most of the articles I published in the next decade related to the translation of early Irish literature into English, data that served as well as the basis for my *Translation in a Postcolonial Context* (1999).

It is important to be open to surprises at this stage of research. One may discover different translation effects from those anticipated in one's hypotheses or sought in one's research design, some of which may occur on the macroscopic level. For example, one may discover that there is a temporal significance in the pattern of publications, or that there are gross manipulations that were completely unanticipated (say, zero translation). Alternatively one may discover no data to support one's hypotheses, necessitating either refinement of the design (say, choice of different texts or different passages within the texts selected) or abandonment of the hypothesis altogether. At the same time, as is the case in most research in the natural sciences, absence of results is itself usually significant and can often be worth writing up.

---

[12] See Sengupta (1990, 1995).

That is, negative evidence is still evidence, though of a hypothesis different from the one motivating the initial research.

What is more typical than lack of data in a well designed research plan is an overabundance of data that must then be organized and analyzed. Usually one also finds textual elements that corroborate one's hypothesis that were not part of the explicit programme of the research design. In working on Irish sagas, for example, I did not set out to look for translation effects in the area of material or social culture, nor did I plan to gather evidence on the treatment of names. But in looking for the data related to my research design, I noted in passing unexpected variance in the translations of those elements and began to collect the additional data as well, though in a less systematic way. The result was ultimately two additional chapters of my book, but these could only be undertaken after a review of the materials in which the new data were collected systematically. In gathering and assessing evidence, it is important to remember that zero translation of texts or segments of texts is usually highly significant, and must be carefully noted and recorded.

The alternate path to research of this sort is to begin on the microscopic textual levels. One might hypothesize, for example, that two languages had vastly different material bases, devising a reseach plan to investigate those differences as expressed in translation. One would then scan specific translations for linguistic anomalies and perturbations related to these linguistic areas and interrogate the resulting pattern in terms of macroscopic cultural significance. One might ask, for example, what do these small-scale textual elements signify in terms of large-scale ideological or cultural positioning? This was the direction I went when I discovered the very peculiar patterns for representing Irish names in Standish O'Grady's *History of Ireland: The Heroic Period* and realized that they were driven by the extreme phonological differences between Old Irish and Modern English. One can often tease out cultural implications from materials that one may at first be tempted to dismiss as random eccentricities of individual translators. In undertaking research that proceeds in this direction, it is often helpful to keep the discourses associated with theories of representation in mind. One should ask, for example, what image of the source text does this textual presentation cast for the receiving audience and what is the ideological or cultural implication of that image? When one works in this direction, from the level of the word to the level of cultural significance, one must also remember to be wary of attributing intention to the translator: one can always argue for the meaning and significance of particular textual elements, but such significance does not necessarily indicate conscious authorial intention in a translation any more than it does in any other text. Thus, translation choices may be a function of cultural norms and textual choices may be driven by unconscious motivations of the translator, as is the case with any author.

Translations like other organized texts tend to be self-referential, establishing their own linguistic norms and conventions. As readers we tend to learn such conventions, adapting and assenting to them with relative ease. Thus our training as readers works against our ability to do research on the microlevels of translations: we must actually work to keep the conventions of a particular translation defamiliarized so as to be able to perceive the translator's norms and choices. Because of the tendency to assent to the self-referentiality of texts, it is often extremely difficult to analyze a single translation perspicaciously in reference to the source text. Comparing two or more translated versions of the same source text or several translations of similar text types may make the norms of any given translation much more perceptible.[13]

Once these steps have been completed, the preliminary data have been amassed. It is wise at this point to identify the emerging patterns that one will concentrate on and then to go back over the texts one is working with so as to check one's data systematically, to make sure that one has correctly noted all instances of a particular pattern, that one has not ignored contradictory evidence, and so forth, before proceeding to analysis of the data and conclusions. It is at this point that one also fills in systematically the data that were not anticipated by the original hypothesis but that were discovered during the process of data collection, as was the case of translations of names in my own research, as I have already mentioned.

A basic requirement of sound research in any field is replicability, and in translation studies this principle is equally valid. A wise researcher will test conclusions by actually attempting to replicate results herself – by examining other relevant passages of the translations being worked with, by looking at translations of other texts presenting similar cultural configurations, and so forth. One can also seek verification of the results of one's research by examining paratextual documents such as translators' introductions, statements about translation from the cultural context, and contemporary reviews of the published translation. And once confirmation comes from these various research strategies, it usually expands the scope of the initial research as well, suggesting further avenues to explore in the texts. Well designed research programmes have a gratifying way of developing positive feedback loops and becoming self-sustaining.

There is a cautionary note to be added here about the type of confirmation to expect. Increasingly it is being realized in translation studies that translation strategies are not consistent. Because of the metonymic aspects of the process of translation, translators privilege certain aspects of the source text over others, just as they privilege certain areas of resistance in their translations while conforming to dominant norms in other respects (see Tymoczko 1999, chapters 1 and 10). Researchers doing studies of translation should be alert to such inconsistencies, expecting to uncover them in the process of research; rather than abandoning a hypothesis when such an inconsistency is revealed, the researcher should analyze and explicate the fragmentary nature of the translation strategy as the hypothesis is pursued.

---

[13] Cf. Pym (1998: 106ff) who sees the comparison of translations as more profitable than the comparison of source text and target text.

There are two other important aspects of research that must be considered in the research design in translation studies, as in all fields. The first has to do with sample size: general conclusions must be based on a sufficiently large sample to justify any extension of conclusions to other situations. Achieving an adequate sample size is not always easy in translation studies, particularly when one is dealing with a unique translation of a source text, translations of the work of a single author, the output of a single translator, and so forth. One reason my own research utilized the example of *Táin Bó Cúailnge* is that there were ten translations of the text ranging over the better part of a century, as well as numerous adaptations, refractions and rewritings. These translations offered a sample of sufficient size to suggest reliable conclusions; few other texts in Irish have been so widely and persistently translated, and there is no other extended Irish heroic narrative that would have served as such a basis of research.

A second principle to keep in mind in making a research design in translation studies, as in other fields, is the necessity for a control group. This is a standard of research that is often difficult to incorporate into one's design in translation studies, because there may be few comparable groups of translations or translators to those one is researching. In certain situations (say when one is investigating a single translation) working with a second translation of the same text will offer a small control sample – and a sample that is often more helpful than using the source text as the control and reference point, because of the issue of self-referentiality of translations that I referred to earlier. In some circumstances a different set of passages within the source text from those one is researching can act as the control group: one can pick passages that are neutral with respect to the issues being investigated. In some cases a control group of parallel texts can be used, either within the same source culture or in an alternate source culture. In the case of translations of early Irish heroic tales, for example, one might use as a control group translations of *Beowulf* or of *La Chanson de Roland* or even of Icelandic sagas. In certain circumstances the control group for such a study might be another genre of the same source literature. But often I have found that for the sort of non-quantified research that is most common in translation studies it is sufficient to use a sort of virtual control group: to draw comparisons with parallel translation situations that are already established in translation studies scholarship. Such comparisons are threaded through my own published research on translation, and they are there in part to compensate for a more rigorous experimental control sample. These issues of sample size and control group are especially essential to address in situations where translation materials are fragmentary, sparse or incomplete.[14]

---

[14] There is an exception that proves the rule: if the structure of the hypothesis that one is pursuing is to establish a counterexample to a position taken as a theoretical or empirical commonplace in translation studies, then obviously a single case study or a very small sample will be sufficient. Such hypotheses are parallel to certain forms of mathematical proof or logical proof, where a

Clearly what I have outlined here is an empirical programme of research, but to be *empirical* is not necessarily to be *objective*.[15] In fact all research, including scientific research, is subjective, influenced by ideas and beliefs related to subject positions, frames of reference, interpretation, mental concepts and received meanings. This realization undermined the philosophical doctrine of positivism in the beginning decades of the twentieth century. In the natural sciences the turn away from positivism is particularly associated with the ascendancy of Heisenberg's uncertainty principle, having to do with the impact of the observer and the act of observation upon the data observed in studies of sub-atomic particles, and Gödel's incompleteness theorem, having to do with frames of reference in mathematics. Moreover, increasingly since World War II, natural scientists have spoken out on issues pertaining to subjectivity, urging, for example, awareness of the social positioning of scientific research and scientific conclusions, and stressing the importance of social responsibility in research. Similar realizations led to the crisis of representation in anthropology and ethnography in the twentieth century, as well as other reconsiderations of basic research in the social sciences, history, and so forth.[16] Translation studies is not exempt from these issues, and it would be a serious intellectual anachronism to aspire to be 'objective' in one's research. One can and should, however, aspire to be self-aware about one's subject position and its influence upon a research programme, as well as to interrogate one's presuppositions. And one can and should try to be a responsible member of the human community as a whole, as well as to have good values within the largest frame of reference one is capable of. Even so, research inevitably will be conducted within intellectual and social frameworks – including the normal intellectual tools of models, theories and paradigms – that will undermine pure 'objectivity' (cf. Kuhn 1962). In this regard, in fact, translation studies may be at an advantage compared to many fields, including most fields of the natural sciences, because translation studies routinely involve not just inquiry but meta-inquiry in the course of research. Hence the field itself

---

single counterexample can either demolish a putative theorem or establish a theorem (if the argument itself proceeds by imagining the contrary case).

[15] The *American Heritage Dictionary* defines *empirical* as "relying upon or derived from observation or experiment", where *objective* is "of or having to do with a material object as distinguished from a mental concept, idea, or belief".

[16] See the discussion in Hermans (1999: 144-50) on aspects of research in translation studies and other fields that make it inevitably partial and, hence, subjective. Hermans argues (1999: 146) that the absence of a clear dividing line between object-level and meta-level is a special feature of translation studies that undercuts its objectivity, but in my experience the same sorts of arguments could be extended to most fields including the natural sciences and even, in some cases, mathematics. Luhmann's argument discussed by Hermans (1999: 150) should be viewed in a sense as a recapitulation of Gödel's incompleteness theorem applied to the humanities and social sciences and, hence, as an articulation of a problem in lay terms that has been delineated even more rigorously in such fields as mathematics and physics.

encourages the interrogation of frames of reference, including those of the researcher, potentially making one's biases more perceptible and making it more possible to enlarge one's frame of reference.[17]

There is a reciprocal relationship between theory and research outlined in the research method under consideration. Theory informs the hypotheses that guide research, but in turn the results of research interrogate and refine theory. Such reciprocity can be expressed in terms of Charles Peirce's three forms of logical reasoning: deduction, abduction and induction.[18] In a sense through a process of deduction, the theoretical framework of the research leads to the initial postulates upon which the research is based. The researcher uses abduction – the only mode of reasoning in Peirce's view to introduce new ideas into intellectual inquiry, the creative force of research – to create the hypothesis that guides the construction of the research design from these postulates.[19] In turn data are gathered relevant to the hypothesis and, through induction from the data, the researcher then tests both the hypothesis and, ultimately, the theory behind the hypothesis as well. Thus a rigorous research programme will be inherently self-reflexive, seeking congruence in theory and data through the exercise of all three forms of logical reasoning explicated by Peirce.[20] This self-reflexive process will be stronger if both micro- and macro-concerns and approaches are integrated at each stage of the research and at each level of logical reasoning.

Much of what I have said here, though taking examples from descriptive studies of translation, can be generalized to other types of research in translation studies also, including empirical research about the processes of translation. And I believe that it has implications for pedagogy as well. Certainly in our era when two new infinite orders have opened to us, it makes little sense to teach students the tools of only one of those orders. When teaching how to do research in translation, a teacher will best serve students by instructing them in the full range of issues and by modeling how to connect microscopic investigations with macroscopic ones, using the two orders of magnitude as mutually reinforcing domains to secure strong conclusions. Similarly in teaching students to translate, it will be helpful to teach them not only microscopic techniques but to teach them to assess the other infinite

---

[17] Pym (1998: 27ff., 123-24, and passim) argues that a researcher's subjectivity is important because it informs the decision to work on specific topics and to choose topics that have importance for the present.

[18] For a convenient summary of these aspects of Peirce's thought, see Gorlée (1994: 42 ff).

[19] One reason that some programmatic research in translation studies seems to issue in "flattened" conclusions may be the absence of abduction – hence creativity – associated with the formulation of a specific hypothesis to be tested.

[20] The domain covered by research is also an essential factor in constructing durable theory that will be applicable to the general or arbitrary case, rather than being restricted to the dominant social conventions of the researcher's context; for a more detailed consideration of this point, see Tymoczko (1999: 32ff).

order as well, so they can best contextualize their own translation processes and products, teaching them to understand the cultural implications of their translation choices and to make informed choices. This will not only permit them to best serve their target audience, but to be self-aware about their ideological commitments and entanglements also.

I will conclude by reiterating the ridiculousness of the refusal to engage with both infinite orders that have opened in our time for examining and analyzing texts and cultures. The essential gesture of those in translation studies who attempt to split cultural studies from linguistics – or vice versa – is such a refusal. This gesture is tantamount to putting on blinders willfully, refusing the views and perspectives of alternate optical instruments. It is as if one of Galileo's contemporaries had used either the microscope or the telescope but denied the validity of phenomena revealed by the other. If one's hypothesis is valid, the different perspectives associated with different orders of magnitude should mutually reinforce each other, acting as confirmation and substantiation of one's conclusions. There is very little to fear here except perhaps one's own ignorance of the range and strengths of the tools and techniques that have been developed in both infinite orders opened by the revolution in knowledge in our time.

I believe that the gesture of refusal is often based on the fact that we do not yet control all the new disciplines and methods that were pioneered in the second half of the twentieth century in particular. In some cases we don't even have definitive names for various approaches to texts, never mind a taxonomy of disciplines that will allow students and teachers alike to survey the field of methods and tools to be mastered. All this is complicated by rapidly changing technologies that often intersect with the expansion of intellectual perspectives. It may take us a while to sort this all out, but awareness of our position between the two infinite orders is a first step in the resolution of the issues before us and in our ability to conduct research in translation studies with the most powerful means at our disposal.

References

Drake, Stillman (1980) *Galileo,* Oxford: Oxford University Press.
Encyclopedia Britannica (1974) 15th ed, Chicago: Helen Hemingway Benton.
Gorlée, Dinda (1994) *Semiotics and the Problem of Translation, with Special Reference to the Semiotics of Charles S. Peirce,* Amsterdam: Rodopi.
Hermans, Theo (1999) *Translation in Systems: Descriptive and Systemic Approaches Explained,* Manchester: St. Jerome.
Kuhn, Thomas (1962) *The Structure of Scientific Revolutions,* Chicago: University of Chicago Press.
Pym, Anthony (1998) *Method in Translation History,* Manchester: St. Jerome.
Sengupta, Mahasweta (1990) 'Translation, Colonialism, and Poetics: Rabindranath Tagore

in Two Worlds', in Susan Bassnett and André Lefevere (eds) *Translation, History and Culture,* London: Pinter, 56-63.

----- (1995) 'Translation as Manipulation: The Power of Images and Images of Power', in Anuradha Dingwaney and Carol Maier (eds) *Between Languages and Cultures: Translation and Cross-cultural Texts,* Pittsburgh: University of Pittsburgh Press, 159-74.

Toury, Gideon (1980) *In Search of a Theory of Translation,* Tel Aviv: Porter Institute for Poetics and Semiotics.

----- (1982) 'A Rationale for Descriptive Translation Studies', *Dispositio* 7 (special issue *The Art and Science of Translation,* ed. André Lefevere and Kenneth David Jackson), 22-39.

Tymoczko, Maria (1999) *Translation in a Postcolonial Context: Early Irish Literature in English Translation,* Manchester: St. Jerome.

The Quest for an Eclectic Methodology of Translation Description

EDOARDO CRISAFULLI

Abstract: *In this article I argue in favour of an eclectic methodology in translation studies reconciling descriptive-empirical and critical-interpretative approaches, even though the former focus on quasi-scientific methods and the latter pursue a historical-hermeneutic understanding of translation. It is argued that descriptive translation studies should make a crucial concession and acknowledge the role of evaluation in translation description. The specific view of empiricism underpinning current descriptive approaches – logical empiricism – is at fault insofar as it promotes a positivistic, value-free conception of research. On the other hand, historical empiricism acknowledges the role of evaluation in research. Methodological eclecticism, however, also requires us to go beyond system-oriented thinking and its search for patterned regularities (or norm-governed behaviour). It is suggested, in particular, that translation scholars should harmonize quantitative analysis (which focuses on patterned regularities) and qualitative analysis (which deals with single choices of a personal-ideological nature). If we are to achieve methodological eclecticism we must enhance the sophistication or explanatory power of descriptive translation studies. But this requires descriptivist empiricists to foreground the human translator and the hermeneutic issues involved in the translation process.*

1. A false opposition: descriptive-empirical approaches vs. critical-interpretative approaches

The predicament of translation studies at the present moment is the lack of an eclectic methodological framework capable of accommodating a wide range of research interests. Declarations of intent in the critical literature stress the need to go beyond a single perspective or discipline, but in actual fact we still have some way to go before a fully-fledged eclectic approach is established. At the same time, no reflection on eclecticism can afford to disregard Mona Baker's caveat: "Translation scholars must recognize that no approach, however sophisticated, can provide the answer to all the questions raised in the discipline nor the tools and methodology required for conducting research in all areas of translation studies" (1998: 280).

In my opinion it is possible to develop an eclectic approach which harmonizes the insights of Gideon Toury (1995), Mona Baker (1993, 1996), André Lefevere (1992), Anthony Pym (1998), Susan Bassnett (1991), Lawrence Venuti (1995, 1998) and Theo Hermans (1985, 1995, 1999) – even though these scholars seem to have totally different methodological approaches.[1] Toury's and Baker's inductive and quasi-scientific methods (required by the search for patterned regularities) seem at odds with Pym's emphasis on the human translator and historical research in general. Bassnett's, Lefevere's, Venuti's and Hermans's ideological concerns with 'manipulation' or the translator's agency demand an historical and critical-interpretative approach rather than a purely scientific one.

In this essay I want to argue that the – in my view, false – opposition between empirical-descriptive and critical-interpretive approaches is a hurdle on the path towards methodological eclecticism in translation studies. The disagreement between empiricists-descriptivists (Toury and Baker) and translation historians (Pym, Levefere, Bassnett, Venuti and Hermans) has more to do with methodological issues than with philosophical foundations. Among the questions relevant to *all* translation scholars are the following: what counts as adequate evidence in translation research? A single target text? A corpus of 'representative' texts? Can a corpus be designed in such a way as to be representative? When we have reached agreement on the nature of the evidence by setting up an adequate corpus, which features of translation behaviour should we single out as relevant or meaningful? Do we look for regularities of behaviour or instances of creativity on the part of translators? In this article I shall attempt to deal with these questions.

The different methodological approaches in translation studies may be reconciled in the context of a unifying epistemological principle – empiricism – provided descriptive translation studies broadens its scope and takes into account the observations of translation historians. A quarter of a century ago Giulio Preti convincingly argued that empirical and historical approaches can be harmonized: historical research has a philological aspect (e.g. explaining agency and causation, that is, linking causes and effects in a given context), which requires empirical verification, while empirical research cannot shun the evaluative judgments that typify historical studies – 'observable facts' may very well be the point of departure for empiricists, but it is the scholar's interpretation that imposes a conceptual order on facts and assesses the significance of empirical data in the first place (Preti 1975: 155).

Therefore, I do not believe that "the empirical bias of the descriptive approach" *per se* is a flaw, as Hermans (1999: 44) seems to contend. Rather, one of the major problems with current empirical-descriptive approaches is their reductionist

---

[1] I make no reference to Even-Zohar's polysystem theory because, as Hermans (1999: 102) argues, "there is no necessary connection" between this theory and descriptive-empirical approaches to translation studies. This of course is not to deny the ground-breaking significance of Even-Zohar's thinking. By the same token, I have not referred to a number of important descriptivists such as, for example, Andrew Chesterman and José Lambert for the sake of economy and conciseness. The position of these (and other) scholars of a descriptive-empiricist persuasion is discussed by Hermans (1999), the most nuanced and comprehensive account of descriptive translation studies to date.

(scientist-positivistic) view of empirical research (further on I shall discuss the other problem of descriptive translation studies, that is, its system-oriented thinking), which is typical of "logical empiricism" (Norris 1997: 67), not of empiricism *tout court*. Logical empiricism posits a radical separation between subject and object, evaluation and fact; it claims that there is a correspondence between statements, predictive hypotheses, etc. on the one hand, and, on the other, "some discrete (observable) state of affairs that would assign them a determinate truth value" (Norris 1997: 72). This view of empiricism has been attacked in many philosophical quarters because "it fails to explain how observation could ever take place – or achieve articulate form – in the absence of some given 'ontological scheme', some pre-existing theory of what should count as an adequate (scientifically admissible) observation statement" (*ibid.*).

A sophisticated version of empiricism that takes into account the hermeneutic dimension – I suggest the term 'historical empiricism' – does not require us to believe that facts are immediately or objectively perceivable, as if there were no pre-existing theories or expectations guiding their selection and categorization. The rejection of logical empiricism does not imply that we have to embrace a radical form of epistemological scepticism. I subscribe to Christopher Norris's anti-relativistic stance: while rejecting a narrow view of empirical inquiry, he makes it clear that poststructuralism is at fault for dismissing "questions of truth, validity and method" as "remnants of an obsolete 'positivist' paradigm with its own covert ideological agendas" (Norris 1997: 7).

Methodological issues are at the forefront of translation studies. I shall focus on empirical-descriptive approaches because I think we ought to enhance their explanatory power and theoretical sophistication within an eclectic view of translation studies. In this respect historical approaches are on safer ground: evaluation and hermeneutics lie at the core of historical studies. The purpose of my proposed eclecticism is to throw out the bathwater (the positivistic slant of descriptive translation studies) without losing the baby (methodological rigour, empiricism and the notion of rational and systematic inquiry). An eclectic methodology is designed to bridge the gap between empirical-descriptive and critical-interpretive (or historical) approaches if it is to shed maximum light on the phenomenon of translation.

2.   Description and evaluation in translation research

But why are empiricist descriptivists under the spell of logical empiricism (and consequently play down the role of evaluation in translation research)? Let us consider the thinking of a leading descriptivist, Gideon Toury.

Toury constructed a diagrammatic representation of James Holmes's sketch of translation studies, according to which the discipline has two branches: pure and applied. The first is divided into descriptive translation studies and translation theory.

Translation theory establishes general principles with the aim of explaining and predicting the phenomena of translating (Holmes 1988: 71). It uses the results of descriptive translation studies together with insights from various other disciplines (linguistics, comparative literature, sociology, etc.) to develop theories and models with explanatory and predictive power. Applied translation studies (applied extensions of translation studies in Toury's revised map of translation studies, see *Figure 1*) are concerned with practical applications like translator training.

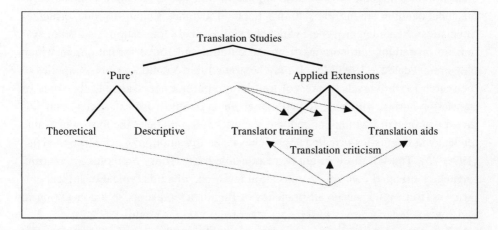

Figure 1: Toury's diagram mapping the "relations between Translation Studies and its applied extensions" (1995: 18)

I agree with Holmes (1988: 71) and Toury (1995: 1) that the study of translation, whether theoretical or descriptive, is an empirical discipline concerned with describing what translation *is* rather than what it *should be*. Toury, in actual fact, seems to posit a gap between theoretical and descriptive studies on the one hand, and their applied extensions on the other (even though he envisages some kind of contact between these branches of the discipline); the latter are concerned with setting norms rather than with explaining or predicting facts of real life. Descriptivists "refuse to draw any conclusions in the form of recommendations for 'proper' behaviour" (Toury 1995: 2). I believe historians should reason along the same lines. Even Hermans, who criticizes the limitations of descriptive-empirical approaches, argues that "the critical task of translation theory does not consist in advocating this or that resistant or oppositional or compliant or fluent or any other mode of translating" (1999: 156; I shall return to Hermans's view of translation theory's critical task).

So far so good. Toury's point of departure, empiricism, is theoretically sound. It is unfortunate, however, that Toury's thinking is at times an obstacle on the path to eclecticism. The fault lies with his belief that an anti-prescriptive stance requires the banishment of evaluation. Let us consider his statement that descriptive translation studies do not establish appropriate translation methods, any more than linguistics determines "appropriate ways of language use" (Toury 1995: 17). I accept the first part of this statement but not the second. The analogy whereby the goals of descriptive translation studies coincide with those of a reductionist conception of linguistics is misleading. Descriptivists, Toury goes on to argue, should "refrain from value judgments in selecting subject matter or in presenting findings" (1995: 2). This highly problematic conviction leads him to adopt a scientistic attitude which emphasizes neutrality and objectivity. And Toury's value-free conception of linguistics, which he applies to translation research, is a source of misunderstanding among translation scholars. Lawrence Venuti, for one, criticizes linguistics-oriented approaches, which, he claims, study translation "as a set of systematic operations autonomous from the cultural and social formations in which they are executed" (1998: 25). It may be argued that Venuti's criticism applies to the search for universals or laws of translation, but not necessarily to the study of translation norms, which are rooted in a given, and thus historical, society and culture. Even though I would not endorse Venuti's assertion that "the most worrisome tendency in linguistics-oriented approaches is their promotion of scientific models" (1998: 25), Toury himself might be responsible for it. Toury promotes a scientific, linguistics-oriented concept of translation research, which is typical of logical empiricism. But by no means all branches of linguistics presuppose a conception in which the scholar's aim is to separate "fact from value" (Venuti 1998: 29).[2]

Let us pursue further the analogy between descriptive translation studies and linguistics. My aim is not to determine the nature of linguistic inquiry, but simply to throw light on Toury's conception of empirical research.[3] As Deborah Cameron (1995: 4) points out, linguists often equate description with the search for objective facts and prescription with a concern for subjective value judgements. But the distinction between norm-observing and norm-enforcing statements is a highly controversial one in linguistics. Linguists like Cameron (1995) and Talbot Taylor (1990) regard normativity as inherent in descriptions. Taylor casts doubt on the

---

[2] Venuti suggests that empirical-descriptive approaches would benefit from certain types of historical and social thinking. He recommends that "empirical approaches, whether based on linguistics or polysystem theory, be qualified and supplemented by the concept of the remainder and the social and historical thinking that it demands of translators and translation scholars" (1998: 29). Venuti, however, focuses on a narrow and politicized concept, the 'remainder', which is unlikely to help in bridging the gap between descriptive-empirical and critical-interpretative approaches. I believe Hermans (1999) is nearer the mark: as we shall see, he emphasizes the importance of a historical-hermeneutic understanding of translation.

[3] The fact that Toury is influenced by a certain conception of linguistics does not mean   we should pursue the analogy with descriptive translation studies any further than necessary. For example, norms are not to be equated with linguistic rules; and even though they condition individual translators, they may be flouted. Moreover, Toury's view of descriptive translation studies is more sophisticated than the linguistic theories separating language and social/historical context (see Milroy 1992).

dualism between descriptive statements, conceived of as purely objective, and normative statements, which rely on authority and power (1990: 21). Statements in authoritative dictionaries, Taylor argues, "are not descriptions of facts, but rather citations of norms" (1990: 24). No matter how neutral the descriptivist considers them to be, their perceived normative force will inevitably affect the linguistic choices of individual speakers. Cameron claims that the point of describing grammar is precisely to establish what the norms are, "so they can be prescribed with confidence to users of the language" (1995: 10).

Milroy's observations are more directly relevant to descriptive translation studies. Milroy, who focuses on the relationship between language and society, believes that language descriptions are normative "because to be accurate they have to coincide as closely as possible with the consensus norms of the community concerned" (1992: 8-9). Yet, he does not equate normative with prescriptive. Unlike Cameron and Taylor, Milroy insists that linguists may distinguish between "*observing* a norm for descriptive purposes and *enforcing* a norm prescriptively" (*ibid.*).[4] But he is also convinced that norm-observing is inseparable from the researcher's value judgments. I too subscribe to this conviction.

I believe that the real obstacle to eclecticism in translation studies is the binary distinction between descriptive statements and value judgments. Toury, it seems to me, is eager to discard value judgments because he equates descriptive translation studies with a reductionist conception of (possibly theoretical) linguistics, whereby evaluation necessarily entails a prescriptive attitude. But value judgments are not always synonymous with prescriptive statements, even though recommendations for proper translation behaviour are obviously based on strong value judgments. Cameron's (1995: 4) and Taylor's (1990: 25) point that an ideologically neutral linguistic science does not exist applies to descriptive translation studies, too.

Toury seems reluctant to accept the implications of his own thinking. Empiricism does not necessarily imply that a descriptive framework can be conceived in a vacuum, that is, without an act of interpretation. Toury, in fact, specifically refers to

---

[4] Clearly, the distinction between norm-observing and norm-enforcing statements is absolute only within descriptive translation studies, and not in translation studies as a whole (the applied extensions of the discipline are concerned with prescribing norms). The point I wish to make is that analogies between descriptive translation studies and (the various branches of) linguistics should be employed and explained carefully, otherwise Venuti's claim that Toury's scientific approach "may well discourage the study and practice of translation experimentalism" (1998: 30) would be justified. But I find it hard to believe that translators may be affected by descriptions of translations in the same way as language users are influenced by language descriptions in authoritative dictionaries. It does not make sense to presuppose (as Venuti does) that Toury's law of 'growing standardization' (or translation conservatism), according to which translators tend to adopt established repertoires, discourages translators from experimenting with the target text, if only because it merely describes what they allegedly tend to do anyway. Toury's law is simply an empirical observation; individual translators may choose to flout it.

"*descriptive-explanatory* studies executed within" descriptive translation studies (1995: 15). And no explanatory study can banish value judgments. One has to acknowledge that no descriptive framework of analysis is immune to interpretive bias. Although there are degrees of bias (the search for universals of translation may be less dependent on value judgments than historical investigations), the fact remains that value judgments influence the selection of data as well as the descriptive categories of analysis and the explanatory theories into which these are organized. This view is widely accepted even by those epistemologists who oppose poststructuralism. Susan Haack, for example, contends that "the epistemologist cannot be a completely detached observer, because to do epistemology at all (or to undertake *any* kind of inquiry) one must employ some standards of evidence, of what counts as a reason for or against a belief – standards which one takes to be an indication of truth" (1993: 13).

It is unsurprising that several influential translation scholars disagree with Toury's scientistic approach. The opposition to Toury's view of objectivity and neutrality is strongest among translation historians. Hermans observes that "the claim to neutrality or objectivity is already an ideological statement in itself" (1999: 36). Translation scholars, Hermans argues, need a critical theory which "tells the observer what to look for and how to assess the significance of what is being observed" (1999: 34). José Lambert has cast doubt on the very distinction between evaluation and description (1991: 31). Anthony Pym, too, stresses that a totally neutral description is a chimera (1998: 9), and Dirk Delabastita is convinced that the selection and description of historical facts "will always be directed by certain *a priori* assumptions" (1991: 140). Venuti makes the same point: "even at the level of devising and executing a research project, a scholarly interpretation will be laden with the values of its cultural situation" (1998: 28-9).

Let us consider the seminal notion of translation norms. Unlike universals or laws of translation (which I shall consider in the next section), these are historically determined and have (a measure of) prescriptive force within a given target tradition. It is beyond the scope of this paper to explain in depth the rationale behind the concept of translation norms (an account is provided in Hermans 1999). Suffice it to say that translation norms allegedly reveal the concept of translation in a given society at a specific moment in time, that is, they are representative of translation behaviour from an historical perspective. Norms "are a product of a tradition of translating in specific ways which can only be observed and elaborated through the analysis of a representative body of translated texts in a given language or culture" (Baker 1993: 240).

However, the assumption that corpora may be representative of translation behaviour is highly problematic. How do we decide on the inclusion in a corpus of a certain body of translated texts in a given language or culture? One cannot escape the fact that the very design of corpora arises out of an act of interpretation. For instance, my selection of the most 'representative' Anglo-American translators of

Dante's *Comedy* (discussed in Crisafulli 2000) was based on implicit theoretical assumptions, which I took for granted. On what grounds did I include certain translations rather than others, and regard them as representative of a specific tradition of rewriting Dante? The design of my corpus was motivated partly by considerations of literary merit (I selected what I regarded as the most poetic translations, *which implies an idealized conception of literature*) and partly by a preconceived notion of what counts as an adequate translation of Dante's *Comedy* in the first place (I eschewed prose translations and included only a select few verse translations, *which presupposes an idealized conception of translation*). The ideologically-biased nature of historical corpora, and consequently of translation norms, casts serious doubt on any strict dualism between description and evaluation.

This is not to say that my corpus does not yield interesting facts about the behaviour of a (more or less representative) group of Anglo-American translators. But can we single out allegedly objective empirical facts, such as translation norms or tendencies of translation behaviour, from such a corpus? I believe we can generalize only in tentative terms: empirical facts do not exist independently of the scholar's viewpoint; indeed, it is the scholar who creates the empirical facts of the analysis by making observable (raw) data relevant to his/her perspective. For example, it may be that one's idealized conception of translation leads one to focus on predominantly mainstream or conservative translators. If this is the case the patterns yielded by the analysis will reflect such an *a priori* or idealized conception and show translation to be a fundamentally conservative enterprise.

It is not only corpus design that is ideologically biased. Venuti provides an excellent example of how the very formulation of translation norms may be ideologically charged. Toury formulates a norm whereby a Hebrew translator of Shakespeare's sonnets censors the text by changing the addressee's gender from male to female. This norm ensured the translation's acceptability in twentieth-century Hebrew culture where homosexuality was unacceptable. According to Venuti:

> Toury's account, even if he doesn't brand the translation homophobic, is nonetheless distanced from homophobia [...] it seems clear that his formulation of the norm is slanted towards liberalism. If he shared the translator's conservatism, Toury might have called the translation a voluntary expression of moral propriety. (Venuti 1998: 29)

The scholar's categories of analysis cannot be neutral descriptions. They imply certain political and ideological assumptions. From this point of view it is correct to say that the researcher's beliefs govern all types of historical scholarship. But the search for methodological eclecticism requires us to proceed further and take a critical look at the notion of 'patterned regularity', which underpins descriptive or system-oriented thinking.

3. Patterned regularities vs. idiosyncrasy and creativity

The problem of translation research is how to achieve a balance between conformity and regularity, on the one hand, and change and creativity on the other; between norm-governed (the trans-individual or collective dimension, which verges on the sociological) and idiosyncratic behaviour (the individual dimension, which foregrounds the human agent); between universal (a-historical) tendencies and personal or text-specific choices.

An eclectic approach integrating quantitative and qualitative types of analysis goes some way towards reconciling these apparent dichotomies. Obviously, this reconciliation will not be successful unless translation scholars of all persuasions become aware that description and evaluation are inseparable. However, this is not sufficient by itself. We must also expose the implications of system-oriented thinking, which is closely linked with empirical-descriptive approaches.

Let us consider Toury's thinking again. Following in Holmes's footsteps (1988: 78), Toury (1995: 11) treats all the branches of translation studies as interdependent but sees the relationship between the theoretical and descriptive branches as lying at the core of the discipline. The findings of descriptive studies lead to the establishment of *"regularities of behaviour"* which in turn will enable theoreticians "to formulate a series of coherent *laws*" (Toury 1995: 16).

Toury's laws are similar to Baker's (1993, 1996) universals of translation, patterns of linguistic behaviour which are inherent in translation. Toury's law of growing standardization, for example, states that translators tend to favour the established or habitual "options offered by a target repertoire" (1995: 268), that is, they tend to be conservative. Baker also notes that translators across a variety of languages have been observed to simplify, disambiguate and make explicit the target text's message (Baker 1993: 243, 246; 1996: 176).

The first problem for translation historians is that the search for universals or laws isolates certain features in an abstract realm where historical problems have no or very little bearing. As Venuti (1998: 25) puts it, the search for laws and universals presupposes a conception in which one should "purify translation practices and situations of their social and historical variables". True, this is only one aspect of descriptive research into translation (the study of translation norms is not a-historical, but it is trans-individual). The second and more serious problem is that scholars of a descriptive-empiricist persuasion tend to subsume all the translator's interventions – even those that occur in single target texts – under the concept of norm-governed or patterned behaviour.

The translator's choices, Toury claims, are not the unaccountable product of idiosyncratic decisions on his/her part. The translator's choices show internal consistency. Toury (1995: 147) in fact asserts that "decisions made by an individual translator while translating a single text are far from erratic. Rather, even though by no means all-embracing, they tend to be highly *patterned*". This implies that one has to look for meaningful regularities in the data yielded by the analysis. Lefevere, who reasons along the same lines, claims that "an isolated mistake is, probably, just that, whereas a recurrent series of 'mistakes' most likely points to a pattern that is the expression of a strategy" (1992: 97). And strategies, I should add, might point to tendencies of translation behaviour either in a given historical context (norms) or across cultures and languages (universals of translation).

Although Toury's point of departure is perfectly legitimate, system-oriented thinking neglects the individual translator. One may argue that this is a price that has to be paid: norms, or tendencies, can only be abstracted from a large number of target texts, by considering the features they have in common. Moreover, how may one document the exceptions, or grasp the idiosyncratic choices of the individual translator, if one does not first establish the norms in the target system and the tendencies inherent in translation behaviour?

There is an element of truth in this observation, but the fact remains that current descriptive-empirical approaches over-emphasize the role of norm-governed or patterned behaviour. As a result, it is undeniable that they document "the conformity, not the exceptions" (Gentzler 1993: 133) precisely because they are concerned with patterned regularities and "the discovery of abstract laws" (Pym 1998: 123). It may well be that translators worldwide tend to be conservative; but the law of conservatism remains purely abstract if we do not constantly apply it to a myriad of – sometimes highly creative – human translators living in historically determined circumstances.

An obstacle on the path towards methodological eclecticism, however, is not only the a-historical interest in laws and universals. In fact, descriptivist empiricists are also concerned with the cultural functions of translation and tend to correlate textual and extra-textual features, which clearly entails a historical perspective (Hermans 1999: 39). Yet when it comes to devising historical studies, descriptivist-empiricists focus on the sociological (the power of institutions, the collective or social forces behind norms), which is detrimental to understanding the individual (or text-specific) dimension of historical research. For example, Delabastita, who subscribes to descriptive translation studies, advocates "a historical and norm-governed concept" (1994: 241) of translation – where the two adjectives seem inextricably linked – and therefore focuses on the study of patterned behaviour in a corpus of target texts rather than untypical choices in one or more target texts.

Descriptivist empiricists should enhance the explanatory power of their historical research. Individual translators are bearers of social meanings, but some of their interventions may be purely personal or rooted in specific aspects of the target tradition. Translators are not simply in the grip of powerful translation and poetic norms; they may have their own ideological agendas. In this respect Pym's observation that Toury's approach, which emphasizes "stability rather than change", overlooks conflict and tension in translation, remains pertinent (1998: 115). No doubt there is both consensus *and* conflict in target traditions. Translation research should consider change, which tends to be norm-breaking, and shifting power relationships, including the question of "who establishes and retains norms" (*ibid.*). Interestingly, the analogy with linguistics is, again, revealing. Cameron (1995: 17), too, believes that conflict should be the object of serious consideration: "conflict renders visible the processes of norm-making and norm-breaking, bringing into the open the arguments that surround rules".

In my research I have focused on an extremely successful translator, H. F. Cary (1792-1844), who complied with coeval norms (Crisafulli 1996, 1997, 1999). It is not surprising that I have tended to subscribe to a predominantly rule-governed view of translation: Cary adhered to mainstream translation practice. I now believe that one should consider disruptive or innovative translators, too. But even if one deals with mainstream translators, it is possible to escape an exclusively norm-governed view of translation. If we intend to pursue methodological eclecticism the solution lies not only in considering conflict and change, but also in focusing on types of translation behaviour ('strategic interventions'), which are not norm-governed or patterned, even though by no means unaccountable or erratic. In other words, we should consider the translator's personal/ideological dimension.

4.   Systematic semiotics

The notion of patterned, norm-governed behaviour, important as it is, cannot in itself throw maximum light on a target text's features. I suggest we employ the term 'systematic semiotics', which harmonizes systematic behaviour (translation strategies are patterned regularities) with the semiotic nature of the translator's choices. The mere act of employing a descriptive framework implies that there are identifiable linguistic features in the source text, which may or may not be transferred to the target text. These may be subjected to a (rational) systematic semiotics, that is, formal features may be subsumed into descriptive categories ('strategies'). Consider, for example, the categories 'zero translation' and 'bowdlerization', which consist in the elimination of tangible features in the source text. Clearly, the analysis of the translator's ideological-personal choices requires a sophisticated hermeneutic approach that does not consider patterns or regularities.

Whereas linguistics tends to be concerned with communities rather than individual speakers, descriptive translation studies should be concerned with both the collective (tendencies of behaviour) *and* the human translator. Descriptive translation studies overlap with linguistics *and* literary criticism and historical studies. Linguists may indeed discard untypical occurrences as idiosyncratic, that is, as irrelevant to the establishment of patterns of language use, but translation scholars cannot avoid considering untypical (that is, individual) choices if their aim is to understand the human translator. A close analysis of exceptions – including instances of alleged 'mistranslations' – might reveal that they are, in fact, strategic interventions revealing certain (unexpected) aspects of the target text's meaning. Although untypical choices occurring only at specific points of the target text are not norm-governed, they may be extremely significant. Even a single instance may shed light on the translator's outlook.

This is not to belittle the notion of typicality, which underpins norms and universals. Corpus-based empirical investigations have shown that translation behaviour is *highly patterned*, and certainly not random. In an eclectic approach the observations of descriptivists-empiricists and translation historians may be harmonized. Lefevere, who was keen on studying the patterns/regularities in the target text, stressed the "importance of the 'human factor' in translation" (1992: 96-7). Perhaps Lefevere was not entirely successful in reaching a compromise between the collective and the individual, but at least he put the human translator at the top of his agenda.

5. Towards an eclectic methodology of translation description

An eclectic approach to textual analysis should describe the interrelationships between trans-individual (socio-cultural, historical and universal) and individual (the 'human element') factors in translation. This requires translation scholars to harmonize quantitative and qualitative types of research. Quantitative, corpus-based research, which is typical of descriptive-empiricist approaches, yields tendencies or regularities of translation behaviour (whether historically determined or universal). These may throw light on a number of strategies used by translators: the universal 'explicitation-disambiguation' has enabled me to account for (rather than criticize) H. F. Cary's frequent explanatory interpolations in his rewriting of the *Comedy* (see Crisafulli 1996) (there are still scholars who take translators to task for adding to the target text). Qualitative analysis, on the other hand, is based on a critical-interpretative approach to the textual evidence. It attempts to link the translator's interventions with the coeval historical context, and aims at revealing the individual translator's politico-ideological outlook.

I suggest a model of textual analysis which considers the target text from three perspectives: poetics, translation-specific factors and ideology. The model, which is particularly suited to the analysis of translations produced before the twentieth century, is deeply influenced by Lefevere's (1992) conception of the role of ideology and poetics in literary translation, by Venuti's (1995) studies on the canon of fluency in the Anglo-American tradition, and by Baker's (1993, 1996) and Toury's (1995) theorizing on laws and universals of translation.

Towards a systematic semiotics of the target (literary) text
(I) Some categories of textual analysis revealing norm-governed/ patterned behaviour

- **Poetic strategies**:
  (1) *bowdlerization* (are there instances of coarse language in the source text which the translator has 'censored'?);
  (2) *euphemism* (is there a tendency to tone down the source text's style?);
  (3) *poeticizing* (e.g. does the translator consistently use poetic markers/ poeticisms? What kind of poetic repertoire does s/he draw from?);
  (4) *archaizing* (is the target text enveloped in an archaic patina – that is, standard archaic usage and/or archaic poeticisms?);
  (5) *zero translation* (are there features/parts of the source text which are omitted in the target text?)

  Most poetic strategies can be accounted for in terms of translation norms and literary values (e.g. the norm prescribing that the translation of an epic poem like Dante's *Comedy* requires an elevated literary style) and/or in terms of a historically determined and culture-specific canon (such as the stategies of transparency and fluency in the Anglo-American tradition).

- **Translation strategies**:
  (1) *Readability* (by what means does the translator achieve fluency?). This strategy is accountable in terms of the historically determined canon of transparency-fluency and Toury's trans-individual law of translation whereby translators tends to simplify the original's textual make-up.
  (2) *Clarification and explicitation* (are there any explanatory interpolations, periphrases, etc. in the target text?): this seems to be a universal feature of translation (trans-individual and a-historical), but surely there must be some variation from one translator to another when it comes to the pervasiveness of these strategies.
  (3) *Generalized compensation*, which is a form of patterned behaviour in the target text (does the translator consistently make intensifying lexical additions throughout the target text, e.g. in order to compensate for the loss of the original rhetorical strength?)

(II) Some categories of textual analysis revealing the translator's outlook: the translator's (political, ideological) interventions in the target text
  (1) *Textual criticism* (does the translator intervene in paratexts and discuss alternative textual variants?). This category describes one possible type of personal interventions – those reflecting the translator's hermeneutics or translation theory (e.g. a translator may want to show the elusive nature of translation and thus take on the function of textual critic).
  (2) *'Mistranslations'* (are there any instances of 'mistranslation' which could be explained in terms of the translator's outlook or political agenda?)
  (3) *Manipulations* (does the translator manipulate certain parts of the source text for politico-ideological reasons?)

(4) *Personal-ideological interventions* (does the translator put forward a non-manipulative politico-ideological reading which, however legitimate, reveals his/her distinctive outlook)?

(III) Types of analysis (see *Table 1*): *quantitative* analysis for regularities of behaviour – translation strategies reflecting norms, canons, universals; and the desire to compensate consistently throughout the target text; *qualitative* analysis for politico-ideological interventions, acts of textual criticism and instances of compensation other than generalized. Generalized compensation is a strategy attempting to make up for the loss of a recurrent, stylistic feature of the source text. Conversely, displaced and contiguous types of compensation occur in specific parts of the target text. Instances of displaced and contiguous compensation are linked to specific losses (e.g. the loss of a pun in the source text) and may be consistent with interventions motivated by the translator's poetics and/or ideology (see Harvey 1995 and Crisafulli 1996).

As Hermans rightly argues, existing models of translation description do not provide "much guidance as to which passages to select for detailed study" (1999: 70). Clearly, when one deals with qualitative analysis "interpretation and judgment" (*ibid.*)

Patterned regularities	Strategic interventions
Realized in the target text's textual strategies, which may be compared with tendencies observed in corpora of translated texts.	Realized in sensitive parts of the target text. Strategic interventions reveal the translator's outlook.
Type of analysis: quantitative	Type of analysis: qualitative
Type of approach: inductive-scientific	Type of approach: critical-interpretative
Focus on trans-individual factors and generalized textual features	Focus on individual translator and text-specific features
Translation norms	Ideological interventions; manipulations
Translation canon(s	Acts of textual criticism
Universals/laws of translation behaviour	Choices of a personal nature; 'mistranslations'
Generalized features of the target text (e.g. generalized compensation)	Interventions located at specific parts of the target text (e.g. displaced and contiguous compensation)

Table 1: Types of investigation and analyses that characterize, respectively, the search for patterned regularities in the target text and the study of the translator's personal/ ideological interventions.

are of the utmost importance. When we select passages for textual analysis, we operate on the assumption that they will yield interesting observations. The very process of selecting data – like the ensuing textual analysis itself – is a complex interpretative act. Therefore, it is simply not possible to lay down hard-and-fast rules for correct qualitative analyses of all target texts. We can only go some way towards developing a methodology facilitating the researcher's task. For example, the translation scholar should consider the translator's biography, his/her declarations of intent and whatever may throw light on his/her background. One should then proceed on the assumption that the translator's outlook will surface at specific sensitive points of the target text (including paratexts). This is the crucial question to qualitative analysis: are there any sensitive parts in the source text that the translator is likely to manipulate, modify or interpret in a specific way, given his/her outlook?

The distinction between poetic and translation strategies cannot be absolute. We can only tentatively categorize the data according to an alleged predominant function. Moreover, the very distinction between trans-individual factors (such as norms) and 'the human translator' is sometimes relative. Even poetic strategies reveal something about the individual translator: his/her unique response to social/cultural pressures or norms; his/her choice of diction within the range of available, that is, permitted options (the translator may be allowed to archaize or modernize the target text). Translators are not simply in the grip of overpowering norms, canons, etc., which are mechanically reflected in the target text. They participate in an intellectual-cultural *milieu* and their choices have to be set within a context, but they also have their own distinctive personalities. Certain interventions in the target text may be highly original or even unique; and, more importantly, single choices may be extremely significant from a politico-ideological point of view.

Clearly, we cannot discard the idea of meaningful patterns when it comes to categorizing all the features in the target text, but I prefer the term 'consistency' when it comes to interventions of an ideological or personal nature, which occur only at specific sensitive points of the target text. If a few choices on the ideological axis are consistent with a certain hypothesis (e.g. a Protestant translator could produce a Protestant-inspired reading of Dante's *Comedy*), we may employ a concept like 'ideological agenda' to subsume them. The qualitative analysis of ideological interventions in particular will always be laden with the scholar's own politico-ideological beliefs.

6.   Conclusions: the critical task of translation theory

Although existing descriptive-empirical models are not totally inadequate, they cannot throw maximum light on the target text without the contribution of historical and critical-interpretative approaches. Toury and Baker have grasped the importance of empiricism – the basic epistemological principle underpinning descriptive research in translation – but their approach is far from uncontroversial. Their emphasis on patterned regularities fails adequately to account for all the phenomena occurring in the translation process.

According to Baker, descriptive translation studies should provide the methodology and research procedures "to enable the findings of individual descriptive studies to be expressed in terms of generalizations about translation behaviour" (1993: 241).

This is an important goal, but it neglects crucial dimensions of translation research. Baker emphasizes the ancillary role of case studies, their usefulness being judged in terms of the contribution they make to uncovering regularities or tendencies. As I have repeatedly pointed out, descriptive translation studies must also provide the methodological principles enabling scholars to study the interrelationship between patterned translation behaviour and the translator's personal choices.

The goal of descriptive translation studies is not only to discover scientific laws with predictive power but also to understand the significance of what I have termed 'text-specific or strategic (personal) interventions', which can reveal a great deal about the human translator. Only by harmonizing system-oriented and critical-interpretative thinking will descriptive translation studies be able to account for the widest range of factors that have a bearing on the target text.

The observations made so far imply that we must broaden the goals of descriptive translation studies. As Hermans points out, empirical-descriptive approaches have focused on "questions surrounding the production, reception and historical impact of translation – especially literary translation" (1999: 44). This is why descriptivist empiricists have developed a sociology of translation, thereby neglecting important dimensions such as "the philosophy of translation, or the mental and cognitive operations of the translation process itself" (*ibid.*). I agree with Hermans (1999: 147) that translation studies as a whole should operate at three interconnected levels: *theory* (which includes the hermeneutics of translation), *analysis* (by which I mean textual analysis) and *history* (translation scholars should strive to maintain a historical orientation).

In fact, one of the major critical tasks of translation studies as a whole "consists in theorizing the historical contingency of different modes and uses of translation" (Hermans 1999: 147). This task requires scholars to focus on the interpretative operations characterizing the translation process. If scholars of a descriptivist-empiricist persuasion aim at understanding translation as a cultural and historical phenomenon, the issue of interpretation should become their central concern. Descriptive translation studies need to develop a hermeneutics of translation and an epistemology (and this is, again, a methodological task) which, besides being compatible with empiricism, has explanatory – *not only predictive* – power. But this should be the object of another article.

References

Baker, Mona (1993) 'Corpus Linguistics and Translation studies. Implications and Applications', in Mona Baker, Gill Francis and Elena Tognini Bonelli (eds) *Text and Technology: In Honour of John Sinclair*, Amsterdam & Philadelphia: John Benjamins, 233-50.

----- (1996) 'Corpus-based Translation Studies: the Challenges that Lie Ahead', in Harold Somers (ed) *Terminology, LSP and Translation*, Amsterdam & Philadelphia: John Benjamins, 175-86.

----- (1998) 'Translation Studies' in Mona Baker (ed) *Routledge Encyclopedia of Translation Studies*, London & New York: Routledge, 277-80.

Bassnett, Susan (1991) *Translation Studies*, London & New York: Routledge.

Cameron, Deborah (1995) *Verbal Hygiene*, London & New York: Routledge.

Crisafulli, Edoardo (1996) 'Dante's Puns in English and the Question of Compensation', *The Translator* 2(2): 259-76.

----- (1997) 'Taboo Language in Translation', *Perspectives* 5(2): 237-56.

----- (1999) 'The Translator as Textual Critic and the Potential of Transparent Discourse', *The Translator* 5(1): 83-107.

----- (2000) '*The Divine Comedy*', in Olive Classe (ed) *Encyclopedia of Literary Translation into English*, London: Fitzroy Dearborn, 339-44.

Delabastita, Dirk (1991) 'A False Opposition in Translation Studies: Theoretical versus/ and Historical Approaches', *Target* 3(2): 137-52.

----- (1994) 'Focus on the Pun: Wordplay as a Special Problem in Translation Studies', *Target* 6(2): 223-43.

Gentzler, Edwin (1993) *Contemporary Translation Studies*, London & New York: Routledge

Haack, Susan (1993) *Evidence and Inquiry,* Oxford: Blackwell.

Harvey, Keith (1995) 'A Descriptive Framework for Compensation', *The Translator* 1(1): 65-86.

Hermans, Theo (1985) 'Introduction. Translation Studies and a New Paradigm', in Theo Hermans (ed) *The Manipulation of Literature. Studies in Literary Translation*, London & Sydney: Croom Helm, 7-15.

----- (1995) 'Toury's Empiricism Version One', *The Translator* 1(2): 215-23.

----- (1999) *Translation in Systems*, Manchester: St. Jerome.

Holmes, James (1988) *Translated! Papers on Literary Translation and Translation Studies,* Amsterdam: Rodopi.

Lambert, José (1991) 'Shifts, Oppositions and Goals in Translation Studies: Towards a Genealogy of Concepts', in Kitty M. van Leuven-Zwart and Ton Naaijkens (eds) *Translation Studies: The State of the Art*, Amsterdam & Atlanta: Rodopi, 25-37.

Lefevere, André (1992) *Translation, Rewriting and the Manipulation of Literary Fame*, London & New York: Routledge.

Milroy, J. (1992) *Language, Variation and Change*, Oxford: Blackwell.

Norris, Christopher (1997) *Against Relativism. Philosophy of Science, Deconstruction and Critical Theory*, Oxford: Blackwell.

Preti, Giulio (1975) *Praxis ed empirismo*, Turin: Einaudi.

Pym, Anthony (1998) *Method in Translation History*, Manchester: St. Jerome .

Taylor, Talbot J. (1990) 'Which is to be Master? The Institutionalization of Authority in the Science of Language', in John E. Joseph and Talbot J. Taylor (eds) *Ideologies of Language*, London & New York: Routledge, 9-26.

Toury, Gideon (1995) *Descriptive Translation Studies and Beyond*, Amsterdam & Philadelphia: John Benjamins.

Venuti, Lawrence (1995) *The Translator's Invisibility*, London & New York: Routledge.

----- (1998) *The Scandals of Translation*, London & New York: Routledge.

What Texts Don't Tell
The Uses of Paratexts in Translation Research

ŞEHNAZ TAHIR-GÜRÇAĞLAR

Abstract: *The paper deals with the relevance of paratextual elements for historical translation research. Exploring the concept of the paratext as it pertains to translation, it argues that considering translation as a paratext restricts the view of current translation studies and impoverishes its conceptual framework. However, a critical description of paratextual elements surrounding translations can be instrumental in bringing to light the divergent concepts and definitions of translation in a specific period within a culture. The paper maintains that paratexts can offer valuable insight into the production and reception of translated texts by drawing attention to concepts such as authorship, originality and anonymity, which are only covert in translations themselves.*

The basic objective of many research projects in translation history is to explore the socio-cultural contexts in which translated texts are produced and received. Contextualization requires a methodology that can take both translated texts and the meta-discourse on translation into account. The present paper deals with the relevance of textual material that does not form part of the actual translated text itself. Researchers involved in a historical project study different types of material. Such material may consist of actual translations, or of such external data as reviews, letters, advertisements, interviews, diaries and public addresses, to name but a few. In between these, there is a third type of material, largely liminal in nature, which often goes unmentioned. This is the terrain of 'paratexts': prefaces, postfaces, titles, dedications, illustrations and a number of other in-between phenomena that mediate between the text and the reader and serve to 'present' the work (Genette 1997:1). The present paper is concerned with the way extratextual and paratextual material can be used in order to reveal translational phenomena that are either absent or only implicit in translated texts themselves. In this study I will use the term 'text' to refer to translated texts, 'extratexts' to refer to the general meta-discourse on translation circulating independently of individual translated texts, and 'paratexts' to refer to presentational materials accompanying translated texts and the text-specific meta-discourses formed directly around them.

When we wish to analyse the conditions that give rise to a series of translations located in a specific place and period in history, we need to develop criteria to be able to select the relevant material. One of the ways to start a project in translation history is through the selection of translations to be included in the project. This constitutes a major problem in itself, as the definition of translation has been tackled in various ways in translation studies. However, there is currently no agreement on how translation can be defined, except perhaps, deciding that the best way to define translation is probably to undefine it. This is the reason why such terms as 'rewriting' (Lefevere 1992) and 'assumed translation' (Toury 1995) have been resorted to. The term 'rewriting' has been instrumental in emphasizing translation's affinity with other activities that are involved in interpretations of text, and are therefore responsible for their survival, such as the writing of anthologies, literary histories and reader's guides (Lefevere 1992: 2). For its part, 'assumed translation' as understood by Gideon Toury makes translation a target-culture dependent concept, deeming all utterances presented, regarded or revealed as translation legitimate objects of descriptive translation studies (Toury 1995: 32). Toury's concept of translation includes such borderline phenomena as pseudotranslations, concealed translations and adaptations. It would be wrong to conclude that he offers a more restricted view of translation than Lefevere's. Rather than giving up the term 'translation', Toury expands its scope and presents it as a relativized concept.

The concept of 'assumed translation' rests largely on the conditions of the reception of texts, since it is the target audience that will mainly determine a text's status as a translation. This process of reception is affected by a number of factors which are not confined to the text assumed to be a translation. Translated texts can offer us a number of clues hinting at their status as translations. The use of foreign names and foreign cultural elements, the subject matter and an unusual syntax may all alert the reader to the possibility of encountering a translation. Nevertheless, the majority of these clues, such as the title of the text, the name of the author, the name of the translator, the name of the source text, identification of a series the book appeared in, are located before the translated text begins. They appear 'around' the translated text, on the cover, on the title page or in a preface; Genette speaks of 'peritexts' in this case (1997: 5). Alternatively, such presentational elements can be located outside the book and can be found in bibliographies, in advertisements in magazines, in review articles or in interviews; Genette here speaks 'epitexts' (*ibid.*). These elements have a strong bearing on how the text will be received, at least at the beginning, before the process of reading the actual text starts. It can be safely assumed that our first impressions of what distinguishes a translation from a non-translation are shaped not by the translation (or non-translation) itself, but by the way texts are packaged and presented.

1. Translation as paratext

In the conclusion to his seminal work on paratexts, Gérard Genette mentions three types of material which he holds exempt from his investigation on the different types of paratexts even though their "paratextual relevance" seems to him "undeniable": translations, serial publications and illustrations (1997: 405). He is aware of the vast scope of each of these three subjects. For our purposes, the omission of translation is telling, showing as it does Genette's reluctance to tackle the problematic

aspects of elaborating translation as paratext. Considering translation as a derivative activity always based on another text that is chronologically anterior to it makes
translation a commentary on the original text, i.e. a paratextual feature presenting
the original. Nevertheless, defining translation in these terms will serve translation
research little, firstly because it leads to a de-problematization of a number of issues
that have surfaced in translation studies in recent years and, secondly, because it
offers a restricted view of translation, excluding pseudotranslations, which have
become important tools in the hands of researchers who investigate concepts of
translation operational in a given society at a given time. Let me tackle these two
points separately.

Regarding translation as a 'paratext' introduces a hierarchical relationship between the source text and the target text, because it foresees more than chronological
ascendancy. For Genette, the paratext is dedicated to the service of something other
than itself, i.e. the text:

> Whatever aesthetic or ideological investment the author makes in a paratextual
> element (a 'lovely title' or a preface-manifesto), whatever coquettishness or
> paradoxical reversal he puts into it, the paratextual element is always subor-
> dinate to 'its' text, and this functionality determines the essence of its appeal
> and its existence. (Genette 1997: 12)

The implications of this statement for translation research are clear. They mean that
translation, when regarded as paratext, will serve only its original and nothing else –
not the target readership who enjoys it, not the target literary system that may be so
influenced by it as to trigger a series of translations of similar texts, not the translator who may enjoy a reputation for having translated that specific text, not the
publisher who may make considerable money out of that specific title, and not the
source text itself whose 'afterlife' (Benjamin 1968) is ensured by translation.

Furthermore, Genette's conception of translation as 'paratext' runs counter to a
perspective that regards translation as initiated in the target culture and intended to
satisfy a need there (Toury 1995: 27). Neither can it be reconciled with the claims
of postcolonial studies which have demonstrated that translation can be used both
as an instrument of 'education' to civilize the colonized and as a means of creating
an image of the colonized (Niranjana 1992: 21, 13). Moreover, Genette's idea of
the literary text appears static; he does not consider how paratexts may enter into a
dialogical relationship with their main text and alter it. He does take account of how
paratexts may influence the reception of a text, but neglects cases where they may
actually cause a change in its textual features. At least in theory, translation may
have an impact on the sending literary system, and even on source authors themselves. It is enough to think of writers who write in non-Western or 'minor' languages
and whose international fame is largely due to translation. For instance, the Turkish
novelist Orhan Pamuk, all of whose novels have been translated into major Western

languages, may, consciously or unconsciously, bear the translatability of his words in mind during the writing process of his new novels.

Regarding translations as paratexts also restricts the scope of translational phenomena, as the source-oriented view provides no room for such things as pseudotranslations. They cannot be treated as commentaries on other texts, since they lack a source. Yet their exclusion from research into translation history means an impoverishment of the methodological framework, because in displaying features common to translations rather than originals, pseudotranslations allow us to glimpse expectations about translation.

In short, viewing translations as paratexts will not serve a broader view of translation based upon a consideration of the textual features, functions, reception or effects of translated texts as well as the relationship between translational phenomena and other elements in the cultural system at large. Nevertheless, Genette's concept of paratext may become a major source of data in a translation history project because it offers valuable insights into the presentation and reception of translated texts themselves.

2. Paratexts in action

In this section I will focus on two test cases from the Turkish system of translated literature in the 1940s to explore some of the ways in which paratexts may be used in historical translation research. Urpo Kovala (1996) has pioneered this line of research in offering an analysis of the position and functions of paratextual mediation in translated texts. His 1996 article presented a detailed study on the paratextual elements employed by publishers of translated literature in Finland in 1890-1939. He linked paratexts with the idea of ideological closure, demonstrating how paratexts, and especially epitexts, contribute to ideological processes in society (Kovala 1996: 141).

In what follows I will limit myself to the way paratexts offer clues about a culture's definition of translation and enable the researcher to ask questions that trigger further thinking and exploration. This is not to say that paratexts did not reflect ideological stances within the Turkish context. The relationship between paratextual elements and westernization and modernization as a dominant ideology of the early republican period will become clear in the paragraphs below. The market-oriented paratextual strategies may also be read as reflecting an ideology of liberalism. Nevertheless, I will not go into the specific ways paratexts interact with or reinforce these ideologies and restrict the scope of this paper to how they can be used in detecting a culture's divergent definitions of translation and original. The paratexts I will specifically deal with are peritextual and epitextual elements that contain names of writers/translators, generic and parageneric indications, the visual lay-out of covers, titles and series titles.

2.1. Paratexts of translated classics

The first case I will present is from the domain of 'canonical literature', namely the translations commissioned by the state-sponsored Translation Bureau and published by the Ministry of Education. The Translation Bureau (*Tercüme Bürosu*), which was launched under the auspices of the Ministry of Education, was active between 1940 and 1966. The Bureau produced around a thousand titles mainly selected from among Western classics. The Bureau is considered to be a part of the general cultural westernization project of republican Turkey. Indeed, the books produced by the Translation Bureau had an educational function and were intended to transfer the ideas contained in the principal literary works of the West to Turkish readers and especially the young.

The translation activity of the Bureau was accompanied by the publication of a journal, *Tercüme*, which offered reviews of translated books as well as articles on translation theory and criticism. Translators who worked for the Translation Bureau were able to voice their views on translation strategies in *Tercüme*. A review of the articles published in the journal reveals that the translators propagated different strategies, but agreed on a few common denominators such as the significance of 'intellectual' and 'literary' value for the selection of works to be translated, the need to create a balance between 'fidelity' and 'freedom' in translation strategies and the importance of rendering a text in full, without additions or omissions (Bogenç Demirel and Yılmaz 1998).

Translators could make themselves heard and strikingly visible in this journal, so much so that the Minister of Education of the time, Hasan Âli Yücel, felt the urge to write that "a good translator is worth a great author" ("iyi bir mütercim, büyük bir müellif kıymetindedir", 1940: 2). A comprehensive analysis of the norms observed by the translators who worked for the Translation Bureau is still to be carried out. However, we can safely assume that the comments coming from translators and critics writing for a state-sponsored journal on translation reflect a canonical view of translation. This view, which was also endorsed by writers and intellectuals who announced their ideas about translation in other (non-state-sponsored) publications, entailed a rigid definition of translation as something that could only be judged in terms of its intellectual and literary merits and its ability to reflect the tone of the original.

This conception of translation was also mirrored in the paratextual elements of the translations produced by the Translation Bureau. The covers of these books were rather plain, printed in white cardboard and featuring no illustration. It was the white colour that these books were later identified with, and the classics translated by the Translation Bureau came to be called 'White Books' or the 'White Series' by the general readership, terms which are still in circulation today. The front cover carried the name of the author, the title of the book and the logo of the Ministry of Education. The spine featured the author's name and the title of the work. The back cover only showed the book's price, without any promotional features or advertisement. The cover layout of Translation Bureau books became a hallmark of translated canonized literature in Turkey. A private publishing house (Yapı Kredi) which launched a series consisting of translated classics in the early 1990s used a very similar layout, indicating the enduring effects of the content and form of the Translation Bureau books.

The Translation Bureau books had two title pages. The half-title page (Genette 1997: 32) mentioned the series in which the book appeared, i.e. 'Translations from World Literature' or 'School Classics'. The former series was usually accompanied by the mention of the sub-series, such as 'Greek Classics' or 'Modern English Literature'. The book title and the Ministry of Education's logo were also on the half-title page. The translator's name only appeared on the title page (Genette 1997: 33) which followed the half-title page. On the title page the author's name was printed in the top part followed by the title of the work. This was sometimes followed by a parenthesis carrying the work's original title in smaller font size and in lower case as opposed to the author and the Turkish title which were printed in large capital letters. The titles of the books translated by the Translation Bureau remained rather close to the original titles. For instance, *Dr. Jekyll and Mr. Hyde,* translated by Zarife Laçiner and published by the Ministry of Education, bore the title *Dr. Jekyll ile Mr. Hyde*, a word-for-word translation of the original. An earlier translation by Hamdi Varoğlu published by Muallim A. Halit publishing house in 1942 was called *İki Yüzlü Adam* ("The Man with Two Faces"). Likewise while Jonathan Swift's *Gulliver's Travels* was translated into Turkish by İrfan Şahinbaş as *Gulliver'in Seyahatleri* ("Gulliver's Travels") and published by the Ministry of Education in 1943-44, a retranslation by Ercüment Ekrem Talu published by Kanaat Yayinevi in 1946 was titled *Cüceler ve Devler Memleketinde* ("In the Land of Dwarfs and Giants").

If we return to the title page in the Translation Bureau books[1], we see that the translator's name came after the original title, in even smaller fonts. The wording followed a certain format across all of the products of the Bureau: "translated into our language by …". 'Tercüme etmek' and 'çevirmek' were the two terms used to refer to 'to translate'. The translator was occasionally introduced with a professional attribute, such as "teacher of English at the Ankara Second Junior High School" (Stevenson 1944), "instructor at the School of Political Science" (Mann 1945), "associate professor at the Faculty of Language, History and Geography" (Swift 1946), etc.

---

[1] These books were not published by the Translation Bureau. The Bureau consisted of a permanent board and freelance translators who translated both for the Bureau and for private publishers. What I call 'Translation Bureau books' were those books whose translations were commissioned and edited by the members of the board of the Translation Bureau and published by the Ministry of Education.

Illustration 1: Cover page of the Translation Bureau's *Gulliver's Travels*

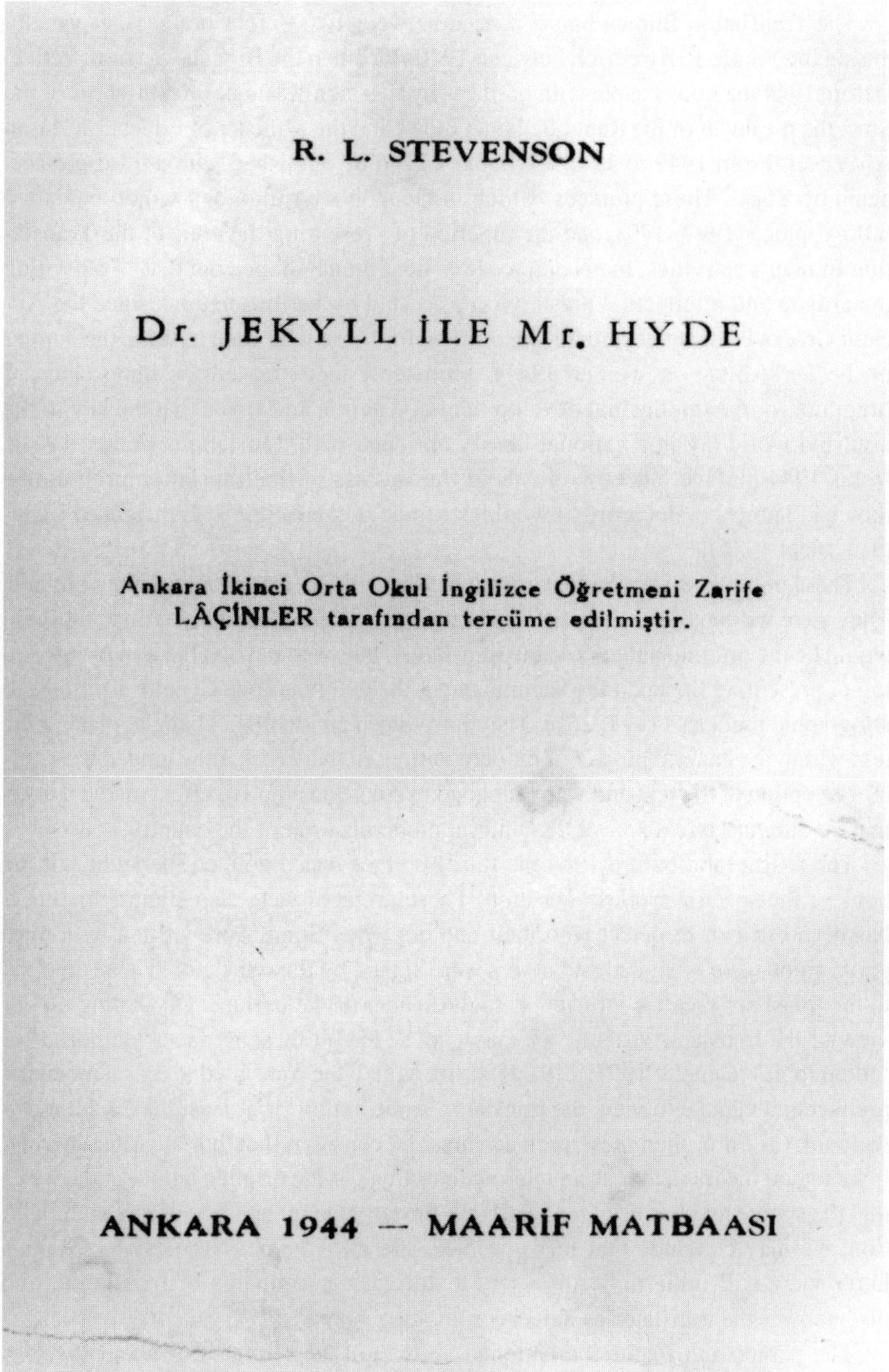

R. L. STEVENSON

Dr. JEKYLL İLE Mr. HYDE

Ankara İkinci Orta Okul İngilizce Öğretmeni Zarife
LÂÇİNLER tarafından tercüme edilmiştir.

ANKARA 1944 — MAARİF MATBAASI

Illustration 2: First title page of the Translation Bureau's *Dr Jekyll and Mr Hyde*

The Translation Bureau books carried between two to four prefaces, especially during the Single-Party period between 1940-46, when the Bureau was most active. Before 1944 the books came with prefaces by two significant political figures of the time, the president of the Republic Ismet İnönü and the Minister of Education Hasan Âli Yücel. From 1943 to 1946 the books would be published with a third preface, again by Yücel. These prefaces, which in Genette's terminology would be called 'allographic' (1997: 179), had the function of presenting the aims of the Translation Bureau's activities. In his preface President İnönü pointed out that "Translating the artistic and intellectual masterpieces created by various nations since the Ancient Greeks is the most valuable instrument for those who want to serve the culture of the Turkish nation" (İnönü 1941). Minister Yücel stressed the importance of literature for the intellectual development of a nation and wrote that the key to the civilized world lay in a national library enriched with translations (Yücel 1941). In his 1944 preface Yücel wrote about the success of the translation programme they had launched, declaring it would continue in the future with increased impetus (Yücel 1944).

These prefaces do not quite conform to Genette's idea of an allographic preface. They were written by senders different from the senders of the text (who in this case would be the original author and the translator), but went beyond the aim of informing or presenting the text they accompanied, the two functions Genette attributes to allographic prefaces (1997: 265). They introduced an ideological angle, placing the text within the general project of modernization. In that sense, they guided the reader's reception of the text and were intended to create an emotive effect on the reader, making him/her feel a part of the cultural modernization of the country.

The fourth (and before 1944 the third) preface was a note on the author of the book or the specific work in question. These prefaces were also allographic but it has been difficult to detect who their authors were. Some were written by a third party, some were unsigned and others were signed by the translator. Those credited to the translator create confusion as to the sender of the preface. Depending on our view of the translator's status, we may choose to call these prefaces 'authorial' or 'allographic' (Genette 1997: 179). If we recognize the translated text as a mediated product and choose to view the translator as the author or at least the co-author of the book (as I do), then these prefaces must be considered authorial. Alternatively, if we regard the translator as an intermediary loyal to the original author and believe that the source text has been rendered into the target language free of any manipulation, we may conclude that these prefaces are allographic. Needless to say, this latter view will undermine the socio-historical determinants of translation and disempower the translator as a decision-making agent.

The paratextual features mentioned above tell us a great deal about the way these translated classics were presented, and possibly received. The paratextual elements also indicate that translators who worked for the Translation Bureau were partially visible. Although their names did not appear on the cover and they were subordinated to the original author in terms of the position and size of their printed names, they were allowed to submit prefaces in which they could inform readers about the text and its author in a manner of their own choosing. However, the frequency with which they were introduced with their 'other' and probably more 'legitimate' professions suggests that translation was not considered a proper occupation and was regarded as a secondary or part-time activity. It is also interesting to see that an overwhelming number of translators were engaged in some form of academic work, teaching at the university or a high school. This indicates how closely the translation of classics was related to education.

Both the articles published in *Tercüme* and the paratextual elements of the translated texts indicate that the Translation Bureau and the translators associated with it conceived of translation within certain parameters which mainly stemmed from translation's relationship with its source text. The publications of the Bureau leave little doubt as to what constituted translation: translation would be a rendering of a specific original text, often identified in the source language in the title pages of the book. The paratextual elements would not accentuate the status of the translation as a mediated text. The cover, as the most salient presentational element of a book's peritext, would first and foremost credit the book to the author of the source text. The translator would be mentioned on the title page only and appear in rather marginal terms, in smaller font and lower case. We can safely assume that borderline phenomena such as pseudotranslations or adaptations fall outside their conception of translation, mainly because these texts are located on the intersection of original writing and translation and defy a one-to-one correspondence between a target text and its source. Indeed the Bureau never published a translation that created uncertainty regarding its source.

When we take a look at translations published by private publishing houses and consider their paratextual elements we encounter a different story. In the following section I will concentrate on the field of popular translated literature, more specifically, the Turkish 'dime' novels of the 1940s. The texts published in this field are dramatically different, not only in terms of the physical features of their paratextual elements, but also the concept of translation that can be deduced from these elements.

2.2. Paratexts of translated popular literature

The extratexts and paratexts encountered around the products of the Translation Bureau reveal that the terms used to refer to translation were mainly "tercüme" and "çevirmek". However, a general survey of other extratextual material published in books, periodicals and dailies as well as paratexts of translations published by private publishers throughout the 1930s and '40s reveals that a variety of terms were used to refer to the act of translation. Not all of these terms would denote the 'canonical' way of defining translation, nevertheless they all refer to products that emerged as a result of contacts with foreign texts.

  Here are some of these terms:
- "tercüme" ('translation' – an Ottoman word of Arabic origin), "tercüman" ('translator');
- "çevirmek" ('to translate' – a neologism introduced in the 1930s), "çevirici"/ "çeviren" ('translator') (the former usage is now obsolete);
- "adaptasyon" (imported from French to refer to adaptation);
- "iktibas" (a word of Arabic origin which means 'quoted after', 'borrowed from');
- "nakil" ('transfer') "nâkil" ('one who transfers') (these two terms, which were operational in the Ottoman and early Republican periods, could refer to both originals and translations and their authors; the mere existence of such a term points to blurred boundaries between the two).

Apart from these, some translations were not presented as translations. This is not to say that they were introduced as originals. There was simply no author's or translator's name on the cover or in the bibliographies covering these works. Yet, the titles of these works leave question marks regarding their origins. For instance, in 1944-45 Güven Yayinevi, a publishing company active mainly in the field of popular literature, published a series called "Meşhur İngiliz Polis Hafiyesi Şerlok Holmes Serisi" ('The Series of the Famous English Police Detective Sherlock Holmes'), which consisted of 83 dime novels offering a mixture of translations and pseudotranslations/originals. Sherlock Holmes was a well-established name among readers of popular literature and there is little doubt that the books would be received as translations instead of originals, although their paratexts did not present the works as translations, even when they were. Let me now present the paratextual elements of one of the novels in this series: *Denizaltının Planı* ("The Submarine Plan", 1944).

  A comparison of the books in this Sherlock Holmes series with original Sherlock Holmes stories reveals that *Denizaltının Planı* was a translation of 'The Adventure of the Bruce-Partington Plans' published in *His Last Bow* (Conan Doyle 1981). Although called a 'book' by its publisher, *Denizaltının Planı* was a booklet of a mere sixteen pages. The price on the back cover was 10 kuruş while books of 150-250 pages published by the Ministry of Education sold for around 100 kuruş. The front cover is rather crowded and colourful. The top part features a promotional statement: "Dünyanin En Zeki ve En Meşhur Polis Hafiyesi Şerlok Holmes" ('Sherlock Holmes, The Most Intelligent and the Most Famous Police Detective of the World'). This part also includes a portrait of a young Sherlock Holmes. The major part of the cover is taken up by an illustration depicting a scene from the story in which Sherlock Holmes is shown as a young, powerfully built man. The illustration features Holmes hitting someone with a stick while an older man is peeping from the door in the

Illustration 3: Cover of Sherlock Holmes Series no. 48, *The Submarine Plan*

background. In the lower left corner we see the serial number of the book which is 48. The book does not have a stripe, perhaps due to the fact that it is not thick enough to have one. The back cover includes the price and an advertisement by the publisher listing other titles in the same series. The bottom part includes the publisher's address. The title page carries the name of the series in which the book appeared "Meşhur İngiliz Polis Hafiyesi Şerlok Holmes Serisi No.: 48" ('The Series of the Most Famous English Police Detective Sherlock Holmes, No.: 48'), followed by the publisher's logo. In the bottom half of the page the story starts.

There is no mention of the writer or the translator. To enquire into the reasons for this anonymity, we have to look beyond the conventional uses of this literary strategy. In his *Paratexts*, Genette mentions the most obvious cases of anonymity and maintains that anonymity takes place if there is an absence of information about the author, if the author is reluctant to give out his name because various forms of anonymity "constituted a precautionary measure in the face of persecution by state or church ... or because they satisfied a doggedly held whim on the part of the author" (Genette 1997: 42-43). In the case *Denizaltının Planı*, rather than an individual decision taken by the translator, anonymity appears as a literary strategy employed in all of the 83 issues of the series. The same strategy was used in another Sherlock Holmes series published in 1955. This information is only available in the paratexts of these stories and anonymity, as a deliberate and widespread strategy, is only apparent in the covers, title pages or catalogues, rather than the texts themselves.

The paratext of *Denizaltının Planı* offers clear indications about the concept of translation which the publishers, or the translator of the story, held. This concept has a much larger scope than the canonized concept reflected in the paratexts issuing from the Translation Bureau. The Translation Bureau paratexts made the text's status as a translation explicit at several stages, starting from the cover. The title, the original author's name, the mention of the original title and the translator's name, together with the name of the series the translations were published in, made it abundantly clear that what we were faced with was a translation. Genette (1997: 11) observes that the paratext "can make known an *intention* or an *interpretation* by the author and/or the publisher: this is the chief function of most prefaces, and also of the genre indications on some covers or title pages (a *novel* does not signify 'This book is a novel', a defining assertion that hardly lies within anyone's power, but rather 'Please look on this book as a novel')". We can also assume that the Translation Bureau paratexts had the specific function of extending a call to the reader to consider the text as a translation. With *Denizaltının Planı* and other books in the series the intention was just the opposite. These works left their authorial origin ambiguous, positioning themselves in a grey area between translation and original writing. One cannot even speak of an authorial visibility here, let alone the translator's visibility. This was the general strategy of the publishers, reflecting an undiscriminating attitude towards translation and original writing, and for that matter towards writers and translators.

The lack of a clear demarcation between translations and original writing can be discerned not only in anonymous works but also in a range of other popular publications which concealed their authorial origins or appropriated the themes or characters of foreign works. Paratexts were manipulated to maintain the same kind of ambiguity concerning the origins of these works. For instance, a sixteen-page book by Selami Münir Yurdatap, writer and translator, titled *Baytekin ile Tarzan* (Baytekin and Tarzan) and printed in 1943, featured an illustrated cover depicting Flash Gordon and Tarzan in front of a spaceship. The title page indicated that the book was written by Selami Münir Yurdatap. Although the book was clearly credited to Yurdatap, the use of Tarzan in the title and the presence of Flash Gordon and Tarzan (who were familiar to the Turkish readership mainly through translations) on the cover revealed the text as being of foreign origin. We are once again faced with a case where the publisher/translator/writer makes a plea to the reader to enter the world of the text without asking about the source of the story.

The paratextual elements of the classics translated by the Translation Bureau made the educational function of these books clear. Or rather, they expressed the intention, the hope, that the books would be received as educational material. This can be deduced from a number of sites, starting with the Ministry of Education's logo on the front cover, including the introductions of teacher-translators and extending to the prefaces. By contrast, the paratexts of popular dime novels did not claim to have any function other than to 'tempt' the reader (Genette 1997: 93). They contained no preface that could guide the reading of the texts and made no effort to assert their cultural and literary merit. The most widespread paratextual practice employed by translated dime novels was to add a 'teaser statement' to the front cover of the books. This statement contained a parageneric designation, offering readers a clue as to the kind of story they were faced with. *Baytekin ile Tarzan* had the statement, "Resimli Heyecanlı Macera Romanları" ('Illustrated Exciting Adventure Novels'), while *Denizaltının Planı* featured a statement identifying the story as a detective novel. Such parageneric designations were rather common, especially in the sixteen-page adventure and detective stories published by a number of publishing houses, among which Güven Yayinevi was the leading name.

This is a significant clue offered by the peritexts about the way these novels were marketed and received. Covers and title pages of canonical works underscored the name of the author as the main presentational element. We can therefore assume that their target readership selected their reading material with reference to the literary origin of the books. The marketing of popular fiction, on the other hand, would be based on genre. This means that readers buying these books would not be interested in who wrote them or whether they were translations or original writing. Rather, they would pay attention to the genre to which the books belonged. This confirms the idea that, unlike readers of 'serious fiction', readers of popular fiction read by 'genre' rather than by 'author' (Roberts 1990: 32).

A review of the textual features of books sold under similar covers reveals that they share several characteristics. These characteristics indicate that the texts may have been manipulated to conform to the parageneric indication appearing in their covers. In other words, paratextual elements may have had a powerful impact on the way the actual texts were written. Translations offer evidence in favour of this idea. Translated texts appearing in the popular dime series were often abridged in order to fit the sixteen-page format. Their plots were usually simplified, a requirement following mainly from the size of the books. In line with their parageneric designation as 'adventure' or 'detective' stories, they emphasized action and adventure-related features over intellectual or emotional ones (see for example *Denizaltının Planı*). This shows that the need to comply with the general concept of the series was a strong factor affecting decisions taken by translators. It further demonstrates the commercial drive behind the observation of specific norms by the translators of these books. Contrary to Genette (1997: 12) who suggests that the paratext is always subordinate to its text, we may conclude that in certain cases paratextual elements may be formed before the texts themselves, and guide not only their reception but also their translation/writing.

3. The methodological relevance of paratexts for translation research

A project on translation history wishing to go beyond what Anthony Pym terms 'translation archaeology' to explore "*why* archaeological artefacts occurred when and where they did, and how they were related to change" (1998: 5-6) will need to devise a model that can enable a contextualization of translational phenomena. This model needs to accommodate a range of historical phenomena and materials, for focussing on a single type of material will hamper the researcher's view. An analysis of norms in translated texts will be insufficient to contextualize these texts within the general cultural system. The shortcomings of an exclusive focus on translations will become evident even before the analysis of the translated texts has begun, for the researcher will need to set herself certain criteria as to what constitutes translation before she can construct her corpus of translated works. The determination of these criteria has to be based not only on current definitions of translation, but also on the concepts of translation that were operative during the period under study.

This requires the researcher to expand her material to cover secondary texts that offer meta-discourses on translation and help to capture the general socio-cultural forces giving shape to translations. Apart from general statements on translation, or from other socio-cultural phenomena that may have a bearing on how translations are produced and received (extratexts), the researcher will come across comments, reviews, criticisms or interviews dealing with specific works (epitexts). The study of such material may offer useful clues not only about how translation was defined, but also about the conditions under which translations were produced and consumed. In the meantime, the immediate paratextual elements surrounding the works, the peritext, can also provide insight into the views of publishers and translators on translation. Peritexts become even more relevant in fields where extratexts and epitexts are rare. Translated popular literature of the 1940s in Turkey is a part of the literary system which has received little attention and almost no written comment from critics. Therefore texts and their peritexts, along with library catalogues and bibliographies providing snippets of epitext, are the only available data in the researcher's hands.

The ideas traced in the peritexts and (where available) epitexts and extratexts will not only complement the description and analysis of the translated texts, but also help revise some of the conclusions arrived at after such an analysis. Likewise, the study of translation norms may yield results which make the researcher question the claims of extratexts and paratexts.

As mentioned earlier, regarding translations as paratexts brings several disadvantages because it imposes a source-oriented and restrictive perspective on translation research. At the same time, analysing the paratextual elements of translated texts will furnish us with interesting information on several points where the texts themselves remain silent. The two case studies sketched above demonstrate that paratexts supply information about the views of publishers and/or translators on what constitutes translation. The paratexts of the classics published by the Ministry of Education in the 1940s brought into relief the 'conventional' definition of translation held by the state-sponsored Translation Bureau. They emphasized the source text and the source author, restricted the translator's visibility in a number of ways, and made explicit the intended function of educating the readers. The paratexts of translated (or original) dime novels showed the publishers and translators active in the field of popular literature positioning themselves in a blurred area between translation and original writing. These paratexts also revealed that parageneric indications and the specific formats of the series had a strong bearing on the way the works were written or translated. The clues found at the paratextual level might prompt questions to be further explored both in the translated texts and their epitexts, as well as in various extratexts: who where the translators translating those dime novels? Were they engaged in other forms of literary activity? Why was there such a gap between the Translation Bureau and publishers like Güven Yayınevi in their respective approaches towards translation? Can the use of anonymity be sufficiently explained by market forces preferring generic indications over originality? The list can certainly be extended.

Exploration through paratexts provokes questions, some of which may never find answers. But then, all we ask of research models is that they generate questions. That is why paratexts deserve more attention in current research models in translation history.

References

Benjamin, Walter (1968) 'The Task of the Translator' [1923], in *Illuminations*, trans. Harry Zohn, London: Jonathan Cape, 69-82.

Bogenç Demirel, Emine and Hülya Yılmaz (1998) Tercüme Dergisinde Çeviri Eleştirisi' (Translation Criticism at the Tercüme Journal), *Çeviribilim ve Uygulamaları* (Translation Studies and Its Applications), December 1998, Ankara: Hacettepe Üniversitesi, 93-106.

Conan Doyle, Arthur (1981) 'His Last Bow', in *The Penguin Complete Sherlock Holmes*, London: Penguin Books.

Denizaltının Planı (1944) Istanbul: Güven Yayınevi.

Genette, Gerard (1997) *Paratexts: Thresholds of Interpretation*, trans. Jane E. Lewin, Cambridge: Cambridge University Press.

Hermans, Theo (1999) *Translation in Systems*, Manchester: St. Jerome.

İnönü, İsmet (1941) Preface to translations by the Translation Bureau.

Kovala, Urpo (1996) 'Translations, Paratextual Mediation and Ideological Closure', *Target* 8(1): 119-47.

Lefevere, André (1992) *Translation, Rewriting and the Manipulation of Literary Fame*, London & New York: Routledge.

Mann, Thomas (1945) *Tonio Kröger*, trans. Mehmet Karasan, Ankara: Milli Eğitim Basımevi.

Niranjana, Tejaswini (1992) *Siting Translation: History, Post-Structuralism and the Colonial Context*, Berkeley: University of California Press.

Pym, Anthony (1998) *Method in Translation History*, Manchester: St. Jerome.

Roberts, Thomas J. (1990) *Aesthetics of Junk Fiction*, Athens: University of Georgia Press.

Stevenson, R.L. (1944) *Dr. Jekyll ile Mr. Hyde*, trans. Zarife Laçiner, Ankara: Milli Eğitim Basımevi.

Stoker, Bram (1940). *Drakyola, Kan İçen Adam*, trans. Selami Münir Yurdatap, Istanbul: Güven Basimevi.

Swift, Jonathan (1946) *Gulliver'in Seyahatleri I-II*, trans. İrfan Şahinbaş, Ankara: Milli Eğitim Basimevi.

Toury, Gideon (1995) *Descriptive Translation Studies and Beyond*, Amsterdam: John Benjamins.

Yücel, Hasan Âli (1940) 'Önsöz' (Preface), *Tercüme*, No. 1, May 1940, 1-2.

----- (1941) First Preface to translations by the Translation Bureau.

----- (1944) Second Preface to translations by the Translation Bureau.

Yurdatap, Selami Münir (1943) *Baytekin ile Tarzan*, Istanbul: Güven Basımevi.

Translation Principles and the Translator's Agenda
A Systemic Approach to Yan Fu

ELSIE CHAN

Abstract: *The three principles of translation which the Chinese translator Yan Fu enunciated in 1898 – xin (faithfulness), da (comprehensibility) and ya (elegance) – achieved canonical status while also being condemned as paradoxical if not contradictory. The essay re-assesses Yan's position and translation agenda in the context of the historical socio-cultural and political crisis in which China found itself at the time. The approach is multi-dimensional and takes its cue from polysystem theory. It is argued that, from Yan's perspective, his sincere purpose of national salvation through translation would only be achieved when his select readership had understood and accepted his sincerity through his deployment of an accessible poetics and the acculturation of otherwise inaccessible foreign ideas. Yan's translation model is construed as a function of power and politics while marshalling literary, institutional, political and ideological accessibility for a definite purpose.*

Lieven D'hulst has argued that the history of translation theory matters not only because our current thinking stems from it, but also because it holds its own interest and complexity, a complexity which becomes apparent when we reflect on the multidisciplinary nature of historical translation theory (cited in Hermans 1999: 99). D'hulst blames the relative lack of interest in older translation theories among contemporary scholars on arrogance and "selective amnesia" (*ibid.*): researchers imagine they have made such momentous progress with their new-fangled paradigms that past thinking has become irrelevant; they tend to look upon past theorizing as a mere offshoot of translation practice, an incidental by-product confined to technical problems (*ibid.*).

This article seeks to address the polarity between historical theories and practices of translation, and to elucidate the relevance of past theorizing about translation. The case under discussion concerns Yan Fu (1854-1921), heralded as the most influential translator and translation theorist in China. Yan's translations of eighteenth and nineteenth-century Western intellectual works effected enormous change in the worldview of his contemporaries. His translation principles have been celebrated by the majority of Chinese translators and in Chinese translation studies anthologies ever since.

I will examine Yan Fu's principles of translation with the help of contemporary functional concepts, more particularly polysystem theory (Even-Zohar 1990; 1997). In view of the criticism levelled at polysystem theory as being too simplistic, determinist, dualistic and reductive (Hermans 1999: 102-119; Lambert 1997), the polysystem concept serves here only as a framework to illustrate the dynamics of a cultural paradigm shift. By historicizing Yan Fu, his translation practice can be analyzed in terms of culture and power, and as functioning in multiple interrelated systems rather than as a conglomerate of disparate elements. The systemic methodology will yield insight into the diversity and complexity of phenomena that have a bearing on Yan's case, and account for its validity and strategic research value in translation studies. Rather than exploring translation as a skill, an art or a science, a position which dominated mainstream translation studies in China until recently, such an approach affirms the multidimensional and interdisciplinary nature of translation studies.

1. Historicizing theory

In the final decades of the Qing Dynasty (1644-1911), the last feudal empire of China, Yan Fu rendered into Chinese a number of Western intellectual works, most of them books originally published in the nineteenth century such as Thomas Huxley's *Evolution and Ethics*, Edward Jenks' *A History of Politics*, John Stuart Mill's *On Liberty* and *System of Logic*, Herbert Spencer's *Study of Sociology* and W.S. Jevons' *Primer of Logic*, but also some from the eighteenth century, notably Adam Smith's *Wealth of Nations* and Montesquieu's *Spirit of the Laws*. However, the distinguished translator is best remembered for propounding, in the preface of his translation of Huxley's *Evolution and Ethics*, three major difficulties of and guidelines for translation: "*xin*", "*da*" and "*ya*", which could be rendered literally as faithfulness (*xin*), comprehensibility (*da*) and elegance (*ya*).[1]

This tripartite model is widely esteemed in China as a logical and sophisticated extension of tenets evolved from ancient Buddhist scriptural translation, which emphasized both faithfulness of content and intelligibility of expression. In his 'Translation Theories in China: A System of Her Own' Luo Xinzhang (1984: 1-19) summarized two millennia of Chinese theorizing about the subject, tracing a diachronic evolution of principles from "original purport" (Dao'an, 314-385, translator of Buddhist scriptures), via "faithfulness" (Yan Fu) and "spiritual resemblance" (Fu Lei, 1908-1966, translator of French literature), to "sublime consummation" (Qian Zhongshu, 1910-1998, scholar and writer). The general consensus in China is that Yan Fu's triad – transferring the source text faithfully [*xin*] in comprehensible language [*da*] and appropriate style [*ya*] – offers a perfect match of past translation principles and an evergreen translation paradigm. The debate concerns the interpretation of what Yan's terms actually cover. Does *xin* mean faithfulness to the form, content, spirit and/or author's intention? Does *ya* necessitate elaborate and recondite language and, if so, does *ya* not run contrary to *da*? There is also debate about

---

[1] For a summary of past views on Yan's theories, see Shen (1998: 65-110). See also Chang (2000) on the current state of translation studies in China.

the relative weight each of the three principles should be accorded by the practising translator. Nevertheless, it is generally held that Yan's tenets, especially *xin* and *da*, constitute the norms of all translation practice and criticism.

There is also a dissenting view, which questions the adequacy of Yan's formula as an account of the complexity of translation. Attempts have been made to foreground his translation enterprise in terms of intended readership and aim (Chau 1986; Chu 2000; Shen 1998), the political function of his translations (Wong 1997), and the role of translation in a period of literary and ideological crisis (Chang 1998: 34-35). The validity of Yan's triad has also been challenged on the grounds that Yan himself violated his own principles and rewrote and manipulated his source texts in esoteric classical Chinese. Nevertheless, most translation criticism after Yan deploys his model as a yardstick: renderings which deviate from his norms are condemned, even though 'special' circumstances will often be invoked to exempt particular translations.

At times, past studies on Yan are slighted as microscopic, impressionistic and repetitious, clogging more macroscopic and systematic investigation. The challenge is particularly embraced by younger contemporary researchers who draw on Western literary and translation studies (e.g. Wang Dongfeng 1999). It has resulted in a debate about theoretical hegemony, with one side rejecting the 'old' as simplistic and ossified, and the other side dismissing the 'new' as iconoclastic and irrelevant. My questions are different. Does the fact that Yan Fu's paradigm has dominated translation discourse in China for a century make it into a significant object of study? Do his principles amount to a theory? How do we conceive Yan Fu's translation practice and his pronouncements about translation in the broader historical context? What is his contribution to translation studies? And, most importantly, what is the significance of his views for future research?

Research on a historical translation theory would be inadequate if alienated from the study of translators and the wider social and historical context, and if confined to the scope and tools of a single paradigm or discipline. In this respect, most existing studies have been limited in scope. Chinese translation studies in the past century have been predominantly philological and hermeneutic, and have taken Yan's triad as a model for translation criticism. There is a lack of in-depth study of the methodological aspects of Yan's principles or of the relation between Yan's purposeful adjustment of the cosmological differences between Chinese and Western cultures and his pronouncements on translation. Sociological, political and comparative literature studies, on the other hand, cast Yan as a great thinker well versed in both Chinese and Western scholarship and as a patriotic scholar determined to acculturate Western progressive thought to enlighten his countrymen. Benjamin Schwartz (1964), for example, has explained Yan's selective reception and importation of modern Western liberal ideas as an attempt to transform the Western military and economic threat into power and wealth for China. However, Schwartz was not primarily interested in translation methods or principles, merely observing that Yan's "paraphrastic translation" and arbitrary commentaries "facilitate occasional serious distortions of meaning" (1964: 96).

2. Poetics and power

Yan Fu, then, has been studied from different but always specific perspectives. What we need is a multidimensional analysis of Yan Fu as a man of his age. The proposal that follows historicizes Yan Fu's principles in the light of the polysystem model.

Let me begin by examining the immediate context. Yan introduced his three principles in the 'General Remarks on Translation' prefaced to his *Tianyanlun* [On Evolution] of 1898, his first published translation, based on T.H. Huxley's *Evolution and Ethics*. The preface opened as follows:

> Translation involves three requirements difficult to fulfil: faithfulness [*xin*], comprehensibility [*da*] and elegance [*ya*]. Faithfulness is difficult enough to attain but a translation that is faithful but not comprehensible is no translation at all. Comprehensibility is therefore of prime importance. (Yan 1973: 4; my square brackets, EC; C.Y. Hsu's 1973 translation is used throughout this article)

The explication here interestingly conforms to home literary conventions. The statement itself is shaped in line with the preference for epigrammatic yet indistinct representation in Chinese literary studies and criticism. Although the three requirements appeared forthwith, Yan did not show his credential until the third paragraph:

> The *I Ching* (*Book of Changes*) says: "Fidelity is the basis of writing." Confucius said, "Writing should be comprehensible." He also said, "Where language has no refinement, its effects will not extend far." These three dicta set the right course for literature and are the guidelines for translation. (Yan 1973: 5)

The Book of Changes ranks among the top five canons (*wujing*) of the Confucian order, the highest institutionalized order of Chinese philosophies. Confucian poetics also form the basis of canonized literary norms, one form of 'repertoire' in Even-Zohar's terminology.[2] It is striking that Yan put forward the same poetics

---

[2] "In the (poly)system it is in the repertoire that canonicity is most concretely manifested [...] Repertoire is conceived of here as the aggregate of laws and elements (either single, bound, or total models) that govern the production of texts" (Even-Zohar 1990: 17). Repertoire designates "the aggregate of rules and materials that govern both the *making* and *handling*, or production and consumption, of any given product", the usability of which may be constrained, determined or controlled by some institution and market (1997: 16). I consider the term 'repertoire' too broad for research purposes; it may include literary norms, cultural conventions and ideological

for home literature and for translation, thus modelling his translation norms on those already established by a dominant type in the target literature. According to Even-Zohar this usually happens when translated literature occupies a peripheral position within the target system and employs secondary models (1990: 48-49). A secondary model governs products that are highly predictable, when a repertoire is firmly in place and all derivative models are constructed in full accordance with it (1990: 20-22).

It is true that in Imperial China translation never played a central role in literary culture. The literary, historical and philosophic heritage of the world's oldest existing civilization with a centralized government and a common written language across an extended stretch of land surrounded by tributary minority states cherished a self-contained and self-sufficient view of itself as the 'Middle Kingdom', largely precluding the need to translate other literary cultures. Translators were known in ancient China as 'tongue men' (*sheren*) or 'imitating officers' (*xiangxu*). Translation was not held in high esteem. Confucius (551-479 BCE) once disapproved of his king's intention to study translation, which he despised as 'petty business' (*xiaobian*) confined to diplomatic affairs to be assigned to 'inverse tongues' (*fanshe*) [translators] who 'transmit the words' (*chuanyan*) (Chen 1992: 11-13). A telling observation by the late Qing scholar Liang Qichao (1873-1929) suggests that Buddhist scriptures were the first foreign texts to be treated with respect, because Buddhist culture at that time had attained a status 'comparable' to that of China (Liang 1988: 85).

The translation of Buddhist scriptures from the second to the tenth century marked the first of three major translation periods in pre-1949 China (the second seeing the importation of Western scientific works in the sixteenth through to the eighteenth century, and the third the translation of Western intellectual and literary works from the late nineteenth century into the 1930s). Although these were periods of exuberant translation activity, translated literature did not play a significant role in the literary system, except after 1919. The reasons are obvious. First, the translation enterprise was carried by a relatively exclusive circle of local translators who often worked in collaboration with foreigners, and involved few if any leading writers. Second, although translation injected new elements into the home literature, it had little impact on major literary trends and mostly followed prevailing literary, cultural and ideological norms.[3] Third, translation often served

---

preferences. I will specify rules and elements as the case may be. For this example, I prefer the term poetics.

[3] Although it might be argued that the pinnacle of Buddhist scriptural translation in the late sixth to ninth century did witness the rise of a unique stratum of Buddhist literature considered to form a genre of its own, I have to stress that Buddhist texts were taken to replace the 'original', from where independent Chinese sects and some pseudo-translations stemmed, and were regarded as a periphery indigenous literature – as is evident from the fact that they receive little or no mention in volumes on the development of Chinese literature – rather than translated literature.

the utilitarian purposes of the politically more open-minded intellectuals in the political or ideological polysystems. As far as literature is concerned, 'translated literature' was largely ignored.

In the second translation period, for example, Jesuit missionaries translated Western scientific and technological works – insofar as these were not incompatible with Christian dogma – as a way of furthering their proselytizing agenda. They collaborated with a handful of Chinese scholar-officials who were not conversant with Western languages but eager to acquire applied Western technology beneficial to their country. The translation of Western works hardly touched Chinese literary culture and failed to affect Chinese thought until Yan Fu. This may explain why, despite the preceding legions of translators and translations of Western works, Yan was considered to be the first student returned from the West to influence Chinese thinking (Liang 1998: 98) and the first Chinese to introduce contemporary Western thought (Hu Shi, 1891-1962, 1979: 194). However, Yan was chiefly commended for his accomplishment in both Chinese and Western scholarship (Liang 1990: 267); his poetics in fact drew severe criticism. He modelled his translations on high-status literary conventions and felt unhappy about his lowly position as a translator. But then, literary culture in pre-1919 China[4] was overwhelmingly monolingual, with translated literature, as suggested above, usually remoulded in conformity with home literary conventions and relegated to the periphery.

The Confucian quotations buttressing Yan's three principles sprang from pre-Han (before third century BCE) sources. Yan stressed the importance of *ya* ('elegance') in his 'General Remarks' in *Tianyanlun* and specified that "in using the syntax and style of the pre-Han period one actually facilitates the comprehensibility of profound principles and subtle thoughts, whereas in using the modern vernacular one finds it difficult to make things comprehensible" (1973: 5). In other words, Yan actually advocated abstruse pre-Han stylistics as the most appropriate vehicle to treat unfamiliar foreign concepts (Chu 2000: 10). His conservative poetics became a means to preserve a traditional repertoire, which ran parallel to the ultra-conservative taste of the ruling mandarin elite whose favour the translator was trying to win. The elite required sophistication and eccentricity to gratify its taste and control the centre of the cultural system; the canonized repertoire exhibited these features in abundance. It becomes apparent that Yan's intended readership and translation purpose determined his translation norms; put differently, the whole

---

[4] In 1919 the May Fourth patriotic democratic movement broke out after the Paris Peace Convention failed to rectify the economic and territorial aggression of the Western powers against China. The movement urged the disbanding of ossified social, political, ideological and literary structures. Many writers then recognized the potential of translated literature to shape a new vernacular and mass literature and introduce innovative ideas from abroad. Thus the disruptive shift in the political (from the Qing monarchy to Republican government in 1911) and ideological (from domestic conservatism to the pursuit of science and democracy) spheres propelled translated literature from peripheral to central status in the home literary polysystem after 1919.

course is governed by the question of power. What Yan strove for is not comprehensible language *per se*, but literary and institutional accessibility.

In his 'General Remarks' Yan Fu indicated that he was perfectly aware of the criticism of his abstruse language, involved style and preference for the eccentric. He defended his conservative option:

> But I must say this is the result of my determined effort at comprehensibility [*da*]. The treatise in the book is largely based upon logic, mathematics and science as well as astronomy. If a reader is not familiar with these studies, even if he is of the same nationality and speaks the same language as the author, he won't be able to comprehend much, far less by reading a translation. (Yan 1973: 5; my square brackets, EC)

His claim that only pre-Han literary norms were adequate for translating serious Western works, however, failed to forestall attack. In his review of Yan's later translation of *Wealth of Nations*, Liang Qichao upbraided him not only for presuming an exclusive readership familiar with classical learning but also for his failure to address the need for long-delayed literary reform and to make difficult and profound treatises accessible to students. He censured Yan's poetics as inappropriate, self-indulgent and at odds with the translator's duty to introduce "civilized thoughts" to his countrymen (Liang 1990: 267). In his response to Liang, Yan pointed out that his translations were meant not for students or the common reader but for the intellectual elite well versed in the Chinese classics (in Yan 1990: 124). That would mean Yan purposefully targeted his translations at the mandarin elite who alone possessed the leverage to effect reforms and change the status quo. It is unthinkable that they would recognize as 'proper' a text carried in a populist container, let alone find it worthy to read and accept the progressive foreign ideas therein. Yan further argued that dumbing down the language to please the uneducated would result in literary blight instead of reform (*ibid.*). The unrefined vernacular would cause the translator to strain the foreign meaning, resulting in gross misinterpretation (Yan 1973: 5) – a reasonable enough claim at a time when vernacular *baihua* was still untried as a literary and intellectual instrument.

As it is, the translator's institutional and ideological position played a key role in shaping his poetics. The *tongcheng* school of literature and learning to which Yan Fu belonged, was opposed to the *bagu* essay form which was tested in the imperial civil service exams but had turned into a hollow bag of stereotyped and hackneyed prose. The *tongcheng* school preferred simple but graceful stylistics to elicit meaningful arguments (poetics), evoking the Confucian tradition (learning) and perfecting social and moral order (ethics). The *tongcheng* school was also critical of the lacklustre utilitarian (*jingshi*) studies as well as the dull and submissive evidential research (*kaozheng*) in vogue among scholars since the beginning of the Qing Dynasty. The political and ideological rivalry is evident. *Tongcheng* masters held that scholarship amounted to more than utilitarianism and submissive studies; good writing should be informed by significant substance and cultured stylistics, as exemplified in the masterly works of the exuberant Tang and Song periods (7th to 13th century CE), which could be traced all the way back to the earlier Han and pre-Han era.

These institutional tenets are clearly visible in Yan's frame of reference and that of his mentor, the notable *tongcheng* master Wu Rulin (1840-1903), who taught in the equivalent of a modern-day university at the imperial capital. Wu approved of Yan's literary taste and stressed, in his foreword to Yan's translation of Huxley (Yan 1998: 1-3), that literary style was essential to preserve the appeal and durability of the content, and that the best form of writing should be rich in both substance and style. Summarizing the development of poetics in China, Wu remarked that only the original expository writings of the pre-Han and Han periods could be considered canonical. He complained that contemporary writers could only produce stereotyped essays prescribed for the imperial civil service exams, pedantic official documents and vulgar fiction, all of which were rigid in form and deprived of ideas. Wu also lashed out at contemporary translators and their rough and ready translations, which intellectuals and the elite found contemptible and which therefore failed to provide enlightenment. In Wu's estimation only Yan was qualified for this demanding task.

Wu's comments allow us to appreciate Yan's translation strategy of resorting to a conservative secondary model. It was an exclusive model that managed to survive, though not without criticism by contemporaries, and succeeded in gaining approval among the intellectuals and even the diehard mandarin elite. But even Wu Rulin seemed to be aware of the instability of the literary system. In his foreword to *Tianyanlun* he cautiously observed that Yan's decorum might be too elevated to win a wide and lasting audience, since Yan's choice of pre-Han poetics was even more remote than that pertaining to the classical literary movement of the Tang and Song Dynasties endorsed by the *tongcheng* school. After the May Fourth Movement in 1919, classical Chinese officially collapsed and Confucianism was toppled in China. The classical and canonized literary models were seriously out of step with the changing needs of the society in which they functioned. This incapacity can also be understood in terms of cultural inadequacy. As the impotence of home traditions and institutions to resist a foreign threat is exposed, obsolescent literary forms may persist but will inexorably be pushed to the periphery where they face growing competition from popular but dynamic subcultures (Even-Zohar 1990: 17). Although the innovative Western thought which Yan transmitted was welcomed, his secondary poetics were condemned as anachronistic and remote. Thus Yan's translations at most achieved static canonicity: the texts were accepted as accomplished products and inserted into a set of sanctified texts that the receiving system was keen to preserve, but the aesthetic repertoire to which they appealed failed to become a productive literary principle.

3. Institution and ideology

Many translation researchers have taken Yan's three principles literally. They either sought to reconcile them with his translation practice or criticized him for not observing them consistently. Most accounts have run into paradoxes.

One such paradox concerns the relation between *da* (comprehensibility) and *ya* (elegance). The argument is that Yan's poetics are too elegant to be comprehensible to a general and certainly to a later readership. The problem here is that Yan was convinced that only adherence to a poetics of elegance would make his renderings acceptable to his intended readership, the mandarin elite with its fierce loyalty to classical and canonized values. Comprehensibility (*da*), therefore, should not be read as meaning straightforward, comprehensible language. Rather, it means political and ideological accessibility to a select readership, recalling Yan's citation of the Confucian canon that required refined language to ensure lasting effect. Yan was undoubtedly a reformist, aiming to influence the mandarin elite who alone had the power to transform the country and restore its self-confidence. At a time when Western imperialist powers were threatening China's very survival, Yan was among the first to see that the source of Western scientific, economic and military superiority actually lay in their innovative thinking and liberal learning, founded in turn on democratic government and an evolutionary outlook. He was particularly influenced by Herbert Spencer's social Darwinism and believed that China urgently needed to be strengthened and enlightened so as to be fit for the international struggle for survival. This is why he first translated Huxley's *Evolution and Ethics*, elucidating, through acculturation and paraphrase, Spencer's thinking on social evolution. Like many of his contemporaries, Yan realized the need to 'translate' progressive Western ideas into wealth and power for China. Translation seemed to him the only acceptable means to challenge the reactionary and chauvinistic elite, unorthodox thinking being more tolerated in translation than in the form of original writing. Yan effectuated his reformist political agenda by wrapping otherwise disagreeably unorthodox ideas in manifestly conservative literary norms.

Yan Fu began his translation of Huxley after China's most humiliating defeat by Japan in 1895. In the same year he released four political critiques in a Tianjin newspaper (*Zhibao*), which made waves in intellectual circles but did not affect the political system, where he held an insignificant position as navy training officer. When still in his teens he had entered a navy school that offered free Western education for the less fortunate; this accounts for his repeated failures at the highest imperial civil service exams in 1885-1893, which blocked his access to officialdom. His excellent Western and quite decent Chinese scholarship, as well as his overseas exposure, was no compensation for his petty position; he was continually snubbed by those in authority. His superior, Li Hongzhang (1823-1901), was displeased with Yan's progressive political stance and daring criticism. Chen Fukang

(1992: 125-6) has argued that Yan decided to embark on his translation career after the aborted Hundred Days' Reform in 1898, which attempted to launch a series of progressive institutional and constitutional reforms. At that point in history, translation appeared to him as Hobson's choice to enlighten the mandarin elite even as he criticized their ignorance and chauvinism and defined his patriotic stance in his *Tianyanlun* preface (Yan 1998: 14-16).

Returning to Yan's justification of his orthodox poetics, both the analogy he drew between the worth of Western intellectual works and pre-Han writings, and his Confucian citation in support of his three translation principles, are thought-provoking. The issue here is more a matter of politics than poetics. Only a handful of the so-called 'hundred schools of thought' prevalent in the pre-Han era maintained their following after Han, the leading school being Confucianism. Confucianism was institutionalized by Emperor Wu in the early Han Dynasty as the state canon governing every aspect of life. Confucian classics formed the basis of the imperial civil service exams and dominated subsequent learning, ethics and poetics. This is crucial to Yan's enterprise: the only path to his Confucian goal of managing state affairs and attaining a peaceful world was through accessible translation. But if 'comprehensibility' (*da*) is more a function of institutional than textual and stylistic accessibility, if *da* never means plain language, there is no reason why it should conflict with 'elegance' (*ya*).

Yan's institutional and ideological concerns were apparently realized by Wu Rulin, who emphasized in his foreword to Yan's *Tianyanlun* that the original work was not only a book on natural science but also a manual for governance. The monolingual Wu further surmised that modern Western works were comparable to Han original expository writings and thus worth translating, and that Yan's eloquent pen had raised Huxley to the same lofty status as the pre-Han classics. It is relevant in this context that Yan apparently asked his mentor for a foreword because the esteemed *tongcheng* literary master's patronage was crucial to raise the translator's status in both literary and political circles (Wong 1997: 52-54).

As regards the paradox that pits 'faithfulness' (*xin*) against 'elegance' (*ya*), the reasoning is that it must have seemed doubtful that abstruse and conservative language would be capable of expressing alien thought in a sufficiently accurate translation. Recalling the Confucian justification for *xin*, I argue that, like many other epigrammatic expressions in the Chinese classics, the meaning of *xin* is indeterminate. The indeterminacy stems from the composite and paratactic nature of Chinese, where new phrases are conveniently formed by juxtaposing existing logographic monosyllabic characters and grammar follows a covert logic allowing volatile parts of speech and punctuation. With it comes an aesthetic which favours equivocal clustering, indefinite representation and evaluative intuition, allowing immense interpretive creativity. As pointed out above, *xin* derives from the *Book of Changes (I Ching)*. It is taken from the representation of the Qian Diagram, the first of the eight divinatory symbols. The representation reads "*xiu ci li qi cheng, suo yi ju ye ye*". The translator's remarks on *Tianyanlun* reads "*xiu ci li cheng*", which Hsu translates as "fidelity (*cheng*) is the basis of writing (*xiu ci*)", itself a very common interpretation. It is extremely difficult to delineate the meaning and even grammar of the *I Ching* quotation. An abstracted crib might be: embellish (*xiu*), diction (*ci*), establish (*li*), one's (*qi*), sincerity (*cheng*), as such (*suo yi*), live (*ju*), enterprise (*ye*), sentence particle (*ye*). *Xiu* and *ci* together can form either a verb phrase, 'refine one's dicton', or a noun phrase , 'rhetoric'; the relationship between the *xiu ci* and *li qi cheng* can be causal, 'rhetoric/refine one's diction to establish one's sincerity', or coordinate, 'rhetoric/refine one's diction and establish one's sincerity'. *Ju* and *ye* can be verbs or nouns and the whole quotation literally means 'rhetoric/refine one's diction to/and establish one's sincerity is the key to living and enterprising'. In addition, the simple decontextualized expression has been subject to multiple interpretations in more than two millennia of annotation and commentary stemming from different periods and schools of thought.

Relating *cheng* to *xin*, 'sincerity' offers the most satisfactory interpretation of *cheng*: sincerity is the basis of refined writing; or, refined writing and sincerity are both important. As for *xin*, it can be a verb or noun and literally means 'true', 'trust' or 'faith'. If *cheng* forms the backbone of *xin*, then *xin* essentially means 'sincere writing with true and faithful intention', *bona fide*. In other words, a translated text should possess a sincere intent, a meaningful and substantial content, which in the Confucian system means anything conducive to cultivation of the self, good governance and harmony with the cosmic order. Yan could achieve his sincere purpose of national enlightenment and salvation by translating that part of the substance of his source texts that contributed to China's well-being. If *xin* means 'sincere purpose', then the circumstances dictated a translation strategy of acculturation. This need not translate into mimetic 'faithfulness' or reproduction of the full content and form of the original text, as the conventional interpretation of *xin* has it.

The title of Yan's first translation is a case in point. Huxley's *Evolution and Ethics* becomes *Tianyanlun*, where *tian* means 'sky, heaven, nature or the higher cosmic order', *yan* means 'evolution or change' and *lun*, 'discussion' – in other words, 'On (Natural) Evolution'! In the book, the passages on natural selection, on the use of art (human force) to domesticate the forces of nature and on the survival of the fittest were selectively 'rewritten' in beautiful and cogent Chinese, consolidated in the form of detailed commentary, annotation and analogy, however arbitrary some of them appeared to be. No doubt these ideas were what he considered truthful and most relevant to the Chinese context and the mandarin elite. And he probably trimmed the part on evolutionary ethics for the same reason, as not conducive to self-strengthening and enlightenment. As Yan himself explained, his translation

> attempts to present its [the original's] profound thought. It does not follow
> the exact order of words and sentences of the original text but reorganizes
> and elaborates. However, it does not deviate from the original ideas. It is

more an exposition than a translation as it seeks to elaborate – an unorthodox
way of transmission. (Yan 1973: 4)

Drawing analogy from the ancient Buddhist translator Kumarajiva (334-413),
known for his popular but acculturated translations, Yan went on to warn other
translators not to use his example as an excuse for their failings. At the end of his
remarks, he wrote:

> The pursuit of truth is akin to the practice of government in that both place a
> premium on the pooling of ideas. Where the present work agrees or differs
> with other books, from what I know I note them in the postscript for the
> reader's reference. Now and then I inject my personal views in the spirit of
> 'Seeking Friends' in the *Shih Ching* (Book of Odes) and 'Mutual Encourage-
> ment and Assistance' in the *I Ching*. Whether my views are sound or not I
> leave to public judgement. I do not insist on my own rectitude. If anyone
> should accuse me of being pretentious and seeking notoriety for myself, he
> misunderstands my *intention* in taking great pains to translate this book. (Yan
> 1973: 6; my italics in the last line, EC)

Mapping his words against the framework of arguments outlined above, his "intention" should be crystal-clear – to produce, based on foreign works, sincere and
cultured writings to influence an elite audience for the restoration of a wealthy and
powerful China. This precludes philological and prescriptive interpretation of his
three translation principles. No wonder he characterized his ideal translation in this
way: "When the translator has understood thoroughly and digested the whole text
he will then be able to rewrite it in the best manner possible" (Yan 1973: 5). His
sincere purpose of national salvation through translation is achieved when his select readership comprehends and accepts his sincerity through accessible poetics
and unavoidable acculturation of otherwise inaccessible foreign ideas. I shall tran-
scribe Yan's theoretical construct in the following formula (in which f means
'function of'):

> *ya*: f (literary/institutional accessibility) + *da*: f (political/ideological accessi-
> bility) → *xin*: f (sincere purpose)

Yan's translation purpose and strategy have often been compared to those of Lin
Shu (1852-1924). Kang Youwei (1858-1927), the scholar official who advocated
the Hundred Days' Reform, acclaimed both men as the outstanding translators of
the period (quoted in Qian 1979: 91). Although Lin, who took up translation after
his wife's death, knew no foreign languages and only translated literary works, he
was also a member of the *tongcheng* school, having also failed several times at the
highest imperial civil service exams. Lin succeeded in giving an impression of the
social, cultural and literary conditions of the Western world in his fiction translations,

helping his monolingual and chauvinistic countrymen to realize that there were indeed civilized, perhaps even 'fitter', cultures and literatures in other parts of the world. Lawrence Venuti has suggested that the two translators were also guardians of the emperor but unexpectedly eroded the authority of imperial culture (1998: 189). He ought to have pointed out as well that these patriotic translators, especially Yan, had wished for a constitutional monarchy and other institutional reforms to reinvigorate China; they did not consider the time was ripe to overthrow the Qing Dynasty and replace it with a Republican government.

But history played tricks on the translators' political agendas. Their reformist translations unexpectedly contributed to the revolutionary ferment, a result they could not have envisaged in their wildest dreams. Lin and especially Yan's acculturating translations attracted a much wider audience than expected; ironically, they were most influential among the not so cultured younger generation whom Yan had scorned. Yan's appeal lay mainly in the imported innovative ideas and in his determined effort to relate them to local conditions. His translations affected the common intellectuals far more significantly than those in power. His work was among the factors leading to the overthrow of the monarchy in 1911 and helped to ignite the May Fourth national protest of 1919 which finally broke with the old institutions, literature and culture.

References

Chang, Nam Fung (1998) '*Yi "zhongshi" wei mubiaode yingyong fanyixue – Zhongguo yilun chuantong chutan* [An Applied Discipline Obsessed with 'Loyalty' – On the Chinese Tradition of Translation Studies]', *Journal of Translation Studies* 2: 29-41.

----- (ed) (2000) *Translation Quarterly* 15, Special Issue on Translation Studies in China: Past and Future.

Chau, Simon S. C. (1986) 'Fanyide zhunze yu mubiao [Standards and Goals of Translation]', *Zhongguo fanyi* [*Chinese Translators Journal*] 3: 46-50.

Chen, Fukang (1992) *Zhongguo yixue lilun shigao* [*A History of Chinese Translation Theory*], Shanghai: Waiyu jiaoyu chubenshe.

Chu, Chi Yu (2000) 'Lun "xin da ya" shuo zai Zhongguo chuantong fanyi lilun zhongde weizhi [The Place of 'xin-da-ya' in Chinese Translation History]', *Translation Quarterly* 15: 1-18.

Even-Zohar, Itamar (1990) *Polysystem Studies* [*Poetics Today* 11, 1], Durham: Duke University Press.

----- (1997) 'Factors and Dependencies in Culture: A Revised Draft for Polysystem Culture Research', *Canadian Review of Comparative Literature* 24(1): 15-34.

Hermans, Theo (1999) *Translation in Systems: Descriptive and Systemic Approaches Explained,* Manchester: St. Jerome.

Hu Shi (1979), '*Wushi nianlai Zhongguozhi wenxue* [Chinese Literature over the Past Fifty Years]', in *Hu Shi Wencun* [*Essays by Hu Shi*], 4 vols., Taipei: Yuandong tushu gongsi, II, 180-261, first published 1922.

Lambert, José (1997) 'Itamar Even-Zohar's Polysystem Studies: An Interdisciplinary Perspective on Culture Research', *Canadian Review of Comparative Literature* 24(1): 7-14.

Lefevere, André (1992) *Translation, Rewriting, and the Manipulation of Literary Fame*, London: Routledge.

----- (1999) 'Composing the Other', in Susan Bassnett and Harish Trivedi (eds) *Post-Colonial Translation*, London: Routledge, 75-94.

Liang, Qichao (1988) *Zhongguo fojiao yanjiu shi* [*History of Chinese Buddhist Studies*], Shanghai: Sanlian shudian, first published 1920-4.

----- (1990) '*Jieshao xinzhu "Yuanku"* [Introducing the New Translation of "Origin of Wealth"]', in Niu and Sun (eds), 266-8, first published 1902.

----- (1998) *Qingdai xueshu gailun* [*Introduction to Qing Scholarship*], Shanghai: Guji chubenshe, first published 1921.

Liu, Ching-chih (1981) *Fanyi lunji* [*Essays on Translation*], Hong Kong: Sanlian shudian.

Luo, Xinzhang (1984) *Fanyi lunji* [*An Anthology of Translation Theory*], Beijing: Shangwu yingshu guan.

Ma, Zuyi (1984) *Zhongguo fanyi jianshi – wusi yiqian bufan* [*A Concise History of Translation in China: Before the May Fourth Movement*], Beijing: Duiwai fanyi chubenshe.

Niu, Yangshang, and Sun, Hongni (eds) (1990) *Yan Fu yanjiu ziliao* [*Research Materials on Yan Fu*], Fuzhou: Haixia wenyi chubenshe.

Qian Zhongshu (1979) '*Lin Shude fanyi* [Lin Shu's Translations]', in *Jiuwen Sibian* [*Four Old Essays*], Shanghai: Guji chubenshe, 62-95.

Schwartz, Benjamin (1964) *In Search of Wealth and Power: Yen Fu and the West*, Cambridge, Mass: Belknap Press.

Shen, Suru (1998) *Lun "xin da ya" – Yan Fu fanyi liluan yanjiu* [*On Xin, Da, Ya: Study on Yan Fu's Translation Theories*], Beijing: Shangwu yingshu guan.

Shuttleworth, Mark and Moira Cowie (1997) *Dictionary of Translation Studies*, Manchester: St. Jerome.

Toury, Gideon (1995) *Descriptive Translation Studies and Beyond*, Amsterdam: John Benjamins.

Venuti, Lawrence (1998) *The Scandals of Translation: Towards a Ethics of Difference*, London: Routledge.

Wang, Dongfeng (1999) '*Zhongguo yixue yanjiu: shiji mode sikao* [Chinese Translation Studies: Century-end Contemplation]', *Zhongguo fanyi* [*Chinese Translators Journal*] 1: 7-11, 2: 21-23.

Wang, Zuoliang (1982) '*Yan Fude Yongxin* [Yan Fu's Intentions]', in *Yan Fu yu Yanyi mingzhu* [*On Yan Fu and His Famous Translations*] (eds. *Shangwu yingshu guan bianji bu* [Commercial Press Editors], Beijing: Shangwu yingshu guan, 22-27.

Wong, Wang Chi (1997) '*Chongshi "xin da ya" – lun Yan Fu de fanyi lilun*' ['Xin, Da, Ya': On Yan Fu's Translation Theories], *Journal of Translation Studies* 1: 36-62.

Yan, Fu (1973) 'General Remarks on Translation' [in *Tianyanlun*, 1898], trans. C. Y. Hsu, *Renditions* 1: 4-6.

----- (1990) '*Yu Liang Rengong lun suoyi "Yuanku" shu* [Reply to Liang Qichao's

Critique on the translation of "Origin of Wealth"]', in Niu and Sun (eds), 123-5; first published 1902.

----- (1998) *Tianyanlun* [*On Evolution*], Zhengzhou: Zhongzhou guji; first woodblock print 1898.

Systems in Translation
A Systemic Model for Descriptive Translation Studies

JEREMY MUNDAY

Abstract: *The essay proposes a systematic and replicable model for the analysis of original texts and their translations, within the framework of descriptive translation studies. The model goes beyond earlier static linguistic models of translation and brings together concepts from systemic-functional linguistics, corpus linguistics and the sociocultural framework. A flexible approach to Halliday's systemic-functional analysis allows analysis of the three main strands of meaning in original and translated texts; the use of tools from corpus linguistics solves the logistical problem of dealing with whole texts, since the computer enables even the non-expert researcher to handle large amounts of data quickly and reliably; and the linguistic findings gain relevance when they are located within the sociocultural framework of the texts. The working of the model is illustrated with reference to translations of an essay by the Colombian novelist Gabriel García Márquez.*

1. Outline of the proposed model

The model proposed in this paper adopts the approach of Toury's *Descriptive Translation Studies and Beyond* (1995), which itself has links to polysystems and systems theory, and has proved extremely influential in recent years. Toury stresses the need for translation studies to develop a proper systematic descriptive branch of the discipline to replace the isolated free-standing studies that are so commonplace:

> What is missing is not isolated attempts reflecting excellent intuitions and supplying fine insights (which many existing studies certainly do), but a systematic branch proceeding from clear assumptions and armed with a methodology and research techniques made as explicit as possible and justified within translation studies itself. Only a branch of this kind can ensure that the findings of individual studies will be intersubjectively testable and comparable, and the studies themselves replicable. (Toury 1995: 3)

Toury proposes (pp. 36-9) the following three-phase methodology for systematic descriptive studies, incorporating a description of the product and the wider role of the sociocultural system:

(1) situate the text within the target culture system, looking at its acceptability;
(2) compare the source text (ST) and the target text (TT) for shifts, identifying relationships between 'coupled pairs' of ST and TT segments; and

(3) attempting generalizations about the underlying concept of translation for this pair of texts.

An important additional step is the possibility (indeed, necessity) of repeating phases (1) and (2) for other pairs of similar texts in order to widen the corpus and to build up a descriptive profile of translations according to genre, period, author, etc. In this way, the norms pertaining to each kind of translation can be identified with the ultimate aim, as more descriptive studies are performed and compared, of stating laws of behaviour for translation in general.

But it is the second step of Toury's methodology which is the most controversial area. The decision of which ST and TT segments to examine and what the relationships are between them requires an apparatus which Toury (1995: 85) feels should be supplied by translation theory. Yet translation theory is far from reaching a consensus as to what that apparatus should be, once influential linguistic models such as Vinay and Darbelnet's (1958/77) and van Leuven-Zwart's (1989, 1990) having fallen by the wayside. Van Leuven-Zwart's two part descriptive/comparative model, while initially promising, suffers from typical problems attached to taxonomies: it is overly complex, comprises far too many categories of translation shift (up to 37) for accurate and replicable classification, and carries out an automatic relation of linguistic shifts to shifts at higher levels of story and discourse without the real recourse to close critical analysis.

Toury (1995: 77), departing from his earlier (1980) use of the invariant concept and in an attempt to add objectivity to the process, proposes a 'mapping' of the TT onto the ST to yield 'a series of (ad hoc) coupled pairs'. This is a type of comparison which Toury admits is inevitably incomplete and which needs to undergo 'continuous revision' (*ibid.*) during the analytical process itself. The result is a flexible and non-prescriptive, if also less than rigorously systematic, means of comparing ST and TT. The flexibility is demonstrated by the fact that different aspects of texts are examined in different case studies. Thus, in one study (Toury 1995: 148-65) it is the addition of rhymes and omission of passages in the Hebrew translation of a German fairy tale; in another (pp. 102-12), it is conjoint phrases of near-synonyms (e.g. *able and talented, might and main*) in literature translated into Hebrew.

However, the flexibility of this approach is achieved by research techniques that are still not as explicit as is necessary for a description to be as objective and as replicable as possible. The alternative to the ad-hoc method is an extensive and more systematic 'repertory of features' approach, although this is potentially 'arduous and tedious' (Holmes 1988: 80). Examples of attempts at such an extensive approach are House's (1977, 1997) adapted register analysis model, Lambert and van Gorp's (1985) descriptive model, and Nord's (1991) text analytic model. However, all still stumble when confronted with the problem of dealing with large amounts of text. An additional criticism of Toury's model (see Hermans

1996, 1999: 39-41) concerns its claim that translations are 'facts' of the target system only. As noted above, Toury first locates the TT in its sociocultural context. However, there seems to be no reason to restrict investigation in this way; the ST obviously also operates in its own sociocultural context, and that too will influence both whether it is selected for translation by the TT culture and also the way it is translated. It follows that consideration needs to be given to both ST and TT sociocultural contexts when studying a translation.

The present paper describes a model I have developed within the framework of Toury's descriptive approach but which proposes a *specific, systematic* and *replicable* means for the analysis of ST-TT pairs, and locates and compares both texts within their own sociocultural context. If successful, this would facilitate the process (suggested by Toury) of deducing the decisions made during translating and the translation 'norms' that were in operation. It would be replicable, enabling further studies to be conducted to test hypotheses. The proposed model examines four interrelated areas of analysis (Figure 1). The ST is located within its own cultural system and compared to the TT's role and reception in its own corresponding TT system; a linguistic profile of the ST is produced, following an extensive yet flexible 'repertoire of features' approach and this is compared to the corresponding profile for the TT. In this way linguistic shifts are identified and an attempt is made to gauge their impact on the cultural level.

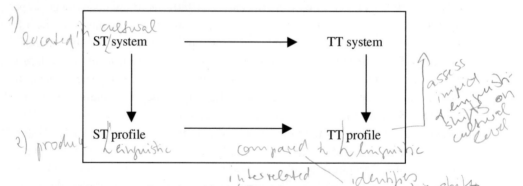

Figure 1: Four areas of analysis

The actual workings of this model brings together ideas and tools from (1) systemic functional linguistics and (2) corpus linguistics with (3) an analysis of the cultural context. The particular relevant strengths and uses of each element are as follows:

(1) *Systemic functional linguistics*: Systemic functional grammar (SFG), pioneered by Michael Halliday (see e.g. Halliday 1970; 1985/94), involves the detailed and systematic analysis of three interconnected strands of meaning in a text.[1] These

---

[1] There is a close link between SFG and what is known as 'discourse analysis' (which may be described as the analysis of stretches of texts or, preferably, whole texts, above sentence level,

three strands, called 'metafunctions', are the *ideational*, the *interpersonal* and the *textual*, which are linked to different linguistic or 'lexicogrammatical' realizations in a text:

- the *ideational* metafunction is broadly 'meaning as representation', often termed "content" (Halliday 1994: 109). Apart from the obvious importance of the denotational component of the lexical items chosen, the major lexicogrammatical realization of this function is the transitivity system: the process described by the verb, the *participants* in the process and the *circumstances* associated with the process (for example, an adverbial group or prepositional phrase).
- the *interpersonal* function involves meaning as "an exchange" (Halliday 1994: 68), whether of goods, services or information. In English, it is realized above all by modality, which is defined as "the speaker's judgement of the probabilities, or the obligations, involved in what he is saying" (Halliday, p. 75). Expressing obligation, probability, usuality and wanting, modality allows the writer or speaker to indicate his or her opinion with great subtlety and, as is stressed by Simpson (1993), in literature it is quite closely linked to the development of narrative point of view.
- the *textual* function deals with meaning as "message" (Halliday 1994: 37), that is, the organization and structure of the clause and the text. It is realized by the thematic structure (the order of elements in a clause and the way information is structured) and by patterns of cohesion (including the use of referents pronouns, as well as collocation, lexical repetition, synonymy, conjunction, amongst others).

Because of the close links between lexicogrammatical patterns and metafunctions, it should be possible, by analysing patterns of transitivity, modality, thematic structure and cohesion in a ST and TT, to see how the metafunctions are working. By following a similar procedure for both ST and TT and by comparing the patterns in the two texts, any shifts on the level of metafunctions should become clear. This approach lends itself well to the analysis of translation shifts and of the decision-making processes of the translator. Indeed, it has heavily influenced work in translation studies by scholars such as Baker (1992), Hatim and Mason (1990; 1997) and Taylor (1990).

Although SFG-oriented analysis has been used in other studies, it is still true that there is a shortage of systematic studies of *complete* published translations

---

with particular attention being given to their communicative role in writer-reader interaction in their given sociocultural context). Halliday makes the case for detailed lexicogrammatical analysis: "a discourse analysis that is not based on grammar is not an analysis at all, but simply a running commentary on a text" (1994: xvi).

(rather than short and isolated passages). The reason for this is mainly the logistical problem posed by the detailed analysis of a long text. The present model proposes that this can be overcome by the use of tools from corpus linguistics to analyse electronically-held versions of the texts under investigation.[2]

2) *handling*
the data
corpus
linguistics

(2) *Corpus linguistics*: Tools used in corpus linguistics are becoming increasingly available to researchers and enable rapid access of linguistic items. The kind of information that can be generated covers on-screen concordances of any search word or other search term, including total text length (the number of 'tokens'), the number of different word forms ('types'), type-token ratios (which give some indication of variety of language), word frequency lists, and so on (see Sinclair 1992 and Baker 1995 for more details of the possibilities). The tools provide two very important advantages: they can reveal phenomena which, because they may be spread over a lengthy text, might escape the attention of a researcher conducting manual analysis; and the analytical process is speeded up and far more reliable (*all* instances of a given term can be called up in a matter of seconds). This frees the researcher to concentrate on close analysis of the phenomena within the immediate linguistic context. Thus, in a detailed computer-assisted analysis of short fiction (Munday 1997), the computer was asked to produce word-lists for each text; these lists were

example

trawled for realizations of the metafunctions (e.g. all verb or process forms in the case of the realizations of the ideational metafunction), which were then called up on screen and checked against the translation using an interlinear form of the ST-TT pair. There are various software packages that can do this; perhaps the most widely available and user-friendly is *Wordsmith* (Scott 1999).

Summary

Therefore the first two stages of the model function as follows: a profile of the ST can be built up by systematically identifying the shifts using an SFG model aided by tools from corpus linguistics. In this way patterns of shifts can be identified throughout a text and the norms adopted (consciously or not) by the translator deduced. This is potentially a very important development.

analysis
within
cultural
context

Then, by (3) *locating the results within the wider publishing, political and sociocultural contexts*, it may be possible to identify factors other than purely linguistic ones which motivate the shifts. In this respect, SFG is useful in that it systematically relates linguistic choices to the sociocultural context. For instance, the lexico-grammatical patterns 'realize' the metafunctions, which in turn are determined by the immediate environment of the text (that is, what is known as the 'context of situation': the field, the tenor or writer-reader relationship, and the mode or form of communication). The context of situation is regulated by what is called the 'context

---

[2] Copyright authorization should be obtained to use the texts for research purposes. As more material becomes readily available on Web, this is less likely to be a problem in the future. Indeed, as web-based publication becomes the norm, so should corpus-based analysis become indispensable.

of culture', which is the higher-level fabric and ideology of the social system and the language genre to which a specific text belongs (Halliday 1978: 189).

The main goal of the present paper is thus to propose a methodology for replicable descriptive studies. The following sections will give an indication of the model in action. The texts used in this illustration are English translations of an essay by the Colombian writer Gabriel García Márquez concerning the case of the shipwrecked Cuban boy Elián González.

2. The model in action: the Elián González story

The six-year old Elián González became headline news in late 1999 when he was taken by his mother and her boyfriend in a small boat in an attempt to flee from Cuba to Florida. The boat capsized and his mother drowned, but Elián was rescued from the sea by the US navy and soon became the subject of a tug-of-war between his relatives in Miami and his father in Havana who was insisting on his return. The political ramifications of the confrontation between human pain and political systems dominated the media around the world at the beginning of the year 2000. This was the context in which García Márquez, a firm supporter of Fidel Castro, wrote a two-page column about the story, 'Náufrago en tierra firme' published initially in the Cuban Communist organ *Juventud Rebelde* and later reprinted in a range of media outlets, including the Spanish daily *El País* on 19 March 2000. Several English translations appeared of this: *The Guardian* published it under the title 'Torn in the USA' on 25 March; *The New York Times* entitled it 'Shipwrecked on dry land' on 29 March; and the Cuban group *Granma International* published another English translation on 21 March, which was made available on the Internet.

2.1. The location of the texts within the sociocultural context

The difference in context between ST and TTs can immediately be seen in the ways in which the story is presented in the different sources. This is especially evident in the photographs that are chosen to illustrate the text: while *El País*, for example, shows (1) the boy with his grandmothers on their visit to see him in Miami, (2) Fidel Castro meeting Elián's father, Juan Miguel, in Havana, and (3) thousands of Cubans demonstrating in the capital in support of his return to his father, *The Guardian* has a less than flattering portrait of the father, arms crossed, described as one of the 'contenders' in the struggle, the other being illustrated by placard-waving demonstrators in Miami "demand[ing] that the boy stays in the US". The contrast between the choice of demonstration photographs may possibly be due to the ease of access to the different language communities, but it definitely has the effect of focussing the reader's attention on the perspective of one of the arguments in the case. Both newspapers, however, print a similar photograph of a bewildered Elián, seen

behind a wire fence, with *The Guardian* posing the question "Stuck in the middle
[...] will Elián González be allowed to go home to his father in Cuba?"

The use of different illustrations places the texts in different frameworks linked
to the ideological contexts of culture in which the texts are published. The Spanish
context merges more with the Cuban perspective. The *Guardian* headline, 'Torn in
the USA', playing on Bruce Springsteen's 1980s polemic hit 'Born in the USA',
shows that its focus is on the human and emotional battle for the child. It also gives
added background to the story ("The plight of a Cuban child washed up on a Florida
beach [...] the battle for custody continues"), information with which the Spanish
reader is expected to be familiar. Both texts are presented as original writing; the
English prints García Márquez's name in bold as part of the headline and gives no
indication anywhere that it is a translation.

This is certainly not the case with the other two TTs. The *New York Times* translation carries the name of Edith Grossman, the famous translator of García Márquez's
fiction since 1985 and stresses García Márquez's status as a Nobel laureate. The
Cuban *Granma International Digital Edition* introduces the text with the downbeat
"Colombian writer Gabriel García Márquez wrote this article in Havana; it has been
published in various Latin American and Spanish newspapers" but at the same time
authorizes reproduction, presumably in an attempt to gain maximum publicity for
the Cuban cause, and invites readers to e-mail their opinions. Such presentation of
the texts may be linked to ideological aims driving publication. The following analysis
will attempt to identify linguistic shifts that occur within this framework.

2.2. Computer-generated statistics of the texts

Analysis will move from general computer-generated statistics to the more specific
close analysis. *Table 1* shows the kind of statistics that serve to suggest further lines
of inquiry for the researcher:

	ST	Granma TT (GIn)	Guardian TT (Gd)	NY Times TT (NYT)
word count (tokens)	3146	2998	2396	1621
different words (types)	1097	1059	866	621
type-token ratio	34.87	35.32	38.16	38.31
average sentence length in words	28.34	24.37	21.59	20.26

Table 1: Word and sentence statistics for ST and TTs

The most striking finding from this table concerns the word count for the different
texts. In all cases the ST is longer than the TTs. This counters conventional thinking
(e.g. Vinay and Darbelnet 1958/1977: 185) which has considered that a TT tends to
be longer than its ST due to explicitation. The differences in *Table 1*, however, go

beyond explicitation or condensation. There are also huge differences between the different TTs: the Granma International text is 600 words longer than the Guardian TT and nearly twice as long as the New York Times TT. Closer analysis of the actual texts in section 2.3.3 will indicate what has occurred.

The statistics for sentence length highlight that the New York Times and the Guardian texts stand out because they have a shorter average sentence length (20.26 and 21.59 words respectively compared to 24.37 in Granma International and 28.34 in the ST). García Márquez's writing is marked by extremely long sentences (see Munday 1997: 187); reasons for the shift in translation will again be discussed in section 2.3.3.

The type-token ratio, an indication of the variety of lexis in the text, has long been known to vary according to text length (Jones 1991: 18). In *Table 1*, it would only be meaningful to compare ratios for the ST and the Granma International TT, which has very few omissions. The type-token ratio for the two is very similar.

[handwritten margin notes: "text length", "Sentence length", "Variety of lexis", "20 most frequent words"]

		ST		GIn TT			Gd TT			NYT TT		
1	de (of)	184	5.85	the	205	6.84	the	165	6.89	the	91	5.61
2	la (the)	106	3.37	to	85	2.84	to	70	2.92	and	48	2.96
3	que (that)	106	3.37	of	84	2.80	and	61	2.55	to	46	2.84
4	el (the)	101	3.21	and	78	2.60	a	51	2.13	in	41	2.53
5	a (to)	86	2.73	a	77	2.57	in	49	2.05	a	35	2.16
6	y (and)	77	2.45	in	68	2.27	of	47	1.96	of	33	2.04
7	en (in/ on)	71	2.26	that	55	1.83	his	37	1.54	his	32	1.97
8	los (the)	59	1.88	his	44	1.47	Elián	34	1.42	was	27	1.67
9	para (for)	50	1.59	was	39	1.3	had	34	1.42	on	24	1.48
10	con (with	44	1.40	on	36	1.2	that	33	1.38	had	22	1.36
11	un (a)	38	1.21	with	34	1.13	was	28	1.17	for	19	1.17
12	se (reflexive)	37	1.18	for	29	.97	for	25	1.04	Elián	18	1.11
13	su (his/ her/ their)	37	1.18	Elián	28	.93	he	25	1.04	he	18	1.11
14	por (for)	33	1.05	had	28	.93	they	23	.96	with	18	1.11
15	lo (it/ him)	31	.99	he	27	.90	Juan	21	.88	Juan	17	1.05
16	no (no)	30	.95	it	24	.80	on	21	.88	Mig-uel	16	.99
17	una (a)	27	.86	as	23	.77	Mig-uel	20	.83	they	16	.99
18	Elián	25	.79	they	23	.77	with	20	.83	at	15	.93
19	ni (nor)	25	.79	is	22	.73	us	19	.79	that	15	.93
20	o (or)	24	.76	be	21	.70	but	16	.67	but	14	.86

Table 2: Word frequency statistics for ST and TTs

What is evident is that the computer-generated statistics highlight areas that may be worthy of close critical analysis. This is especially the case with word frequency lists. *Table 2* shows the twenty most frequent words in each text. To the right of these words is the number of times they occur in the text and the percentage this represents of the total words in the text. A typical English correspondent of the Spanish words is given in brackets. Thus, *de* (often with the meaning *of*) is the most common word in the ST, it occurs 184 times and represents 5.85% of the total word forms in the ST.

Many of these common word-forms such as *de* or *the* will be the most frequent in any text in Spanish or English. More interesting are the comparative frequencies which can be followed up by close examination of instances. It would also be possible to extend the study considerably to look at very many different word-forms; because of space considerations, I shall limit myself to just two examples. First, the occurrence of the name *Elián* is, in percentage terms, far more frequent in the Guardian TT compared to the ST or the other TTs. Proper name referents are important for the cohesion of a text, so this discrepancy will be examined in section 2.3.3 on cohesion and the textual metafunction. A second example is the word *that*, which is most common in the Granma International TT. It is sometimes predicted (e.g. Baker 1995: 236) that the overuse of the relative pronoun *that* is a characteristic of translations from languages such as Spanish where the corresponding pronoun *que* cannot be omitted as it can in English. Computer-assisted analysis draws attention to the different frequencies and then allows all the instances to be accessed and examined quickly onscreen.

Analysis of our examples reveals that only four of the instances of *that* in the Granma TT can be discarded as demonstrative pronouns (e.g. "*that* Friday"). Of the others, there are several occasions where the Granma International TT closely follows the ST structure and includes the translation *that*. Example 1 is a comment from the Elián's father complaining about interference when he phones his son:

> 1a. *A veces le hablan a gritos al niño mientras conversamos, suben al máximo el volumen de los dibujos animados en la televisión o le ponen un caramelo en la boca <u>para que no se le entienda</u> lo que dice.*
> 1b. Sometimes they talk to the boy in loud voices while we're having a conversation, they turn up the volume of the cartoons on the television as high as possible, or put a candy in his mouth <u>so that I can't understand</u> what he's saying. (GIn)
> 1c. Sometimes they shout at the boy while we're talking, or turn the volume all the way up on television cartoons, or put a candy in his mouth <u>so it's hard to understand</u> what he's saying. (NYT)

Here, translation 1c, omitting the word *that*, is more informal and perhaps better suited to the translation of speech.

The admittedly restricted number of examples presented in this section is designed to indicate some of the possibilities offered by computer analysis, which allow relatively rapid access to features of whole texts and bring features to the attention of the analyst that might otherwise go unnoticed. As will be seen in the following sections, the computer is also a powerful tool when combined with the systemic-functional framework to look at all examples of the different metafunctions in two texts and to compare the markedness of the profiles in ST and TT.

2.3. The metafunctional analysis of the texts

An analysis of the metafunctional profiles in the two texts reveals differences. For reasons of space, the focus will be on comparing patterns between the ST and the Guardian TT, but, where particularly relevant, comparison will be made with the other TTs.

2.3.1. Ideational metafunction

Transitivity patterns are often altered in the TT, as can be seen in example 2, describing Elián's fellow fugitives' use of a drug to counter sea-sickness:

2a. la mayoría de los pasajeros se inyectaron gravinol intravenoso
2b. most passengers were injected with Gravinol (Gd)

While 2a suggests the passengers did the injecting themselves, 2b removes responsibility for the action. The implication is that this was an action done to them, presumably by those in charge of the crossing, who stood to gain a large sum of money were it to be successful. Yet example 2 is atypical because the majority of shifts in ideational profile in the Guardian TT deflect responsibility from the relatives in Miami. Thus, a passive is used in the TT when the heavy outboard motor is thrown overboard (a blunder that causes the boat to capsize), whereas the ST clearly describes it as an action committed by those in charge (*los responsables del viaje*):

3a. los responsables del viaje desmontaron el motor desahuciado
3b. the engine – a write off – was dismantled (Gd)

Furthermore, the responsibility for the change in Elían's character while he is in Florida is also shifted. This is seen in the report of his grandmothers' return from their visit to him in the United States:

4a. De modo que [las abuelas] volvieron a Cuba escandalizadas de cuánto lo habían cambiado.
4b. They [the grandmothers] returned to Cuba outraged at how much the child had changed. (Gd)

The ST's 'lo habían cambiado' ('they had changed him') shows that it is the Miami-based relatives who have provoked the change; the passive in the TT again obscures this responsibility.

2.3.2. Interpersonal metafunction ~ modality

Many markers of the interpersonal metafunction, especially what Halliday (1994: 354) terms 'interpersonal metaphors', are omitted in the TT. One such example is *parece que* ('it appears'):

> 5a. <u>Parece que</u> habían zarpado el 20 de noviembre…
> 5b. They sailed on November 20… (Gd)

This omission of such hedging makes García Márquez's account far more factual. On some occasions, this can have the effect of removing emotion. This occurs in the following description of what happens in the sea when Elián's mother, Elizabeth, somehow managed to help her son:

> 6a. <u>Lo que es difícil de entender, aunque merece ser cierto</u>, es que ella tuvo la serenidad y el tiempo para darle al hijo una botella de agua dulce.
> 6b. <u>She is said to</u> have had the foresight and time to give Elián a bottle of water. (Gd)

In the ST, García Márquez emphasizes the astonishing feat this action represents, if it is true ("Lo que es díficil de entender, aunque merece ser cierto" – "what is difficult to accept, although it deserves to be true"). The TT's "she is said to" removes the astonishment altogether by a replacement of interpersonal elements with a passive and neutral reporting verb.

A reduction in the interpersonal force of the text is also evident in the omission of attitudinal epithets (for an explanation of these see Halliday 1994: 184): Elián's father is described as "de buen carácter" ('of good character') whereas he is just "laidback" in the TT, and "anfitriones interesados" ('self-interested hosts') in Miami are merely "hosts" in the English. Such omissions affect the relative merits of both sides of the family as they face each other across the straits. Another example concerns the situation of the father, with whom Elián lived until he was taken away:

> 7a. Juan Miguel, por su parte, se casó más tarde con Nelsy Carmeta, con quien tiene un hijo de seis meses <u>que fue el amor de la vida de Elián hasta que Elizabeth se lo llevó para Miami.</u>
> 7b. Juan Miguel had married Nelsy Carmeta: the couple have a six-month-old baby. (Gd)

The whole of the last clause has been omitted in the TT. It is translated in the Granma International TT as "a six-month-old son who was the love of Elián's life until

Elizabeth took him off to Miami". The selection of such detail in the ST obviously adds a positive light to the Cuban family and a strongly negative one to the albeit luckless mother who was prepared to destroy Elián's happiness. The same occurs with the later suggestion that the United States will suffer a "pérdida jurídica e histórica". The "legal and historical loss" of the ST becomes the "overall loss" of the TT. While *jurídica* and *histórica* might normally be classed as descriptive and not attitudinal, their collocation with *pérdida* adds a negative evaluation because of the connotations of infringing the law and being tainted in the eyes of history. Those connotations disappear in the Guardian TT, although they are all retained in the Cuban translation.

2.3.3. Textual metafunction

In the statistics in section 2.2 above, we noted the increased frequency of the name *Elián* in the Guardian TT, the difference in sentence length and overall text length between the different texts. These points all fall within the ambit of the textual metafunction, especially of the cohesion of the texts. Closer examination of specific instances using a computer-generated concordance to cross-check occurrences gives an indication of what is happening. Thus, the search-term *Elián* brings up the 34 occurrences in the Guardian and the 25 in the ST. Those which appear in the TT but not the ST can quickly be identified, as in example 8, where Munero, the mother's companion, threatens Elián:

> 8a. *Se ha dicho también que Elián tomó conciencia allí mismo de los peligros de la travesía, y lloraba a grito herido para que lo dejaran. Munero, temeroso de que los descubrieran por* el llanto*, amenazó a* la esposa*: "O lo callas tú, o lo callo yo".*
> 8b. Elián also became aware of the dangers of the crossing and screamed, begging to be allowed to stay in Cuba. Munero, fearful they would be discovered because of Elián's crying, threatened Elizabeth: "Either you shut him up, or I'll do it myself." (Gd)

The TT shows greater cohesion, with the translation *Elián's crying* instead of simply *the crying* or *the screaming*. Elsewhere in the TT, *Elián* is used to replace a synonym such as *the boy* or *the child*. Interestingly, example 8b indicates the increased use of Elizabeth's name (rather than *his wife*). The same translation occurs in the Granma International TT:

> 8c. Munero, fearful of being discovered due to the child's wailing, threatened Elizabeth: "Either you shut him up, or I will." (GIn)

Increased cohesion is generally felt to be a characteristic of translated texts (e.g. Blum-Kulka 1986); computer-assisted analysis provides a tool to enable cohesive ties to be checked.

Similarly, shifts in sentence length were revealed by the computer, the most evident differences being between the ST and the New York Times TT. Specific examples were checked. Typical is example 9:

> 9a. *Elizabeth quedaba encinta pero sufría abortos espontáneos en los cuatro primeros meses de embarazo. Al cabo de siete pérdidas, y con una asistencia médica especial, nació el hijo tan esperado, para el cual tenían previsto un nombre único desde que se casaron; Elián.*
> 9b. Elizabeth would conceive but miscarry in the first four months of pregnancy. After seven miscarriages, the child they had longed for was born. They had decided on a unique name for him: Elián. (*New York Times*)

The ST comprises two sentences of 14 and 29 words; the TT in 9b carries this information into three chunks of 12, 11 and 10 words.

Sentence length is closely linked to punctuation; the formal use of the semicolon in 9a and the colon in 9b prompted an investigation of their frequency in all the texts. The ST contains one semi-colon and ten colons (which mainly introduce quotations); the New York Times TT has one semi-colon and five colons, Granma International uses four semi-colons and eleven colons, whereas the Guardian text contains ten semi-colons and sixteen colons. Punctuation conventions do vary between Spanish and English, and it would be worth investigating how much they differ between British and US English, but for the moment it can certainly be stated that the Guardian TT demonstrates greater formality, as in example 10b where first a colon and then a semi-colon punctuate the translation:

> 10a. *Estas artimañas fueron sufridas también en carne propia por Raquel Rodríguez y Marcela Quintana, las abuelas de Elián, durante su tormentosa visita a Miami, cuando un agente de la policía a órdenes de una monja frenética les arrebató el teléfono celular con que ellas daban noticias del niño a sus familias de Cuba. La vista que había sido prevista para dos días se redujo al final a noventa minutos, con toda clase de interrupciones provocadas, y con no más de un cuarto de hora a solas con Elián.*
> 10b. Raquel Rodríguez and Marcela Quintana, Elián's grandmothers who made a stormy visit to Miami had the same problems: at the order of a frantic nun, a police officer snatched their mobile phones so that they could not pass on news to the family in Cuba. Their two-day visit was eventually reduced to 90 minutes, with all kinds of manufactured interruption; they only had a quarter of an hour on their own with Elián. (Gd)

Sentence length and punctuation may seem relatively minor differences, but they do indicate that one characteristic of García Márquez's writing is shifted in translation. Alterations to the cohesion and coherence profiles of the two texts can also have repercussions for the reading of the article. Thus, reference to the two countries involved through the use of synonyms reflects the perspective from which the story is told. In the ST, the United States is once referred to as *la otra orilla* ('the other shore') and the Cuban régime as *la revolución*. In the Guardian TT, the first loses any emotive or poetic referent to become *in the US*, and the positive connotation of the revolution is turned into the dictatorial sounding *Castro's Cuba*.

Although, for ease of analysis, SFG analyses the different metafunctions separately, the following extract demonstrates how many of the phenomena discussed in this paper (ideational and interpersonal as well as textual) interact within the same passage:

> 11a. <u>Según ellos</u>, a la medianoche del 22, <u>los responsables del viaje des montaron el motor desahuciado</u> y lo tiraron en el mar para aligerar la carga. Pero la barca, descompensada, dio una voltereta de costado <u>y</u> todos los pasajeros cayeron al agua. <u>Sin embargo</u>, una suposición de expertos es que la voltereta pudo haber roto las frágiles soldaduras de los tubos de alumnio, <u>y</u> la barca se hundió.
> 11b. At midnight on the first day out, <u>the engine – a write off – was dismantled</u> and thrown into the sea to lighten the load. But the boat was destabilized and turned over on to its side. All the passengers fell into the water. Experts suspect that the capsize may have broken the fragile soldering on the aluminium tube, <u>causing</u> the boat to sink.

The first line, as was discussed in example 3, exhibits a shift in transitivity structure, removing responsibility for the accident from those organizing the trip (*los responsables del viaje*) to an agentless passive (*was dismantled*). The omission of *según ellos* ("according to them") in line 1 also affects the interpersonal profile and truth value of the TT. Furthermore, the cohesion of lines 3 to 5 of the Spanish is altered in translation. The frequent use of the conjunction *y* ("and") is characteristic of García Márquez's writing, especially in his fiction where a fairy-tale type frame is often followed, and where extremely long sentences and paratactic, non-causal structures typify the language and thinking of children. The structure alters completely in the TT: the *y* conjunction of line 3 is replaced by a full stop, a stronger break that requires greater cognitive work on the part of the reader to establish the links between the two sentences. There is also no translation of *sin embargo*, fronted in line 4 of the ST, where it functions as a discourse marker and guide to the reader to expect a contrast. It is possible that the translator felt that there was no real contrast here, that the breaking of the soldering was a logical result of the capsizing. Finally, the TT again avoids use of 'and' to translate the *y* of the last line, this time preferring a hypotactic present participle (*causing*) which strengthens the links between the ideas and clauses. The result of such pattern changes in English is a dislocation of García Márquez's style in translation.

In addition to such differences, the model also reveals more striking shifts. Analysis of the New York Times TT version of example 10 surprisingly shows the omission of the underlined segment in 10a:

10c. These kinds of stratagems were also suffered in person by Raquel Rodríguez and Marcela Quintanta, Elián's grandmothers, during their turbu-lent trip to Miami. Their visit with him, scheduled to last two days, was reduced to 90 minutes, with all kinds of intentional interruptions, and they said they spent no more than a quarter of an hour alone with Elián. (NYT)

The detail that has been omitted ("at the order of a frantic nun, a police officer snatched their mobile phones") paints an extremely negative picture of the US authorities. Closer examination of the rest of this TT shows that the many omis-sions fall mainly into two categories: first, mention of geographical place names such as Cárdenas or the names of the hotels in which Elizabeth had worked; sec-ondly, the final 800 words which discuss the history of Cuban-US relations and the possible political damage to Al Gore's presidential campaign in November 2000. This explains the word count statistics for the text in section 2.2 above.

2.4. Possible motivations for the translation shifts

That there have been substantial shifts between ST and TTs is not open to doubt. The question is what has caused this and here further reference needs to be made to the sociocultural and political framework in which the translations have been pro-duced. There are a number of possibilities: the translator of the Guardian TT has followed a non-systematic translation strategy that has produced a non-systematic and somewhat distorted translation; the shifts might be related to the skirting of specific translation problems in the text (thus, in 3, the word *responsables* is not easy to translate succinctly, and, in example 6, the translator may have been sur-prised by the wording of "lo que es difícil de entender, aunque merece ser cierto"); some of the punctuation changes may well have been carried out by a copy-editor, while the omissions in the TTs may have been down to the constraints of space in the media and the need to cut the original, but then the question would be, why these cuts and not others? Ideologically more exciting is the possibility that the shifts have been intentionally motivated by a publisher or even a translator to create a different image of the story in the minds of its readers. It may not be far-fetched to suppose that omissions of certain anti-US sentiments in the New York Times TT were motivated by a desire to reduce the possible political fall-out from the publication of a polemical text written by the enemy. Not surprisingly, the TT published by the Cuban Granma International is a full translation of the ST and retains the anti-US comments.

3. Conclusion

Although I have attempted to locate the two texts in their immediate sociocultural framework, there is more investigation that can be done. Interviews with the newspaper editors and translators, if possible, would illuminate some of the reasoning behind the translation decisions, and the reception of the two texts might be gauged by looking more closely at the subsequent reactions in the media. It is noteworthy that the week following the publication of this article saw a series of letters in the UK and the USA supporting or attacking the Cuban position, none of which referred to the English TT as anything other than García Márquez's writing even though some quoted his words in English. These readers would probably have no access to the fuller Cuban translation.

This SFG analysis of ST-TT pairs has successfully identified important aspects that have undergone shifts in translation. The analysis has been assisted by the use of corpus linguistic tools that enable rapid manipulation of text and an uncovering of trends that may not be obvious to manual analysis. Finally, the setting of the results within the sociocultural and political context of the texts has enabled some conclusions to be drawn as to the norms at work in the translation process. Of course, some areas of the model may need to be adapted to the subjects under investigation; thus, strict SFG analysis, especially of textual and transitivity structures, may not work so well with non-European languages, while detailed analysis of shorter texts can be carried out without the use of a computer. That is why I stress the flexibility of the model: by examining the relative markedness of the metafunctional profile of text pairs (rather than merely listing the specific lexicogrammatical realizations) adjustment can be made for languages that are differently structured. Importantly, too, it means that the model is still replicable. That is, other studies can and should be undertaken to test the hypotheses: do translations of the Elián González text into other languages exhibit the same phenomena as the English translation? Is García Márquez's non-fiction generally subject to greater shifts in translation than his fiction? If so, what are the reasons? Are these ideological reasons? Is non-fiction generally treated differently in translation? In this way, with a model designed to be replicable, testable and applicable to other texts and language pairs, we can begin to build up a more systematic picture of translation phenomena that can lead to the testing of further hypotheses and to a refining of what Toury terms as 'laws' of translation.

References

Baker, Mona (1992) *In Other Words: A Coursebook on Translation*, London & New York: Routledge.
----- (1995) 'Corpora in Translation Studies: An Overview and Suggestions for Future Research', *Target* 7(2): 223-43.
Blum-Kulka, Shoshana (1986) 'Shifts of Cohesion and Coherence in Translation', in

J. House and S. Blum-Kulka (eds) *Interlingual and Intercultural Communication*, Tübingen: Gunter Narr:,17-35.

Brown, M. (1994) *The Reception of Spanish American Fiction in West Germany 1981-91*, Tübingen: Niemeyer.

García Márquez, Gabriel (2000a) 'Náufrago en tierra firme', *El País* 19.3.2000: 6-7.

----- (2000b) 'Torn in the USA', *The Guardian Review* 25.3.2000: 1-2.

----- (2000c) 'Shipwrecked on dry land', *The New York Times* 29.3.2000: Op. Ed.

----- (2000d) 'Shipwreck on dry land', *Granma International Digital Edition*, 21.3.2000.

Halliday, M.A.K. (1978) *Language as Social Semiotic*, London & New York: Edward Arnold.

----- (1985, 2nd edition 1994) *An Introduction to Functional Grammar*, London: Edward Arnold.

Hatim, Basil and Ian Mason (1990) *Discourse and the Translator*, London & New York: Longman.

----- (1997) *The Translator as Communicator*, London & New York: Routledge.

Hermans, Theo (1995) 'Toury's Empiricism Version One', *The Translator* 1(2): 215-23.

Holmes, J.S. (1988) *Translated! Papers on Literary Translation and Translation Studies*, Amsterdam: Rodopi.

House, Juliane (1977) *A Model for Translation Quality Assessment*, Tübingen: Gunter Narr.

----- (1997) *Translation Quality Assessment: A Model Revisited*, Tübingen: Gunter Narr.

Jones, S. (1991) *Text and Context: Document Processing and Storage*, London: Springer.

Lambert, José and Hendrik van Gorp (1985) 'On Describing Translations', in T. Hermans (ed) *The Manipulation of Literature: Studies in Literary Translation*, London & Sydney: Croom Helm, 42-53.

Leuven-Zwart, Kitty van (1989) 'Translation and Original: Similarities and Dissimilarities, I', *Target* 1(2): 151-181.

----- (1990) 'Translation and Original: Similarities and Dissimilarities, II', *Target* 2(1): 69-95.

Munday, Jeremy (1997) *Systems in Translation*. Unpublished PhD thesis. University of Bradford.

Nord, Christiane (1991) *Text Analysis in Translation*, trans. C. Nord and P. Sparrow, Amsterdam: Rodopi, originally published 1988.

Scott, M. (1999) *Wordsmith* (software), 3rd edition, Oxford: Oxford University Press.

Simpson, P. (1993) *Language, Ideology and Point of View*, London & New York: Routledge.

Sinclair, J.M. (1991) *Corpus, Concordance, Collocation*, Oxford: Oxford University Press.

Taylor, C. (1990) *Aspects of Language and Translation: Approaches for Italian-English Translation*, Udine: Camponette.

Toury, Gideon (1980) *In Search of a Theory of Translation*, Tel Aviv: Porter Institute.

----- (1995) *Descriptive Translation Studies and Beyond*, Amsterdam & Philadelphia: John Benjamins.

Vinay, J-P. and J. Darbelnet (1958/1977) *Stylistique comparée du français et de l'anglais. Méthode de traduction*, Paris: Didier.

A Model of Structuralist Constructivism in Translation Studies

JEAN-MARC GOUANVIC

Abstract: *The article proposes a theory of translation based on Pierre Bourdieu's structuralist constructivism. By constructivism Bourdieu means a twofold social genesis, one constitutive of what he calls 'habitus', the other of social structures. The habitus of a translator is a durable, transposable disposition acquired by the socialized body, by which the translator exercises his practice in a field to which a text to be translated belongs. The field is the locus where the translator posits the text's action, at the conjunction of a subjectivity and an historicity. Two cases of translators' habitus are taken as illustrations, with reference to Maurice-Edgar Coindreau and Marcel Duhamel. Their respective habitus appear profoundly different, although their translations appeared with the same publisher, Gallimard. The heuristic status of the notions of habitus and field and the conditions of historicization are examined with respect to translation. Following Bourdieu's structuralist constructivism, translating agents are seen as playing the role of practical operators who exercise their power in a relational way, i.e. competitively as well as cooperatively.*

To be fully understood, literary production has to be approached in relational terms, by constructing the literary field, i.e. the space of literary *prises de position* [position-takings] that are possible in a given period in a given society. *Prises de position* arise from the encounter between particular agents' dispositions (their *habitus*, shaped by their social trajectory) and their position in a field of positions which is defined by the distribution of a specific form of capital. (Bourdieu 1983: 311)

1. Introduction

In translation studies a distinction is usually made between studies which deal with extant products and those which attempt to analyze determinations specific to the process of translation. The distinction between process and product, first introduced by James Holmes in 1972 (Holmes 1988),[1] has become classic. It is useful in that it denotes different states of reflexivity. The study of translation as process can concentrate more particularly on mental operations or on discourse analysis in

---

[1] To this distinction between product and process Holmes added a third possible option, function-oriented research, which does not quite work on the same level of pertinence, since the study of translation both as product and as process may be functional.

translation, or on more programmatic concepts aimed at understanding what translation can or must be. Studying translation as product means investigating from a
descriptive angle the social and historical factors bearing on translation in a given
time and work. As a result, process-oriented approaches are much less concerned
with the historical dimension of the activity and much more with synchronic aspects of translation, whereas product-oriented studies aim to reconstruct the historic
logic which has presided over its emergence. The study of translation as product is
geared – this is its final horizon – towards the historical knowledge of a cultural
segment of a given space at a given time, and it seeks to posit translation as one of
its determinants in this space at this given time.

There is another theoretical possibility, even though it does not quite amount to
a new view on translation. It consists in viewing translation in terms of 'production'. It is on this problematic of translation as production that I wish to concentrate
here. In doing so, I will simultaneously elucidate what is at the heart of this approach, the model of *structuralist constructivism* as developed by Pierre Bourdieu.

Before dealing with *structuralist constructivism*, it may be useful to recall that
Bourdieu has begun to attract the attention of translation scholars. For example,
Daniel Siméoni, in his article 'The Pivotal Status of the Translator's Habitus'
(1998), examines the issue of the specialized habitus of the translator and the
primary role it might play in translation studies. In his *Translation in Systems*
(1999) Theo Hermans reviews André Lefevere's contribution to a discussion particularly on Bourdieu's notion of 'cultural capital'. For my own part, my book
Sociologie de la traduction (1999) addresses the history of the translation of American science fiction in the French cultural space in the 1950s from the viewpoint of
Bourdieu's sociology of culture.

Bourdieu's theory of culture, then, is definitely gaining ground in translation
studies. I will now briefly examine the foundations of this theory and its possible
application to translation. Bourdieu defines 'constructivism' as follows:

> There is a twofold social genesis, on the one hand of the schemes of per-
> ception, thought, and action which are constitutive of what I call habitus,
> and on the other hand of social structures, and particularly of what I call
> fields and of groups, notably those we ordinarily call social classes.
> (Bourdieu 1989: 14)

Bourdieu's model of constructivism (the structuralist component of it will be
discussed at the end of this article) can readily be applied to translation. Furthermore, it sheds light on aspects which are frequently overlooked in translation,
as we will see.

A *sine qua non* of social constructivism is that it deals with actual states of affairs in a given society and at a given moment in the history of that society. Social
constructivism cannot be content with vague periodizations of disparate corpora.

For an analysis which claims to draw its inspiration from this model, it is imperative that it places the activities it investigates in a social milieu, in the full meaning of this term. In other words, this type of analysis will focus, on the one hand, on interventions by agents who are the producers of the texts under discussion, and, on the other, on the structural and institutional conditions which are at the origin of the production in question. The social milieu is here anything but a mere framework in which to lodge a text that would somehow predate the milieu or exist independently of it. Any text, translated or not, results from a social production process. It is impossible to consider it divorced from the social, for that would take away what makes it into a text, with all it contains, from the creativity of its producer to the stereotypes which it rehearses and which are anchored in the prevailing *doxa*. The corpus possesses characteristics that are specific, and for the purpose of contrastive analysis, distinct corpora will be compared so as to determine those specificities. How does translation define itself in this context?

2. Habitus and translation

Translation, like other forms of written production, is open to a scholarly analysis. But it is unlike other written works in that at least four elements intervene in its operation. These are the source text (and its determinants), the target text (and its determinants), the translator as a subjectivity, and the translator as historicity. These elements entertain relations which tie them together, and which can be described in Bourdieu's terms through the notions of *habitus* and *field*.

The habitus (Bourdieu 1990: 53) of a translator as producer may be defined as a durable, transposable disposition acquired by the socialized body, which invests in practice the organizing principles that are socially constructed in the course of a situated and dated experience. In today's world it would appear as natural, for example, that a French translator working on American literature has learned English at secondary school. The skills needed for the exercise of translation will typically have been acquired in a translator training institution. These acquired dispositions however do not turn him or her into a translator. To become a translator, s/he will have to implement his/her activities with respect to a given field. The relationship between the actualized dispositions of the translator's habitus and the translator's position vis-à-vis a text to be translated, that is vis-à-vis a text belonging to a given field, this relationship takes shape as the activity of translating becomes a matter of routine, when the habitus has been internalized as an integral part of the operation of translation in the field.

Translation as production is here considered in the very moment of its genesis, the instant of its emergence, not *a posteriori* as a product viewed in terms of the use subsequently made of it in a given framework according to norms reconstructed with the benefit of hindsight. The practical operator that is the translator locates his or her action at the conjunction of a subjectivity and an historicity, as the site of an historicized subjectivity or subjectified historicity. The translator's practical sense[2] is the ease with which s/he produces a translation that is inscribed in a given field. The field as historicity gives way to subjectified practices which are themselves simultaneously produced in the exercise of activities stemming from the field, an exercise that builds up subjective dispositions specific to the translator as agent. These subjective dispositions, shaped in the historic practice of the field and embodied in a habitus, are then re-invested in the field which at first presided over its genesis, and they find there conditions favourable to their expression.

What is constitutive of experience *in abstracto* is related to a habitus acquired in a particular field, which is also the field to which the text to be translated belongs. Fields however are not hermetically sealed. Due to their relative permeability, the translation habitus may be transferred from one field and from one text to another, for example from sociology to ethnology. Very distant fields that do not share adjacent stakes, such as physics and philosophy, do not show connecting traits expressed in the form of transferable dispositions acquired in a field and valid in another one.

3.   Two cases of translator's habitus: Maurice-Edgar Coindreau and Marcel Duhamel

How does a translator acquire the translation habitus? Put differently, how is the disposition to translate internalized? Let us take the example of the literary field, and two of its most renowned Francophone translators. Maurice-Edgar Coindreau, the translator of William Faulkner, took a degree in Spanish and at first showed little interest in the literatures of North America. In Madrid in the early 1920s he struck up a friendship with Pepe Robles, who introduced him to John Dos Passos. In 1923 Coindreau emigrated to the United States, where he taught French at Princeton. He undertook the French translation of *Manhattan Transfer* (published in 1928) in order, as he said in an interview, to learn American slang (Coindreau 1974: 36-37). This is one of the characteristics of his constructed habitus: he had to learn American slang so as to be able to translate it subsequently, and he learned it through translation. His knowledge of slang and colloquial English is at the outset bookish. After this first experience he was hooked, becoming the main propagator and translator into French of a particular American literature, the literature of the southern states of the USA. Contemptuous of the so-called *lost generation* writers (a designation coined by Gertrude Stein), Coindreau turned with gusto to the southern United States. He compared the southern states' experience in the American

---

[2] The *sens pratique* of the translator is a necessary coincidence between a habitus and a field, by which one finds immediately, without deliberating, things to be done and to be done in a proper way in the situation of translation (Bourdieu 2000: 135-6).

Civil War and its aftermath to that of the *Chouannerie*, the Vendée's failed counter-revolution at the time of the French Revolution. This is deeply constitutive of Coindreau's habitus and it is at the core of his social trajectory: he had a very clearly marked preference for southern states writers (William Faulkner to begin with) due to the similarity of their *Weltanschauung* with that of the *Chouans*, a *Weltanschauung* characterized by *failure overcome*. Had he possessed the talent of a writer, he reflected, he would not have translated but would have written about the *Chouans* instead (Coindreau 1974: 103).

For a sharply contrasting case, let us take the example of Marcel Duhamel (1972). The comparison is natural since Coindreau and Duhamel 'jointly' translated John Steinbeck's *The Grapes of Wrath* in 1947.[3] Duhamel is very much a self-taught translator. His formal education ended with elementary school and he did not know a word of English when he was fifteen. In 1915 he found himself in Manchester, where he learned English on the job, working for a time in a hotel owned by an uncle of his. After the First World War he did his military service, mainly in Istanbul, where he met Jacques Prévert. During the 1920s he became the manager of his uncle's hotels in Paris and lived in the rue du Château with Jacques Prévert and the painter Yves Tanguy, enjoying the bohemian lifestyle of the Surrealists. He tried his hand at translating detective novels, *Green Ice* by Raoul Whitfield and subsequently *Little Caesar* by W. R. Burnett (the latter published by *France-soir*). The translation of *Little Caesar* made his name and he joined the Tobis Klangfilm company as an Anglo-American film dubber. One day Marcel Achard gave him three books to read: *This Man is Dangerous* and *Poison Ivy* by Peter Cheyney and *No Orchid for Miss Blandish* by James Hadley Chase. In a fit of enthusiasm he translated all three without having any prospect of seeing any one of them appearing in print. They eventually became the first three titles of the *Série noire* which Gaston Gallimard agreed to publish from 1944 onwards. Gallimard sent him to England to negotiate the translation rights of works by Erskine Caldwell, John Steinbeck, Dashiell Hammett and Raymond Chandler, in addition to Chase and Cheyney whom he met in person. Following a trajectory in keeping with his past history, his career of translator and publisher of American authors and of *Série noire* writers had taken off.

The main feature of Duhamel's translations is his use of slang and colloquial linguistic forms, which was quite an original way of translating at the time. Until after the Second World War, and whatever the kind of literature to be translated, French translations invariably amounted to a heightened 'literarization' of the original texts, raising – Antoine Berman (1986: 70) aptly speaks of *exhaussement* – the

---

[3] Coindreau translated approximately the first fifty pages; Duhamel then took over, trying to mimic Coindreau's style (Duhamel 1972: 533). Coindreau plays a dominant role here, since it is his way of translating that Duhamel strives to adopt in the translating that remains to be done. For more details see Gouanvic (2000).

original's stylistic level. Duhamel, by contrast, adopts a decidedly plebeian way of rendering style. This is undoubtedly related to his primary habitus, acquired in the practical learning of English in Manchester during World War I and in the 1920s when he and his companions were living in the Surrealist commune of the rue du Château.

4. The translator's habitus and the literary field in translation

It is not hard to appreciate the distance separating Coindreau, a university graduate (he was an *agrégé* of Spanish) and professor, who assigns a quasi-philosophical function of overcoming historical failure to literature, from Duhamel, for whom literature offers above all pleasure, even jubilation and a rather poetic enjoyment. The gap is inscribed in the choice of texts to be translated, in the translated texts and in the ways they actually translate them. Whereas Coindreau translates William Faulkner, eminently high-brow realistic literature, Duhamel tackles low-brow genres such as the detective novel. This different choice of texts is obviously connected with the translator's tastes based on their acquired habitus. In Coindreau's case, his habitus drives him homologically towards texts demonstrating a tragic image of life, an image he imposes on the text in translation beyond its original significance.[4] In Duhamel's case, his habitus (constituted of colloquial English learned and *used* on the job, his participation in the Surrealist movement, his professional activity of a film dubber) predisposes him towards the genres and authors he actually translated.

The translation determinants and the hierarchies of socio-aesthetic taste they convey are expressed through the actualization of the translators' habitus. But, beyond these determinants, it is a certain image of translated literature and of literature *per se* that the translator's habitus calls for and that the translator chooses to translate, actualizing his habitus. The literary translators' habitus influences the field of literature, i.e. the space which acts as a scene for the struggles between different literary producers to determine the shape of literature to come.

Now, a translation is not an indigenous work, a work deemed to inscribe itself in the continuity or discontinuity of a national literary tradition. As a rule, translations are brought out in special series, recognized as 'foreign authors' series with titles like *Du monde entier* or *Prosateurs étrangers modernes*. In this way publishers keep translations at a respectable distance from the indigenous literary field and its

---

[4] Annick Chapdelaine (1994) has analyzed how the translations of Faulkner (especially *The Hamlet* by René Hilleret) into French did not see the comic effects of the text and obliterated the sociolects specific to the Black vernaculars in the Southern states. This observation also applies to Coindreau's translations.

tradition, and at the same time they classify them within the indigenous literary field. The principal effect of this classification into 'in' and 'out' is that translations are not allowed to upset the hierarchy of literary taste in the target field. Instead of provoking violent and sudden upheaval, translations bring about exogenous change by stages, in the form of gradual, progressive influence in the midst of endogenous change. Their workings are not recognized as exogenous since they are mixed with local, ongoing, undifferentiated change.

5. The heuristic status of *habitus* and *field*

The examples will have made it clear that the notions of habitus and field are inextricably related. One cannot be conceived without the other. What is the theoretical model these notions convey? The objectivation they give rise to is that of an investigative tool. The status of habitus and field is heuristic, which is to say that these concepts do not aim strictly speaking at attaining the real but at providing a vantage point from which to view the real. Their production mode is that of an 'as if'. The notions of habitus and field operate on the plane of this 'as if', which is of course the very condition of scientific discourse. In other words, we behave – and write – 'as if' there existed a field of literature in France in which cultural producers, including translators, struggle to impose their production as preferable to that of others, and their struggle is supported by the dispositions they have acquired in previous struggles.

In actual fact it is incorrect to say that the producing agents 'struggle to impose their productions as preferable to that of others'. The struggle does not take place on a conscious, deliberate level; rather, it is 'as if' agents were struggling to impose their vision and division on the reality of the field. In Bourdieu's model, the power of habitus, the driving force that moves things, is located not at the level of consciousness but of beliefs, that is to say, it operates "at the deepest level of bodily dispositions" (Bourdieu 2000: 177).

6. Source field, target field and historicization

Among all cultural producers, translators have a special role to play owing to the fact that the work which is to emerge in the field already exists as a foreign text in the source field. The struggles of translators to impose themselves in the target field are not entirely of the same sort as those engaged in by a writer in the literary field. Once a publisher has taken the decision to translate, the work to be translated is not subject to the same intense struggles in which original writings are involved. Of course there are numerous examples of works to be translated which are discovered by translators who then act as series editors or literary directors. But translators *qua* translators are cultural agents who take charge of a foreign text and put it into the target language; their translating practice is oriented towards both the source text and the target text.

The link tying the translator to the source field is momentarily obliterated in the translation operation: the text is decontextualized from the source field and dehistoricized, then re-contextualized and re-historicized in the target field. Translation effectuates a break with the source field, its struggles and the stakes of those struggles. But this does not mean that the source society is absent from translation. In fact it is present under a certain guise in the target text. From the moment the text is recognized as having been translated from a foreign language and culture, from the moment its foreign provenance is flagged by the indication 'translated from *x* by *y*' on the title page, a relation is established with the original society, producing a view of that society as perceived through the eyes of the target society. As soon as 'translated from *x* by *y*' appears on the title page, the legitimacy of the source society in the target society is actualized, i.e. historicized and subjectified. In the case of the translation of American literature in the context of postwar French culture, it is fair to say that if legitimacy can be assessed by (among other things) the number of translations made, American society commands considerable legitimacy in French society – compared, that is, with the volume of translations of non-American work published during the same period.

It is the image of a whole society which comes into view through translation. The image can be erroneous, fair, or partial. Of course, no text offers a full view of its society, not even Balzac's panoramic *Comédie humaine*; a text holds up a partial image, valid only for the section dealt with in the particular enunciation framework which the text itself establishes. The image created of a source society by means of translation taken in its entirety is worth a certain amount of symbolic capital, which circulates among those target social groups who use this literature in translation.

7.   A structuralist constructivism

Bourdieu's constructivism is not idealized: it is a structuralist constructivism. "By structuralism or structuralist, I mean that there exist, within the social world itself and not only within symbolic systems (language, myths, etc.), objective structures independent of the consciousness and will of agents, which are capable of guiding and constraining their practices or their representations" (Bourdieu 1989: 14). It is a constructivism in which symbolic power is exercised with the collaboration of those who are subject to it. But an 'awareness' of this collaboration is not enough for symbolic power to be effectuated. Power, we have seen, is expressed in fields through the body socialized by beliefs. What we have therefore is a constructivism which takes account of the unconscious dimension in human action.

At this point it is useful to remind ourselves of another component of Bourdieu's model, one which highlights the relational nature of power. In fields, it is competition which institutes the game that is being played out between various agents, all of them eager to acquire the best position for themselves and their allies. Cooperative competition or conflictual cooperation between agents is what brings the field into existence in the first place. This is visible in the struggle among publishers to obtain the texts for translation and to have exclusive contracts signed by foreign authors and agents. For example, a hard-headed competition took place between the publishers Stock, Delamain et Boutelleau on the one hand, and Gallimard on the other, in which the translation rights were acquired by the former as regards Scott Fitzgerald's *Tender is the Night*. The novel was translated by Marguerite Chevalley and published in 1951 under the title *Tendre est la nuit,* with a preface by the literary director André Bay.

The translating agent deploys his or her know-how on a text in accordance with the given target field to which that text belongs. And the text's belonging is negotiated in the target field through the translator's particular manner of translating. As a result, the economy of symbolic exchanges is also differential in that the translator's manner of translating represents a form of negotiation between the 'possible' which the field affords and the distinctions which it allows. The differential dimensions of translation can be studied when there are several translations for one text, i.e. when a text has been retranslated after a while for reasons that remain to be examined. In that case contrastive analysis of translations is feasible, and the positions taken by a publisher and by a translator in his/her translation appear clearly. The novel *1919* by John Dos Passos was first translated by Maurice Rémon as *1919* and published by Éditions sociales internationales in 1937, and re-translated by Yves Malartic in 1952 as *L'An premier du siècle (1919)*. This version was published in Gallimard's series *Du monde entier*. A comparison of both translations reveals quite different positions in the French literary target fields.

8. Conclusion

In the approach outlined here translation as production is not viewed through the uses that are made of it, the functions to which it corresponds, or the factors which determine it. The study of translation as production investigates the moment of the translation's emergence according to the habitus of translating agents active in the fields for which the translations are destined. Translation as production therefore rests on the empathy between, on the one hand, the mode of socialization embodied in a habitus that supposes the social practice of translation, and, on the other, the historicized subjectivity resulting from the translated text's belonging to a given field. This empathy or, in Berman's terms, this "drive to translate" (*pulsion à traduire,* Berman 1986), is to be found in the translators' subjectivity, as expressed in biographies and autobiographies, prefaces, introductions, afterwords, translator's notes and the like. But, as we all know, there is a painful shortage of documents in which translators explain how they perceive themselves and ply their trade. The lack relates to what Lawrence Venuti (1995) terms the 'invisibility' of translators. But then, translation studies will not reach maturity until translators too have acquired their rightful place in the field of cultural production and feel free to give voice to their particular experience of translation.

References

Berman, Antoine (1986) 'L'essence platonicienne de la traduction', *Revue d'esthétique*, Nouvelle série 12: 63-73.
Bourdieu, Pierre (1983) 'The Field of Cultural Production, or: The Economic World Reversed', trans. Richard Nice, *Poetics* 12: 311-56.
----- (1989) 'Social Space and Symbolic Power', trans. Loïc J. D. Wacquant, *Sociological Theory* VII(1): 14-25.
----- (1990) *The Logic of Practice*, trans. Richard Nice, Cambridge: Polity Press.
----- (2000) *Pascalian Meditations*, trans. Richard Nice,Cambridge: Polity Press.
Chapdelaine, Annick (1994) 'Transparence et retraduction des sociolectes dans *The Hamlet* de Faulkner', *TTR/Études sur le texte et ses transformations* VII(2): 11-33.
Coindreau, Maurice-Edgar (1974) *Mémoires d'un traducteur. Entretiens avec Christian Giudicelli,* Paris: Gallimard.
Duhamel, Marcel (1972) *Raconte pas ta vie*, Paris: Mercure de France.
Gouanvic, Jean-Marc (1999) *Sociologie de la traduction: La science-fiction américaine dans l'espace culturel français des années 1950*. Arras: Artois Presses Université.
----- (2000) '*Polemos* et la traduction: la traduction de *The Grapes of Wrath* de John Steinbeck', *Athanor*, new series, X(2): 268-79.
Hermans, Theo (1999) *Translation in Systems*, Manchester: St. Jerome.
Holmes, James S (1988) 'The Name and Nature of Translation Studies' [1972], in his *Translated! Papers on Literary Translation and Translation Studies* (ed. R. van den Broeck), Amsterdam: Rodopi, 67-80.
Lefevere, André (1998) 'Translation Practice(s) and the Circulation of Cultural Capital. Some Aeneids in English', in S. Bassnett and A. Lefevere (eds) *Constructing Cultures. Essays on Literary Translation*, Clevedon: Multilingual Matters, 25-40.
Siméoni, Daniel (1998) 'The Pivotal Status of the Translator's Habitus', *Target* 10(1): 1-39.
Venuti, Lawrence (1995) *The Translator's Invisibility. A History of Translation*, London & New York: Routledge.

Translatability between Paradigms: Gramsci's Translation of Crocean Concepts

DEREK BOOTHMAN

Abstract: *Thomas Kuhn's* Structure of Scientific Revolutions *(1962) posed, among other things, the problem of whether and how it is possible to translate between scientific paradigms. Thirty years earlier a similar problem of translatability between philosophical and scientific languages had been raised in Antonio Gramsci's* Prison Notebooks, *then published in the immediate postwar years. This paper examines how Gramsci undertook a translation into his own realist-materialist paradigm of certain key concepts used in the philosophically idealist one of Benedetto Croce, the dominant Italian professional philosopher of the first half of the twentieth century; for purposes of illustration and clarity, a reconstruction is given of these terms translated between the paradigms. Additionally, a comment is offered on Gramsci's approach to the differences between national cultures, and his view of what leads to greater or lesser exactness in such intercultural translations. Finally, some examples are briefly discussed of interparadigmatic translations involving either Gramsci's paradigm or other similar and compatible ones.*

1. What does it mean to translate between paradigms?

In the first number of the new series of *New Left Review* Luisa Passerini comments on the "break-down of any common tradition or transmission of meanings" in one specific area of the social sciences, involving historians of different political generations; this suggests, she goes on to say, "not only a multiplication of different intellectual languages, but great difficulty in translating between them" (Passerini 2000:140). The late Thomas Kuhn made a rather similar point in his *Structure of Scientific Revolutions* (1970: 203), then going on to comment in the debate on that book that much of the social sciences seems typified by "claims, counter-claims and debates over fundamentals", just as in Presocratic discourse, with the result that it does "not at all resemble science" in his conception of the 'normal science' phase of the so-called hard sciences (Kuhn 1974: 6). Between such types of 'critical discourse' there exist, in Kuhn's view, not only problems of the translatability of the same homophonic terms, or of terms that play equivalent roles in the structure of rival paradigms, but sometimes real untranslatability because of the conflicting descriptions of reality offered by what he calls incommensurable paradigms.

This 'incommensurability' is easy enough to understand in some cases in the exact sciences: there is quite evident incompatibility, for example, between the old heliocentric system and the Copernican one that replaced it. But whereas Kuhn was dealing with formal languages, some authorities, for a variety of motives, take a similar view for natural languages too. We may here point to the Sapir-Whorf anthropological hypothesis and to Quine's view that rival conceptual schemes are under-determined by experience: in the limit of someone landing in an alien culture with no knowledge of its language, the resulting radical translation becomes indeterminate.

What I should like to do in the following pages is try to link some aspects of the above to the short group of paragraphs headed the 'translatability of scientific and philosophical languages' in the eleventh of Antonio Gramsci's *Prison Notebooks*. Approaching the matter from a different angle, Gramsci too uses the concept and even the actual term 'paradigm', but in his case as referred to the human sciences. It may seem strange to some to quote Gramsci on matters regarding language and translatability, given that the interest shown in his *Notebooks* has been largely political, but his writings go far wider than that. It should not be forgotten that his university training was in linguistics and, indeed, since the integral version of the *Notebooks* became available in Italy in the mid-1970s, linguists there and now elsewhere have begun to take up a number of the insights contained in his writings. In the English-speaking world, among other things, three separate versions of some or all the notes he wrote on translatability have now been published.[1]

Gramsci starts from the premise that for translation to be possible between languages, natural or otherwise, or between cultures, there must be some fundamental underlying similarity. However, caution is here necessary in specifying what the nature of the translation actually is. Gramsci's own words come in useful: "translatability is not 'perfect' in every respect, even in important ones (but what language is exactly translatable into another? what single word is exactly translatable into another language?), but it is so in its basic essentials" (Gramsci 1995: 309). Typical of his overall approach, he does not take up a rigid and absolutist position on whether concepts can be translated or not, and in this seems to adopt a different stance from Kuhn's implied approach on the human sciences as stated in the brief quote above.

What Gramsci has in mind is, in effect, three different types of translation, which renders his notes on the subject not entirely easy to condense or comprehend immediately. First as regards 'orthodox' interlingual translation, he later on expands his comment here in an aside of a fairly standard nature. In speaking of high school translation exercises from the classical languages he notes that

---

[1] The versions are due to Carl Marzani (Gramsci 1957), Steven R. Mansfield (Gramsci 1984) and the present writer (Gramsci 1995); for purposes of convenience all references in the text to the translatability notes will be made to this latter volume, which also gives information on when these and other notes were written and where to find them in the Critical Edition of the Notebooks. Here dates have been mentioned only where strictly necessary; for further information the reader is referred to Francioni (1984).

what identity there seemed to be at the start of the exercise (Italian 'rosa' = Latin 'rosa') becomes increasingly complicated as the 'apprenticeship' progresses, moves increasingly away from the mathematical scheme and arrives at a historical judgement or judgement of taste, in which nuances, 'unique and individualised' expressiveness prevail; this also applies in a single language to diachronic semantic variations and to functionally determined variations within a sentence. (Gramsci 1985: 384-5)

Secondly, Gramsci speaks of what now we might call intralingual translation, not so much as this term is used by Jakobson (1971: 261) in the sense of reformulation in a natural language, but as interparadigmatic translation, i.e. translation between paradigms. By way of example he cites the comments of the liberal economist Luigi Einaudi on the ability of the pragmatist philosopher Giovanni Vailati to furnish proofs of the same theorem in the languages typical of different schools of economic thought (Gramsci 1995: 308). In a slightly earlier note on the same subject he describes this process as a "mutual translatability of these languages" (Gramsci 1995: 183). He goes on in the latter note to cite another example: whether, using the marginal utility economic paradigm, one may arrive at the same explanation of profits as that given by the labour theory of value.[2] Gramsci here refers to Engels's assertion that the marginalist economist Wilhelm Lexis's formulation of the theory of profits "amounts to the same thing as the Marxian theory of surplus value" and "in reality [...] is merely a paraphrase of the Marxian" (Engels 1967: 9-10). In these examples, different conceptual schemes are seen to cover the same reality in different ways. As such we are dealing with translations of concepts between different paradigms, rather than from one natural language to another.

The third step that Gramsci takes is that of sketching out the conditions whereby a translation may be effected from the culture of one country to that of another (an intercultural translation). Here one is dealing with whole discourses which may be in superficially unrelated fields, but which reflect deeper-level social processes, a point with which no one with a nodding acquaintance with Marx (or Lévi-Strauss) should have difficulty. His own description of the process is "two fundamentally similar structures have 'equivalent' superstructures that are mutually translatable, whatever the particular national language" (Gramsci 1995: 312), where 'fundamentally similar' is to be understood as referring to societies that have reached comparable socio-economic stages of development .

The present contribution attempts principally to look at the second of these types of translation in probably the main example treated by Gramsci himself. This is the

---

[2] For the economists of the post-1870 'marginal utility' school the value of a given commodity, which then has somehow to be related to its market price, is determined by its utility to the individual, i.e. by the significance the individual subjectively attaches to the commodity for his/her want-satisfaction; for Marx, on the other hand, a commodity's value is determined by the different quantities and qualities of labour used in its manufacture (Roll: 321 and 269).

translation into his own Marxist paradigm of concepts taken over from the Italian idealist philosopher Benedetto Croce. In Gramsci's own terminology, the operation is sometimes referred to as a translation from speculative into historicist, or realist historicist, language, rather than the more normal terms of idealist and Marxist respectively. By exploring this area and then citing certain other translations between paradigms, I hope to indicate possible ways in which differences or similarities between paradigms might be shown up more clearly, thus leading to a better understanding of problems of compatibility between different conceptual schemes.

2.   The Gramscian paradigm

It is not accidental that, in the second half of 1932, while Gramsci was giving final form to his notes on translatability, he was also engaged in doing the same thing to his notes on Benedetto Croce. In the Italy of the first half of the twentieth century, Croce was the major representative of the philosophical idealist tradition and a key figure for non-Marxist democratic culture, dominating the fields of philosophy, history and literary aesthetics. Gramsci says of himself (1995: 355) that he had been "tendentially somewhat Crocean" during and just after his university years; his settling of accounts with Croce takes place through the interparadigmatic translation he carries out on Croce. Textual justification for this claim comes at the start of the second part of the tenth notebook, which Gramsci headed 'The Philosophy of Benedetto Croce'. We there find two brief paragraphs in which he comments that his notes on the 'translatability of scientific and philosophical languages', in the adjoining eleventh notebook, should be brought together with those on the relationship between his 'philosophy of praxis'[3] and 'speculative philosophies', meaning principally Croce's (Gramsci 1995: 306). He also makes the explicit claim that the former of these philosophies is able to translate the latter into its own terms. Gramsci's work on Croce is, then, to be considered his translation into the paradigm of the philosophy of praxis of the high point reached in Italy by idealist philosophy.

In speaking of translation a problem does arise, however, for a writer like Gramsci. At first sight his approach seems highly eclectic; indeed the concepts he uses are drawn from a wide range of thinkers, especially those coming after the turning point that he identifies in the French Revolution, but also going back to earlier theorists such as Machiavelli. What Gramscian scholars of the last generation have noted is that when he incorporates into his discourse a term taken from elsewhere, without

---

[3] The formulation 'philosophy of praxis' has often been taken as merely a circumlocution for 'historical materialism' to avoid censorship problems. Maria Rosaria Romagnuolo (1987-8: 123-66) demonstrates that, after about the middle of 1932, 'philosophy of praxis' substitutes the term 'historical materialism' even in rewritten versions of first draft notes. This conscious change testifies to Gramsci's emphasis on the aspect of human intervention as against positivist and mechanistic readings of Marxism.

changing the words used, its meaning is often modified. On other occasions he may take a term from elsewhere and, under a different label, reinterpret it for developing a concept that has a similar or equivalent function within his own discourse. Both are examples of translation between paradigms, with the common property that, whether the terms incorporated are the same or different, the concepts undergo a semantic shift on being carried across ('trans-lated') from one paradigm to the other; simultaneously the position they occupy in the hierarchy of one paradigm may not automatically be the same as in another (see also Kuhn 1970: 200).

A whole number of such 'translations' appear in Gramsci's discourse,[4] but here we shall concentrate on certain terms that Gramsci adopted and adapted from Croce, namely 'ethico-political history'(see section 3 below); and the 'dialectic of distincts' (section 4) and, with it, the general question of the dialectic; and the relationship between 'error' and 'ideology' or 'illusion' (section 5).

3. Ethico-political history, historical materialism and hegemony: empirical canons and hierarchical rank

The importance of Croce within Italian culture has already been commented on above and, indeed, Gramsci's Notebooks contain more references to Croce than to anyone else, bar none. Of the notions developed by Croce that of 'ethico-political history' was of particular interest to Gramsci. Indeed two books which Gramsci received in prison, Croce's *History of Italy 1871-1915* (1928) and his *History of Europe in the Nineteenth Century* (1932), which applied this concept, were regarded by Gramsci as "destined to become the paradigm of Crocean historiography", his "crowning achievement" (Gramsci 1995: 348 and 367 respectively).

What Croce meant by the term 'ethico-political history' is explained in the essays he published in book form in the mid-1920s (Croce 1926) and available in English under the titles 'Economico-political history and ethico-political history' and 'The unending struggle between Church and State' (Croce 1946); here the representatives of the 'Church', incidentally, are to be understood in the broad figurative sense of "those who, in modern and lay society, are represented by [...] the custodians of ideas" (Croce 1946: 129), i.e. a moral élite of 'intellectuals', using a noun not then in common use in its Italian form. In these essays Croce explains that what he means by his concept of ethico-political history is a 'moral' history, seeing the main trend in human history as the expansion of morality as represented by these élites. Commentators are agreed that Croce's concept of morality is then intimately linked

---

[4] With no great effort, one can pick out at least three dozen major items that characterize Gramsci's discourse, of which about a third seem borrowings from the lexis of other thinkers. Some of these are listed in a recent paper discussing the concepts implicit in the notions of 'historical bloc' and 'hegemony' (Boothman 1999: 58-9).

to liberty, and that further liberty for him is linked substantially and not just etymologically to liberalism (Bobbio 1998: 39-40). It is this notion of liberty that characterizes 'ethico-political' history, as indicated below.

In discussing Croce's two paradigmatic ethico-political histories Robert Caponigri notes that the "positive and effective ethico-political force in the nineteenth century was liberalism, which supplies both the ideality and the effective moral will of the century", and that one of the central themes of these histories is how liberty, defining liberalism, is translated into the institutions (Caponigri 1955: 175). In Croce's own words the object of ethico-political is "not only the State [...] but also that which is outside the State, [...] namely the moral institutions" (Croce 1946: 73). He tends to gloss over the Marxist historiography with which he (Croce) had flirted at the close of the nineteenth century, accepting – acritically in Gramsci's view – a version of Marxism of which at the turn of the century he had written scathingly (Gramsci 1995: 415-6). Thus, true to the revision – or renunciation – of Marxism announced in the preface to the 1917 edition of *Materialismo Storico ed Economia Marxistica* (one of a number of things not in the English translation of that book), Croce observes that "as regards political theory, the concept of power and of struggle, which Marx had subtracted from States and handed over to classes, seems now to have made its return from classes to States" (Croce 1917: preface, xvi). Caponigri draws the double conclusion that, for Croce, firstly, "liberty is the concept which defines the human spirit in its ontological character; through this concept [of liberty] the human spirit is discerned in its ultimate quality of being [...]. Ethico-political history [...] is the history of human freedom, because liberty is the constitutive form of the human spirit itself" and that, secondly, the "concept of history as the history of liberty had as its necessary practical complement liberty as a moral ideal, that is, as an end, the chief end of all practical activity" (Caponigri 1955: 176-7 and 186).

This view is confirmed by Croce, who makes all "histories pertaining to practical activity [...] lose their autonomy and become part of moral [i.e. ethico-political] history" (Croce 1946: 75). Liberty or freedom is both the moving force and the outcome or end of history. While Croce does not ignore times of stress, of poverty, etc., he does not include them in his model, limiting himself to noting that there are "times of poverty and hardships, or of frenzied mammonism, of tyranny and slavery; during such times the moral or religious spirit [...] can hardly breathe. Yet that spirit is never absent and inactive" (Croce 1946: 127). And indeed this spirit is always uppermost in Croce's mind, assuming a real form and substance. The conclusion he arrives at as regards the relationship between ethico-political history and historical materialism is that just as he was "among the first to recommend the study of the concepts of historical materialism, [he] always advised that its dictates be treated as simple empirical canons of research" (Croce 1946: 68, where the more precise 'canons' substitutes 'rules' in Castiglione's translation), thereby relegating historical materialism to a subordinate position in the structure of ethico-political history.

Croce's approach here has the weight of a considerable intellectual tradition of, in particular, German nineteenth-century historiography behind it, and as such is not to be dismissed lightly. It modifies this tradition by including both what the German school "in too narrow a manner" considered the State (Croce's 'political' member; see Gramsci 1995: 372) and "what is considered society" (the 'ethico' member, see Croce 1946: 72-3). The ground covered is much the same as in Gramsci's paradigm but, for him, Croce stops short. Crocean historiography consists of a reconstruction of what, in analogy with Kuhn's concept of 'normal science', might be called 'normal history'. But just as we cannot fully understand aspects of, say, today's normal science, such as quantum mechanics or relativity, without knowing the background to the failures of the previous paradigms (classical mechanics applied at the sub-atomic level or certain aspects of Newtonian gravitation) and the revolution that ushered in the new ones, so Gramsci similarly makes the point, in one of his most rhetorically impassioned passages, that the histories of nineteenth-century Europe and of post-1871 Italy cannot be understood without the French Revolution and the Napoleonic wars in the former case and the struggles of the *Risorgimento* in the latter (Gramsci 1995: 348-9 and 330).

All this is far from suggesting that Gramsci rejects Crocean ethico-political history. Two of Gramsci's statements are of interest here. In his reading, Marx's approach contains "in a nutshell the ethico-political aspects of politics or theory of hegemony and consent, as well as the aspect of force and of economics" (Gramsci 1995: 399). The implications of the latter phrase emerge more clearly and are better integrated into the Gramscian paradigm elsewhere: "ethico-political history, in so far as it is divorced from the concept of historical bloc,[5] in which there is a concrete correspondence of socio-economic content to ethico-political form in the reconstruction of the various historical periods, is nothing more than a polemical presentation of interesting philosophical propositions, but it is not history" (Gramsci 1995: 360). Here there are two of what M.A.K. Halliday calls semantic discontinuities or leaps (Halliday and Martin 1993: 82-84). In the first quotation Gramsci is obviously speaking of the base-superstructure metaphor, it being well-known that for Marx "the economic structure of society [is] the real foundation" of a given society "on which arises a legal and political superstructure" (Marx 1970: 20) which would, for Gramsci, include Croce's 'ethico-political history' as one aspect. The second semantic gap is the partial equivalence between 'historical bloc' and the

---

[5] The 'historical bloc' is a concept taken principally from the French political theorist Georges Sorel, with an unacknowledged input from Marx's *Theses on Feuerbach*. Gramsci's fundamental definition of it is the unity of structure and superstructure (Gramsci 1971: 137), but it differs from the static structure-superstructure metaphor in emphasising the aspect of diachronic historical movement. For a more detailed philological study see Boothman (2000).

'base-superstructure' model. This latter metaphor progressively disappears between 1932 and 1933, to be replaced with that of '*blocco storico*' (Cospito 1990), except when the division into the two parts is being made for purposes of analysis.

The major points that follow from the above are that, as long as account is taken of the element of force, Croce's ethico-political history is compatible with Gramsci's paradigm. Here force may be a type of external constraint, such as the relations into which men and women enter, independent of their will, for Marx's "social production of their existence", or it may be the force that creates a new situation, such as the struggles of the *Risorgimento* or the Napoleonic period, both missing from Croce's histories. Hegemony in a broad definition is like Machiavelli's centaur, half-beast and half-man, that symbolizes both force and consent, while in the narrower definition of hegemony as consent, "ethico-political history is the mechanical hypostatization of the moment of hegemony, of political leadership, of consent in the life and development of the activity of the state and civil society" (Gramsci 1995: 343).

A second point is that, whereas Croce states in his main essay on ethico-political history that it "alone seems to be History, history *par excellence*", the conception of ethico-political history for Gramsci "may be adopted as an 'empirical canon' of historical research which needs constantly to be borne in mind [...] if the aim is that of producing integral history and not partial and extrinsic history (history of economic forces as such etc.)" (Gramsci 1995: 358 and, in a slightly different formulation, 332). There is compatibility between ethico-political history and Gramsci's paradigm, but it is of interest to note that in the reciprocal translations one thinker does of the scheme upheld by the other (with Croce of course giving his reading of Marx rather than of Gramsci) there is an inversion of rank. On the one hand, for Croce the dictates of historical materialism are "simple empirical canons of research" and Marx's historical materialism "an interpretative canon of history" (Gramsci 1995: 335). If the German school wrote an "integral history" (Croce 1946: 72), ethico-political (or 'moral') history, in going beyond it, is even more of an "integral history", while other "histories pertaining to practical activity [...] lose their autonomy and become part of moral history" (Croce 1946: 73-4); indeed anything that is not ethico-political history is inevitably partial and one-sided (Croce 1946: 130). For Gramsci, on the other hand, ethico-political history is, as we have seen, not rejected; however, unless firmly sited within the historical bloc, it is a "polemical presentation of interesting philosophical propositions, but it is not history" (Gramsci 1995: 360).

In this entire dialogue, Croce's contribution to which is in his historical writings themselves and partially in his post-war reviews of Gramsci's *Prison Letters* and *Notebooks*, each side accepts a certain partial validity of the stance of the other. Ethico-political history is accepted by Gramsci as forming part of his concept of hegemony, while historical materialism is accepted by Croce as a subordinate part of his brand of historical research. There is however an inversion in hierarchical rank, in which one thinker's concepts form merely a subordinate part of the other's overall view.

4. Distincts, their dialectic and the question of superstructural rank

Another reinterpretative translation of importance is that made of the Crocean concept of the *dialettica dei distinti*, i.e. the dialectic of four 'distincts' or 'distinctions', depending on the context. Outlines of what is meant are given by Mure (1967), H. Wildon Carr (1917: 136-52), Orsini (1961: 19-21) and Roberts (1987: 77-8). Orsini (1961: 317) further notes that the *Nuovi Saggi di Estetica* (Croce 1920), available in English as *The Essence of Aesthetic* (1921), provides a good commentary by Croce himself on what is involved, and this has been drawn on here.

As Croce sees it, the human spirit is divided two-fold into the theoretic (knowing) and the practical (doing), the former being subdivided into aesthetic (intuitive, 'the beautiful') and concrete conceptual thought ('the true'), and the latter into the ethical ('the good') and the economic or utilitarian, which represents Croce's specific addition to the three categories that have come down to us from classical Greek thought. The category of the economic or utilitarian is broad enough to deal with anything – including, as Gramsci points out, love – that may have a bearing on the production and reproduction of the existence of humanity. Croce's dialectic of the distincts allows circulation among these categories that characterize all human activity.

Gramsci's concept of historical bloc likewise aimed at being all-embracing and likewise had the problem of finding a mechanism of actively correlating one sphere of activity with another. It is only after quite some hesitation regarding, for example, whether the dialectic of the distincts can be regarded as really dialectical (Gramsci 1995: 369; April-May 1932), that he concludes there is something of importance in it. While certainly it is for him merely a verbal solution, it does indicate "a real methodological exigency" (Gramsci 1995: 399, dating to the last few months of 1932).

More or less at the same time as writing this latter paragraph Gramsci was beginning to revise the notes on political theory he had sketched out in the early months of the year and gave their final form some time between May 1932 and the end of 1934. It is here that Gramsci starts to explore the application of the Crocean distincts to his own schema, "translating speculative language into historicist [i.e. Marxist] language [...] seeing whether this speculative language has a concrete instrumental value, superior to previous instrumental values" as he says elsewhere (Gramsci 1995: 344).

First of all, for the 'translation' into his paradigm of the Crocean concept of distincts/distinctions, Gramsci observes in his notes on political theory that the 'distinction' will be between "the ranks [*gradi*] of the superstructure", the problem being that of "establishing the dialectical position of political activity (and of the corresponding science) as a particular level of the superstructure" (Gramsci 1971: 137). He goes on to say that such activity constitutes "the first moment or first level; the moment in which the superstructure is still in the unmediated phase of a merely confused assertion of the will [*affermazione volontaria*] at an elementary stage". He then asks: "can one really speak of a dialectic of distincts, and how is the concept of a circle joining the levels of the superstructure to be understood?" (*ibid.*). The answer he suggests is through the "concept of 'historical bloc', i.e. unity between nature and mind (structure and superstructure), unity of opposites and distincts" (*ibid.*). Similarly he asks "what relationship [...] will there exist between the politico-economic moment and other historical activities? Is a speculative solution of these problems possible or only a historical one given by the concept of 'historical bloc' presupposed by Sorel?" (Gramsci 1995: 399-400).

Once again Gramsci is carrying out a translation. The Crocean concept of the dialectic of distincts is reinterpreted so as to apply to the levels or ranks of the superstructure rather than the aspects of the human spirit, but it may be noted that the function in the two paradigms is the equivalent one of satisfying the need to actively correlate the different sectors of human activity. We thus would seem to have an example of what Kuhn describes as a coming together of members of different language communities, at least one of which has "learned to translate the other's theory and its consequences into his own language" (Kuhn 1970: 202).

5.   Ideology and error

Within the historical bloc, where "material forces are the content and ideologies are the form" (Gramsci 1971: 377), another question of translation between Gramsci and Croce arises, this time regarding 'ideology' and 'error'. Here 'ideology' is often for Gramsci "the whole ensemble of the superstructures" (Gramsci 1995: 413) that relate to a given economic structure of society. But different from some readings of Marx, and maybe from what Marx himself intended, Gramsci's 'ideology' is not a simple reflection of the economic base of society. It can be the ensemble of ideas consonant with that base, but it can also be those ideas that derive from the states of affairs in previous stages of society, or alternatively it can represent a sublimation at another plane of current states of affairs. Ideology and the superstructures are for Gramsci an objective part of operative reality, and anything but arbitrary constructs (Gramsci 1995: 395). However they are not permanent and universal, but transient due to these practical origins (Gramsci 1971: 445).

In the 1917 preface to his *Materialismo Storico ed Economia Marxistica* (as noted above, not in the English translation) Croce had rejected the position that the superstructures have an 'objective and operative reality' for Marxism, claiming instead that Marxism considers them as mere appearance.

There is however a point of contact. A concept that plays for Croce a similar role to one aspect of Gramsci's 'ideology' is 'error', which consists in mistaking for permanent, real thought (philosophy) those mental facts that are transitory or fleeting, unmediated products of practical activity (Gramsci 1995: 413). Indeed Croce himself poses the rhetorical question "[…] in what way is error born except as the interference of practical activity in the theoretical spirit?" (Croce 1926: 89), i.e. an unwarranted intrusion of the lower levels of his hierarchy of distincts into the higher ones. While Gramsci is not convinced by the rigid distinction between ideology and philosophy, he does see here an influence of, if not the actual derivation from, Marxism. Crocean 'error' occupies the place of the Marxist concept of 'illusion', which, as part of the superstructural phenomena and thus of ideology, is nothing other than a "historical category transient in nature because of changes in practice" (Gramsci 1995: 413).

In terminology introduced at the end of Section 1 above, he sums this up in his claim that "Croce's philosophy is to a quite notable extent the retranslation into speculative language of the realist historicism of the philosophy of praxis" (Gramsci 1995: 355).

6. Intercultural translation

It may be, as Gramsci speculated, that there is an "instrumental value" in Croce's principle of distinctions; there certainly is in a type of dialectic that allows one to pass from one hierarchical level to another. Here the wheel turns full circle and we go back to the problem, posed at the beginning of this paper, of the reciprocal translation of different cultures. This might appear in the guise of interlingual translation but is – as translation between languages must of necessity be – an intercultural translation.

For Gramsci what is being dealt with is a cultural homologue. He notes the fact that different societies, citing France and Germany at the turn of the nineteenth century, express basically the same ideas in the different cultures that characterize them (Gramsci 1995: 310-3). His immediate source here was an article of Croce's (1950 reprint: 291-302) referring to a pamphlet by the academic lawyer Adolfo Ravà (Ravà 1909). The principal reference point for Gramsci was, however, Marx's youthful work *The Holy Family*, which extends the comparison by classing French political practice and literature and classical German philosophy together with English economics (David Ricardo): all of them in their specific time expressed similar underlying movements in their societies. The implications of Gramsci's position are that each of these currents of thought in the 'superstructure' of society is connected to the 'base' by a chain running through the different levels (ranks) of the superstructure (Gramsci 1971: 137), and probably, in his view, running through different levels within fundamentally equivalent structures, i.e. the ensemble of productive relations which people enter into. He is thus making use in his paradigm of the reinterpretative translation of Croce's dialectic of distincts discussed in Section 4 above.

While Gramsci was here taking as his paradigm the Europe of the French Revolution and of the first industrial revolution, his model is of course far more general in its scope. If his reasoning is anywhere near correct, it would seem to go at least some way towards explaining why similar social and cultural movements spring up more or less simultaneously in differing countries at the same stage of civilization. More modern examples of this are the Modernist movement in its various manifestations, followed chronologically by minimalism, deconstructionism, neo-liberalism, 'weak thought' as the refusal in contemporary Italian philosophy of great metaphysical systems, all of them forms of the postmodern reaction to past overarching doctrines. Factors like these, and their relative strengths in one country or another, help define the hegemonic discourse that in part characterizes the 'national-popular' analysed by Gramsci.

Where caution needs to be applied is in addressing Gramsci's non-rhetorical question "whether one can translate between expressions of different stages of civilization in so far" as he claims "as each of these stages is a moment in the development of another" (Gramsci 1995: 307). How far, for example, one can actually translate the experience of a colonial society from a position within the culture of an imperial country is open to doubt; their relations of production and superstructural factors are widely different. An analogous comment also applies in the case of trying to translate the experiences of gender and ethnic groupings. Probably we have to use the fall-back position cited in Section 1 above, that "translatability is not 'perfect' in every respect, even in important ones [...] but it is so in its basic essentials" (Gramsci: 309). As Gramsci wisely reminds us, "the intellectual element 'knows' but does not always understand and in particular does not always feel" (Gramsci 1971: 418). Without that understanding and feeling no community can come near to 'translating' another's experience. To go further than that means pushing his model beyond its limits of applicability and arriving at a situation of untranslatability; 'going native', in the concepts of Kuhn, Quine and others, has been a solution proposed by Marxism regarding participation in class and anti-imperial movements, but this solution is not always possible and perhaps not always relevant.

7.   Some tentative conclusions

In this paper the term paradigm has been used quite frequently in a familiar Kuhnian sense, and we have seen that Gramsci too uses it in a similar way to describe what Croce was attempting to do in two of his histories in particular. The term is not used inappropriately by or of Gramsci. Recently the linguist Stefano Gensini has observed that in Gramsci "every keyword [...] is organized at the formal level thanks to its relationship [...] with the rest of the system" (Gensini 1991: 72), and the philosopher of language Ferruccio Rossi-Landi (1983: 26) makes a similar general point. The various terms of Gramsci's discourse do in fact 'hang together' in the way described, each piece interacting with others and being normally definable only by calling into play the others in a way that is consonant with the features of a Kuhnian paradigm.

Initially those who invoked a strict definition of paradigm were sceptical of what, for example, Hilary Putnam calls the "sloppiness, the lack of precise theories and laws, the lack of mathematical rigor" of the social sciences (Putnam 1975:152). For what we are faced with is a mix of fundamentally a natural-language system with elements of formal language. Putnam is to my mind quite right, but only if one recognizes the difference between, in semiotic terms, the 'signals' used to denote concepts in the exact sciences and the 'signs' used in the human sciences. Here 'signals' are technical means for indicating the objects, actions, processes and such-like which generally reflect the non-ideological or at least minimal ideological content of most established theories in the 'hard science'. The social sciences are couched more in terms of 'signs' that indicate an ideological theme. Signs "reflect and re-fract another reality [...] the domain of signs coincides with the domain of ideology" (Vološinov, 1973: 10). It is the 'sloppiness factor' inherent in ideological discourse that perhaps until relatively recently has obscured for many people the paradigmatic nature of discourses such as Gramsci's.

One aspect of such a paradigmatic discourse is, as has been noted, that in passing from one discourse to another it is not enough for a given term in one paradigm to be translated as either homophonically the same, or as a rather different term in another paradigm. The location of the term within a hierarchical structure can also be of importance. When a term or concept is incorporated from outside, there may also be other differences. Either its intension or its extension may be modified. Such is the case of "ethico-political history as the history of the moment of he-gemony" (Gramsci 1995: 345).

It is to be emphasized at this point that we are not primarily concerned here with whether Gramsci's or Croce's (or someone else's) paradigm gives a better result, but rather to indicate, as Kuhn says in his 'Reflections on my critics', that "lan-guages cut up the world in different ways", which is one reason why translation "between theories or languages" is "so difficult" (Kuhn 1974: 268). And, as Kuhn constantly reminds us, there is "no neutral observation language to appeal to" (1970: 146 and 201; 1974: 266 and 268). The only appeal that can be made is to the human praxis of a 'discourse community', understood not as an academic community but as society itself through, according to Gramsci, the identity of history (practice) with philosophy (theory) and therefore with politics (Gramsci 1995: 382-3): indi-vidual translators may translate words on a sheet of paper but such a sign, inserted, it must be remembered, within its own social and ideological context (Ponzio 1976: 6) can only be incorporated into a culture and thus be fully translated by the mem-bers of the target culture.

The importation of terms into a paradigm is theorized by Gramsci quite explicitly in his Eleventh Notebook. Thus it is not merely a turn of phrase that was being used when Carl Marzani, the first translator into English of the notes on translatability, entitled his Gramscian anthology *The Open Marxism of Antonio Gramsci* (Gramsci 1957). Gramsci, without being aware of it, was methodologically distancing himself from the rigid system, closed to outside influences, of what became codified as 'Marxism-Leninism', in effect decreeing its demise as a theoretical edifice over half a century before the socio-economic system on which it was built finally collapsed. At the same time it may be noted that he rejects certain notions put forward by fellow Marxists, not easily reconcilable with his own humanist and Hegelian dialectical approach, as in his polemic against Bukharin (Gramsci 1971: 419-72). There is an 'incommensurability' factor between these rival paradigms, not easy to isolate but most likely due to a determining position in the conceptual hierarchy of their relative paradigms.

The Gramscian paradigm covers much of the ground covered by other paradigms such as Crocean idealism, some other tendencies within Marxism, and at least some types of post-Marxist deconstructionism. The situation is akin to what Herbert Butterfield says of the transpositions early modern scientists had to carry out: here too one is "handling the same bundle of data as before, but placing them in a new system of relations with one another by giving them a different framework" (Butterfield 1949: 1). Metaphorically, we might conceive the paradigms as consisting of three-dimensional webs which are spread over the same terrain but which may sometimes invert the vertical, i.e. hierarchical, position of a concept in one paradigm as compared with that of a like concept in another.

The implications of this include the possibility of translating other paradigms, in the sense of seeing what terms correspond, where they fit into a hierarchy, and how reasonable is the resulting structure. A case of this type that springs readily to mind is that of another great indirect debate of the twentieth century. The late Lucien Goldmann comments that in *Being and Time* Heidegger differentiates himself from three other philosophers, but names only two of them. Heidegger's subject matters leave minimal doubt that the third philosopher is Lukács (Goldmann 1977: 27). In Goldmann's analysis, there is between Heidegger's phenomenologist *Being and Time* and Lukács's Marxist *History and Class Consciousness* an identity of or at least a very close relationship between concepts that express at times nearly identical ideas. For Goldmann the "radical difference of terminology" between the two works can be resolved "by respectively *translating* the developments of each thinker into the terminology of the other" (Goldmann 1977: 10-11; my emphasis, DB).

A much more recent example is provided by the leading Afro-American pragmatist intellectual Cornel West, who has acknowledged a debt to Gramsci regarding the nature of his philosophical engagement. On the important question of the role of intellectuals West first uses the Gramscian division between traditional intellectuals who see themselves as an independent social group, and 'organic' ones, more intimately linked to a social class. There then turns out to be near-identity between the two thinkers on the nature of the relationship established between the elaboration of ideas by the organic intellectuals and the culture of the socially oppressed to whom these latter relate (West 1997: 312-3). On this non-trivial point, Gramscian Marxism – though not necessarily other types of Marxism – 'translates' through identity of concepts into the discourse of 'prophetic pragmatism', as West calls his own development of pragmatist thought.

Then, taking the case of deconstructionist post-Marxism as exemplified by Ernesto Laclau and Chantal Mouffe, we can ask: is there a fit or is there incommensurability between Gramsci's view, which makes a social class playing a fundamental role within a socio-economic formation into the "*single* unifying principle" in all hegemonic formations (Laclau and Mouffe 1985: 69), and their own deconstructionist position, which does not allow for an organizing centre of this type? Or, again, what sort of compatibility is there between Gramsci's historicist Marxism and Althusserian structuralist Marxism?

The last point to make returns to intercultural translation. In 'translating' into his schema Croce's dialectic of distincts, Gramsci provides a means of linking the various ranking levels of the superstructure one to another and thence to the base, in Marx's metaphor. If, for given societies, the bases (i.e. relations of production in an extended definition of production according to Marx's 1859 *Preface*) are 'fundamentally similar', then, by ascending upwards in terms of the base-superstructure metaphor, these societies "have 'equivalent' superstructures that are mutually translatable" (Gramsci 1995: 312), where the ensemble of the superstructures correspond to the 'broad' definition of Gramsci's 'ideologies'. Thus a model is furnished to explain homologous cultural movements in different national societies. It may be crude, but as realist philosophers of science observe, such models, without necessarily being complete, can explain important phenomena. One of the tasks of Kuhnian 'normal science' is then to improve the fit of theory to facts – often by reinterpreting 'theory-laden facts'.

It must be noted, however, that the Gramscian model proposed for intercultural translation depends on the existence – within a complex and contradictory Hegelo-Marxist totality – of an organizing centre, provided by the base (hence the reservations on compatibility with deconstructionist post-Marxism and anti-Hegelian post-structuralism). The more similar the societal bases, the more exact and convincing the intercultural translation. Can theories, like deconstructionism, that depend on infinite regression and reject the notion of an organizing centre, provide a model that also furnishes an explanation of the mutual translatability of superstructural phenomena? Or, as Gramsci claimed, is it "only in the philosophy of praxis" that "the 'translation' [is] organic and thoroughgoing" (Gramsci 1995: 307)? It is an open question and one that is, to my mind, worth pursuing.

References

Bobbio, N. (1998) 'Croce maestro di vita morale. Conversazione con Norberto Bobbio', in P. Bonetti (ed.) *Per conoscere Croce*, Napoli: Edizioni Scientifiche Italiane, 35-43.

Boothman, Derek (1999) 'Ipotesi linguistiche sui *Quaderni del Carcere*', in R. Medici (ed.) *Gramsci e i linguaggi della politica,* Bologna: CLUEB, 39-62.

----- (2000) 'L'Uomo' (editorial title), supplement to *Rinascita della Sinistra*, II (12): xvii.

Butterfield, Herbert (1949) *The Origins of Modern Science 1300-1800*, London: Bell.

Caponigri, A. Robert (1955) *History and Liberty, the Historical Writings of Benedetto Croce*, London: Routledge & Kegan Paul.

Carr, H. Wildon (1917) *The Philosophy of Benedetto Croce*, London: Macmillan.

Cospito, G. (1990) *Struttura-sovrastruttura nel pensiero di Gramsci. Variazioni sul 'problema fondamentale' della filosofia della praxis*, unpublished degree dissertation (supervisor Eduardo Sanguineti), University of Genova.

Croce, Benedetto (1917) *Materialismo Storico ed Economia Marxistica* (3rd edition), Bari: Laterza. English version (1966 reprint) *Historical Materialism and the Economics of Karl Marx*, trans. C.M. Meredith, London: Cass.

-----(1920) *Nuori Saggi di Estetica*, Bari: Laterza. English version *The Essence of Aesthetics* (1921), trans. D. Ainslie, London: Heinemann.

----- (1926) *Cultura e Vita Morale* (2nd edition), Bari: Laterza.

----- (1946) 'Economico-Political History and Ethico-Political Hiltory' and 'The Unending Struggle between State and Church', in *Politics and Morals*, trans. S.J. Castiglione, London: Allen and Unwin, 67-77 and 125-30.

----- (1950, 4th ed.) 'Reminiscenze ed interpretazioni', in *Conversazioni Critiche*, Second Series, Bari: Laterza, 291-302.

Engels, Friedrich (1967) *Preface* to Vol. III of Marx's *Capital*, New York: International Publishers.

Francioni, G. (1984) *L'Officina Gramsciana,* Napoli: Bibliopolis.

Gensini, Stefano (1991) 'Modernità e linguaggio in Gramsci', in V. Calzolaio (ed.) *Gramsci e la modernità*, Napoli: Cuen, 71-81.

Goldmann, Lucien (1977) *Lukács and Heidegger*, trans. W.Q. Boelhower, London: Routledge & Kegan Paul.

Gramsci, Antonio (1957) 'Translation of Scientific and Philosophic Idioms', in *The Open Marxism of Antonio Gramsci*, trans. C. Marzani, New York: Cameron Associates, 59-64.

----- (1971) *Selections from the Prison Notebooks*, eds. and trans. Q. Hoare and G. Nowell Smith, London: Lawrence & Wishart, and New York: International Publishers.

----- (1975) *Quaderni del carcere,* ed. V. Gerratana, Torino: Einaudi.

----- (1984) 'Notes on Language: Translatability of scientific and philosophical language (*linguaggi*)', trans. Steven R. Mansfield, in *Telos* 59, 136-40.

----- (1985) *Selections from Cultural Writings,* eds. David Forgacs and G. Nowell Smith, trans. Boelhower, W.Q, London: Lawrence & Wishart.

----- (1995) *Further Selections from the Prison Notebooks,* ed. and trans. Derek Boothman, London: Lawrence & Wishart, and Minneapolis: Minnesota University Press.

Halliday, M.A.K. and J.R. Martin (1993) 'Some Grammatical Problems in Scientific English' in *Writing Science: Literary and Discursive Power*, London & Washington

D.C.: The Falmer Press, 69-85.

Jakobson, Roman (1971) 'On linguistic aspects of translation', *Selected Writings Vol. II*, The Hague & Paris: Mouton, 261-66.

Kuhn, Thomas (1970), *The Structure of Scientific Revolutions*, Chicago: Chicago University Press (2nd ed.).

----- (1974), 'Logic of discovery or psychology of research?' and 'Reflections on my Critics', in A. Musgrave and I. Lakatos (eds.) *Criticism and the Growth of Knowledge*, London & New York: Cambridge University Press (corrected edition), 1-23 and 231-78.

Laclau, E. and C. Mouffe (1985) *Hegemony and Socialist Strategy*, London: Verso.

Marx, Karl (1970) '1859 Preface' to *A Contribution to the Critique of Political Economy*, trans. S.W. Ryazanskaya, London: Lawrence & Wishart, 19-23.

Mure, G.R.G. (1967) 'The Economic and the Moral in the Philosophy of Benedetto Croce', occasional paper, Centre for the Advanced Study of Italian Society, University of Reading.

Orsini, Gian N.G. (1961) *Benedetto Croce, Philosopher of Art and Literary Critic*, Carbondale: Southern Illinois University Press.

Passerini, Luisa (2000) 'Discontinuity of history and diaspora of languages', *New Left Review (II)* 1: 137-144.

Ponzio, A. (1976) 'Introduzione' to V.N. Vološinov, *Il marxismo e la filosofia del linguaggio*, trans. N. Cuscito and R. Bruzzese, Bari: Dedalo.

Putnam, Hilary (1975) 'Is Semantics Possible?', in *Mind, Language and Reality (Philosophical Papers Vol. II)*, Cambridge: Cambridge University Press, 139-52.

Ravà, Adolfo (1909) *Introduzione allo studio della filosofia di Fichte*, Modena: Formiggini.

Roberts, D.D. (1987) *Benedetto Croce and the Uses of Historicism*, Berkeley & Los Angeles: California University Press.

Roll, E. (1949) *A History of Economic Thought*, London: Faber & Faber.

Romagnuolo, M.R. (1987-8) 'Questioni di nomenclatura: Materialismo storico e filosofia della prassi nei Quaderni del Carcere', *Studi filosofici* X-XI, Napoli: Bibliopolis.

Rossi-Landi, F. (1983) *Language as Work and Trade*, trans. M. Galli Adams *et al.*, South Hadley (Mass.): Bergin & Garvey.

Vološinov, V. N. (1973), *Marxism and the Philosophy of Language*, ed. and trans. L. Matejka and I.R.Titunik, New York: Seminar Press, (first published Leningrad, 1929 and 1930).

West, C. (1997) *La filosofia americana*, trans. F.R. Recchia Luciani, Roma: Editori Riuniti; originally *The American Evasion of Philosophy. A Genealogy of Pragmatism* (1989).

Translation as *Terceme* and *Nazire*
Culture-bound Concepts and their Implications for a Conceptual Framework for Research on Ottoman Translation History

SALIHA PAKER

Abstract: *This paper questions the de-problematization, in scholarly discourse, of* terceme *as a culture-specific concept covering a wide range of Ottoman translation practices from the thirteenth to the twentieth century. It proposes a conceptual framework for research to break through restrictive approaches that arise from ideological concerns or modern concepts of translation. It calls for research to engage in in-depth investigation into the activity of poet-translators and their texts which have been identified as translations or which researchers can assume to be translations, depending on the evidence in tradition or in modern scholarship. In this way not only* terceme *but also the concept and practice of* nazire, *or parallel and competitive poetry, is incorporated in the framework. A context for the study of both is found in the notion of an Ottoman interculture conceived as a site where Ottoman poet-translators engaged in intertextual operations in the overlap of Turkish, Persian and Arabic cultures. It is argued that Ottoman interculture evolved into an autonomous system through a process of linguistic and literary hybridization, and that research within this context calls for a recognition of overt and covert changes in the dynamics of culture over the centuries as well as in practices and conceptions of translation.*

1. Introduction

In the following pages I propose a conceptual framework for the historical-descriptive and interpretative study of Ottoman literary translation practices. The framework is intended to help define the field of research in terms of three concepts: *terceme* (translation practice of a very wide range), *nazire* (*imitatio* in the form of parallel and response poetry) and Ottoman interculture. I argue that *terceme*, which was practised from the thirteenth century onwards, and *nazire*, which became prominent from the fifteenth century, are culture-bound concepts of translation and should be recognized as such, and designated as *terceme* and *nazire* in translation discourse. I also suggest that since poets were the primary agents of Ottoman literary translation and transmission, their activities could be profitably studied in terms of an 'interculture'. Ottoman interculture is conceived as a hypothetical site where poet-translators[1] operated in the overlap of Turkish, Persian and Arabic cultures, an

---

[1] 'Poet-translator' is my designation in this paper. Latifi (d.1582) in his literary-biographical

overlap that should be distinguished from the generally held notion of a 'common Islamic culture'. My final argument is that by the end of the sixteenth century Ottoman interculture can be characterized as a literary-cultural system, which had acquired autonomy as a result of hybridization. In this framework, the concept of interculture can open up a perspective for researchers to observe the changes in Ottoman (inter)culture through the study of changes in the *terceme* and *nazire* practices of the poet-translators. It would also facilitate questioning certain established paradigms in Turkish literary-historical scholarship.

The issues raised here will be of relevance to researchers who seek to problematize 'translation' both in English and in the language(s) of the culture(s) in and on which they work. Questioning and theorizing in English, which in my case means working outside the home language, can have a liberating effect on the researcher who is perhaps looking for an alternative forum for discussion and feedback. It can also have revitalizing effects on the home (research) context to which these discussions generally travel back, in English (as lingua franca) or in translation.

Doctoral research formulated in English but with a historical focus on Turkish translation discourse and on translations into Turkish has gained considerable momentum in recent years.[2] In Şebnem Susam-Sarajeva's (2002) and Şehnaz Tahir-Gürçağlar's (2001) theses primary sources cover translations belonging mainly to the republican period (1923-). Academic research into the history of translation into Turkish is still largely confined to this period. Implicit is the need for further serious research on the long tradition behind modern notions and practices. The history pre-dating the modern period (presumed to have started in the second half of the nineteenth century), in other words, at least five and a half centuries of Ottoman translation history,[3] has hardly been touched upon in the current paradigm of research in translation studies.[4] The Ottoman Turkish language and script are not accessible to all researchers in the field,[5] which makes interdisciplinary

---

dictionary of poets (*tezkire*) writes about "plain-speaking translator poets (*mütercim, sade-gu şairler*) [...] numerous" in the fifteenth century (in Tolasa 1983:276). Latifi also mentions poets who followed the "path of translation (tarik-i terceme)" which, in the case of Ahmed Paşa (d.1497), "was regarded favourably by some, but not by others" *(ibid.)*.

[2] See, for instance, the Ph.D. theses by Özlem Berk (1999), Şebnem Susam-Sarajeva (2002) and Şehnaz Tahir-Gürçağlar (2001).

[3] There are some excellent critical editions of the works of early poets who translated Persian narrative poetry for the pleasure and instruction of Turkish princes in the fourteenth and fifteenth centuries while Persian continued its dominance as the literary language. But scholarship has not particularly focused on such works as translations. The period is generally held to be important because the early poet-translators who, in Zehra Toska's words "were the creators of the language of Turkish literature" served as models for later poets (2001: 3).

[4] Taceddin Kayaoğlu's (1998) work on translation institutions from the seventeenth to mid-twentieth centuries is important in providing the existing data for those who do not have access to Ottoman script, but remains a documentary history without analytical concerns.

[5] The Arabic script of Ottoman Turkish was officially replaced by Romanized letters for Turkish

collaboration between translation scholars and Ottoman cultural and literary historians the more pressing. Nevertheless, very few scholars have actually stressed the
need for collaborative studies. Contemporary historian Cemal Kafadar is one of the
few, although he does not particularly have translation studies in mind (1995: 64).
In his insightful analysis of the medieval Anatolian warrior epics which figure as
Turkish versions of Persian and Arabic sources, Kafadar observes that

> (t)he transmission of these narratives over time, place, milieux and media
> presents many problems that have not been dealt with. The currently rather
> sharp boundaries that exist in Turkish studies between historical and literary-
> historical scholarship must be crossed in order to deal with some important
> questions that arise from the existence of this intricately interrelated body of
> narratives. *(ibid.)*

The diversity in the pre-Ottoman and Ottoman translation tradition and its multiplicity of variants[6] calls for rigourous research into foundations, from which a plurality
of "histories" of translation can be reconstructed (Tahir-Gürçağlar 2001:1). Secondary sources that can offer historical data on concepts and practices of translation
are scant. Examining this long-standing translation tradition will reveal much about
continuity and change in culture and literature and language.

A certain illusion has been dominant: that Turkish translation history began with
renderings from European sources in the middle of the nineteenth century, and that
the preceding five hundred or more years of Ottoman intertextual and intercultural
tradition involving Persian and Arabic were not really about translation. The fact
that it was easier to observe differences between the source texts stemming from the
European 'other' and the Turkish target texts naturally played a part. But the republican ideological revolution, with its emphatic focus on westernization, also had a
role in constraining retrospective analysis on translation to go back no further than
the mid-nineteenth century *Tanzimat*, the period of extensive reforms brought about
as a result of Turkey's first major political and socio-cultural encounter with Europe. However, now that the paradigms of cultural and historical criticism are
changing, it is time that rupture with the Ottoman past and subsequent alienation
are seen as challenges to rethink discontinuity in terms of both change in tradition
and continuity. The now archaic term *terceme* itself is telling in this context. Adopted
from Arabic into Turkish before the thirteenth century, it did not drop out of the
translation discourse immediately with the republican purist language reforms in
the 1930s, but remained in currency as a technical term well until the 1960s.[7]

---

following the republican alphabet reform of 1928. See Tahir-Gürçağlar (pp. 78-92) for a discussion on the cultural consequences of the change in script and the subsequent language reform.
[6] Walter Andrews, for instance, describes Ottoman culture as "a culture of variants" (1997: 8).
[7] *Terceme*, of Arabic origin, appears as an older form in written Turkish than *tercüme*, its modern
orthographic variant. In modern literary-historical discourse on Turkish literature they can be

2.   Translation as *terceme* and *nazire*

The need to problematize *terceme* was prompted by thoughts and discussions arising from two interconnected sources: from the research seminars in the History of
Translation in Ottoman/Turkish Society in the Department of Translation and Interpreting at Boğaziçi University, which materialized thanks to the contributions of
specialists in Ottoman Turkish literature, and from the joint interdisciplinary projects
initiated by the same department and that of Turkish Language and Literature.[8] In
order to view the range of Ottoman translations for observations of their functions,
we began by computerizing a catalogue of texts from all centuries, which was followed by a subsidiary project to form a corpus of translations of romance narratives
in the *mesnevi* genre of poetry from the fourteenth and fifteenth centuries.[9] While
some of these works were paratextually designated as translations (in terms of *terceme*
and of related verbs of Arabic, Persian and Turkish origin), many others could only
be characterized as having some intertextual relation with Persian/Arabic sources.[10]
In retrospect, the problem can be formulated as follows: what would our criteria be
for 'assuming' certain texts as translations in Ottoman culture? In other words, we
were faced with the problem of defining Ottoman notions of what we call 'translation' in English, and *çeviri* in Turkish today?

---

used interchangeably. *Tercüme*, gradually lost its place to *çeviri*, a modern Turkish neologism,
which denotes (like *tercüme*) the concept, process, and product of translation and derives
from the verb *çevir-mek*, to turn (transitive). Such neologisms began to gain ground with the
Turkish language reform movement for purism in the 1930s. *Çeviri* has displaced *tercüme* in
modern discourse on translation, but *tercüme* is still in use e.g. with reference to commercial
translation, and to indicate a traditionalist stance, which sometimes, not always, implies also
a certain ideological antagonism towards republican reforms. In Levend's literary history
(1984: 80-90) the section on translation combines all three, the archaic, the modern and the
traditional: it is headed *"Tercüme"*, and discusses translation in terms of both *terceme* and
çeviri. See Tahir-Gürçağlar (pp. 154-167) for examples of the use of *tercüme* in early republican discourse on translation.

[8] *Translations and their functions in the continuity of Ottoman culture: fourteenth – nineteenth
centuries* and *Early Ottoman translations and their functions in the formation of Ottoman literary models*. Both projects are conducted by members from the Translation & Interpreting and
Turkish Language & Literature Departments of Boğaziçi University, and were supported by the
Boğaziçi University Research Fund in 1997-1999 and 1999-2001 respectively. The present paper is a contribution to both projects.

[9] *Mesnevi* is a team of Arabic origin for narrative poetry in rhymed couplets.

[10] For the first project we examined secondary sources such as catalogues, Ottoman poets' biographies, literary histories and critical editions to see if certain unidentified works were in any way
assumed to be translations either by tradition or by modern scholarship; if sources could be traced
or established for certain so-called "adaptations"; or if versions claimed to be of "original" quality had been identified in any way as translations or related to translational practice.

3.   The problem of definition: problematizing *terceme*

I take as my point of departure the brief but significant statement by the eminent
literary historian Agah Sırrı Levend in his *Türk Edebiyatı Tarihi* (History of Turkish Literature): "In our old [i.e.pre-Ottoman & Ottoman] literature, *terceme* signifies
more than what we mean by *çeviri* today" (1984:80). The statement is immediately
followed by Levend's classification of four "forms of *terceme*" : (a) "Literal", as in
the interlinear, earliest translations of the Kur'an; (b) "faithful", as in the later renderings of the Kur'an and in many literary translations; (c) literary translations
involving "the transfer of subject matter"; and (d) "expanded (literary) translations".
This classification, in which groups (c) and (d) are not clearly demarcated, is not
meant to be analytical but merely descriptive. Fortunately, Levend has more to say
on group (d), thus giving us the chance to form a critical opinion of his views on
terceme. In the case of expanded literary translations, he writes,

> the poets never think of translating the source text as it is; they do not con-
> sider themselves dependent on the source text. They transfer some pieces,
> translate others as they are. Those parts they consider important are trans-
> ferred in an expanded form, to which they have added their own thoughts and
> feelings. They transform the work in such a way that it would not at all be
> right to name such work a translation (*çeviri*)". (ibid.)

Here, Levend seems to draw our attention to the distinction he made in his initial
statement between Ottoman *terceme* and the modern Turkish sense of *çeviri*. His
explanation for "expanded translations" is intended to define *terceme* as an Ottoman practice of translation in opposition to *çeviri*, which in his mind seems to stand
for something like 'translation proper'. But we have to be careful, for Levend's
explanation lacks in terminological precision. His often indiscriminate reference to
çeviri, as in the following statement, generally leads to confusion if not read carefully: "Although they [poets] sometimes call their work a translation [designated
first as *çeviri*, but in the second instance as *terceme*], this is out of deference for the
source author" (1984: 81). As examples of this practice, Levend cites three works
by three poet-translators: Gülşehri's (14th century) translation of *Mantıku't Tayr*
by Attar (d.*ca.*1220), Kutb's (14th century) translation of *Husrev ü Şirin* by Nizami
(*ca.*1141-1203/17) and Seyf-i Serayi's (14th century) translation of *Gülistan* by Sadi
(*ca.*1213-*ca.*1292). None of these is, in his view, "translation proper" (*tam bir çeviri
değildir*, ibid.). A fourth example, Nevai's (1441-1501) *Lisanü't Tayr*, a version of
Attar's Persian work mentioned above in Chagatai Turkic, "cannot even be considered a translation" (*çeviri bile sayılmaz, ibid.*).[11] At this point it becomes fairly clear
to me that Levend's explanation of this particular form of *terceme* practice is

---

[11] Kutb, Seyf-i Serayi and Nevai wrote in Turkic dialects different from early Anatolian Turkish.

indeed formulated in opposition to the notion of *çeviri* as 'translation proper'. We can conclude that groups (a) and (b) in his classification conform with his notion of 'translation proper', the modern Turkish concept of translation, but group (d) does not. In other words, according to Levend, in groups (a) and (b) *terceme* and *çeviri* are understood to overlap as concepts and terms, but this is not the case in group (d), where *terceme* is described as Ottoman culture-bound.

Levend's group (c), literary translations which "transfer subject matter", also turns out to be problematica. In his section headed *"Tercüme"*,[12] Levend says about this group that "authors do not translate the work sentence by sentence, but transfer the meaning in the manner they have grasped" *(ibid.)*. However, in the preceding section headed *Nazire* and *Cevap* (parallel and response poetry) he apparently had more to say on the subject, but without any cross-reference to his *"Tercüme"* section (1984: 70-80). Having stated that "in Islamic literature *nazire* is not imitation in the modern sense of the word, but a similar poem written in the same metre and rhyme as the work of another poet, in order to honour that poet,"[13] Levend goes on to explain how poets practised *nazire* "on a much broader scale in their romance narratives (*mesnevi*)" by drawing on "common themes", i.e. the same subject matter as those of acknowledged Persian masters (1984: 70).

Zehra Toska (2002: 65) has pointed out that the sixteenth-century literary biographer Latifi praised the poet Şeyhi's (d.*ca*.1431) romance narrative *Hüsrev ü Şirin* as a *nazire*. But we also know that the same work was identified as *terceme* by other biographers, like Aşık Çelebi (1520-1572) who had some words of praise for it, and Taci-zade Cafer Çelebi (d.1515) who criticized it sharply (cf.Timurtaş 1980: 89-90). What is intriguing here, in view of following arguments on *nazire* in this paper, is that a fifteenth-century work could be described in terms of both *terceme* and *nazire* in the sixteenth century, and that it could be criticized as *terceme* but praised as *nazire*.

In Levend's view *nazire* romances treat "common themes", such as the romance of Leyla and Mecnun, of Hüsrev and Şirin, which "should not be studied in terms of theft, but in terms of differences in treatment and of personal contributions by each poet" (1984: 70). In some cases "only the same metre, rhyme and essence" are adopted, in others the same form of textual segmentation too (1984: 71). Among the many examples which Levend gives in this section of his book, there is also a significant one which is described as "exactly similar" to its Persian source. "It would not be wrong to call this a translation (*çeviri*)", Levend writes *(ibid.)*.

In view of his explanations on the Ottoman practice of *nazire* as imitation in the form of parallel or response poetry, *terceme* forms in Levend's group (c) gain a much wider scope or dimension. They are now understood to include *nazire*. But

---

[12] See footnote 4.

[13] For the intertextual workings of *nazire* in lyric poetry, see examples in English translation in Toska (2002:67-10) and Andrews (2002:19-24).

once more it depends on the reader to make this connection. It is also up to the reader to tease out of Levend's words the opposition between his conception of Ottoman *terceme* and his notion of 'translation proper' expressed in his use of the term *çeviri*. One of the greatest difficulties for today's researchers is that this opposition has not been clearly identified or explained by Levend. We have to deduce it from his brief comments, loose explanations and list of examples.

To make matters worse, there is hardly any chronological framework in Levend's above-mentioned sections to guide the student or the non-specialist through his examples. For instance, in the "*Tercüme*" section there are numerous critical comments on *terceme* made in verse by individual Ottoman poets, which obviously reflect the practitioners' time-bound notions. But these comments are far from being informative for lack of context and chronology. For example, the following prose quotation from the sixteenth-century chronicler Nergisi is also included by Levend among the verse comments. It provides us with an important description of two strategies in *terceme* practice, 'word for word' and 'sense for sense': "some express the translated words in exactly the same word order" (*elfaz-ı mütercemeyi bi'aynihi terkibi ile ta'birdür*) but are "dull in expression" and lack "clarity" and "rhetorical elegance" (Levend 1984: 83). "The second takes the sense of the (source) language (*me'al-i kelamı ahzidüp...*) and, in order to pour the inner meaning of the (artistic) language of the original author into the mold of beautiful expression, gives it an attractive polish by means of appropriate words and phrases and compounds and metaphors, so as to confirm and represent the desire of that (original) author in a pleasant form and worthy manner" (ibid.; in Walter Andrews' translation, quoted in Holbrook 2002: 98). In the same extract in Levend, Nergisi also claims that he himself practises the second type of *terceme* because he wants to "serve his friends" who, he expects, will not revile him but tolerate his lapses once they have grasped the reasons for any expressions added to or omitted from his translation *(ibid.)*. However, there is no indication in Levend's section that Nergisi was not a poet but an eminent chronicler of the sixteenth century, who wrote in ornate poetic prose. This is yet another instance of lack of context. We must also bear in mind that although Nergisi's description of two basic types of *terceme* is helpful, it cannot be taken as *the* norm that applied to all Ottoman poetic and prose *terceme* practices over several centuries; it stands as one understanding of translation in the sixteenth century.

Levend's other example in prose is Latifi, who was a poet but also a critic-biographer of poets (1984: 83). About his sixteenth-century contemporaries Latifi wrote: "some poets translate (*terceme*) and crib (*tı raş*) from poets in another language or they observe a meaning and deal with it in a better way, borrowing (*iktibas*) it. Some distinguished people look favourably on such theft and prefer it to pieces that the poet was following [rendering]". Although there is reference above to two forms (*tıraş* and *iktibas*) of intertextual transfer not mentioned before or after in his section, Levend does not comment on either of them or on their relation to *terceme*.

Nevertheless, it is of prime significance for us that Levend has given us a description of what type of texts in his view can be assumed as representing *terceme* and *nazire*. Despite the lack of analytical rigour which mars Levend's presentation and discourse, his statements, groupings and examples are still the principal authoritative source on which we can rely for a definition, however loose, of *terceme*. Or, to be more precise, they constitute, as a whole, *his* definition of *terceme*, which seems to me to be the most useful working definition to be adopted in a study of the Ottoman practice of translation – the most useful, because it provides us with authoritative criteria to make assumptions on what *terceme* might be, in a very broad field where many instances of *terceme* appear to lie concealed (Toury 1995: 31-35, 70-71; cf. Paker and Toska 1997: 80,87-88).

There are a few more points to be clarified at this juncture, with special reference to *translation* (in English). In describing the field of of *terceme* – from which, I conclude, emerges a culture-bound concept – Levend identifies some forms of Ottoman translational behaviour as conforming to the modern Turkish concept of *çeviri*, others as not. That is, his criterion for identifying *terceme* has recourse to *çeviri*, which is the closest Turkish term to correspond to the modern concept of *translation* (in English) but which itself is a culture-bound concept. Şehnaz Tahir-Gürçağlar (2001: 150-226) has recently demonstrated in her analysis of the Turkish discourse on translation from 1923 till the 1960s, that the modern Turkish notion of translation was construed over at least four decades of debate and discussion on the functions, definitions and strategies of translation, using both the old terms *terceme* or *tercüme* and the modern verb *çevir-mek* and its various derivatives. This culminated in what I conclude to be the consensus on the modern concept as *çeviri*. As researchers, therefore, we have to bear in mind that there are two principal notions of translation in the continuity of Turkish culture. The relationship between *terceme* and *çeviri* is similar to that between *traductio* (corresponding to *terceme*) and *translatio* (corresponding to *çeviri*) as discussed by André Lefevere (1990). But it is also different in one significant respect: the Turkish distinction has to be connected to a modern nation-building process and a concomitant ideological revolution which aimed at a political and cultural break with the past. *Terceme* and *çeviri* are to be taken as both culture-bound and time-bound, each pointing to the other's cultural otherness. Recognizing this seems to be part of the process of rethinking rupture in terms of changes in cultural continuity.[14]

In revisiting Gideon Toury's *In Search of a Theory of Translation*, Theo Hermans raised the question: "If we are trying to gauge Amharic *tirgum* [which incidentally is identical in etymology with *terceme*, SP], do we take *translation* [i.e. the culture-bound "concept of translation as it exists in modern English usage"] or *translation₂* [as an assumed universal, supra-lingual concept] as a basis?" (1995: 221). Before

---

[14] See footnote 4, on the co-existence of the old and the new as *tercüme* and *çeviri*.

commenting on this question, I would first like to focus on Hermans' own response, which is centred on "we as researchers", that is, "we" as the subject, who will

> have to account for the fact that we have no option other than to approach
> *tirgum* – or whatever terms are used, say, in medieval European cultures or
> by the Nambikwara of the Amazon region – as members of a particular cul-
> ture who have construed the concept of translation in a certain manner. *(ibid.)*

For me, the question here is who is "we"? If "we" refers to the community of scholars who operate in a monolingual area by taking English as their sole or most
important basis of reference, then this would signify a one-way, Anglo-centric importation and interpretation of data from lesser known or ancient cultures (and one
that would give weight to the way they are processed in English). But if we think of
the subject as scholars representing different cultures who offer their data both in
the language of that culture and in English, this would mean that we expect *those*
scholars, rather than the Anglo-centric 'observer'-cum-interpreter, to contribute to
(at least) a bilingual discussion, by providing a context, a definition or an interpretation of *tirgum* or any other concept they are dealing with. I am inclined to think it
is the latter condition Hermans has in mind when he draws attention to the need for
"renewed questioning of exactly what kind of cultural translation they [i.e. "translation scholars, who are constantly dealing with cultural otherness"] are performing
when they are *interpreting* – I use the word advisedly – different concepts of translation" (1995: 222).

The need for "renewed questioning" in this respect applies not only to thinking
and formulating in English, but also in Turkish. In view of the proliferation of historical translation studies carried out both in English and in Turkish, we have to
bear in mind that the cultural specificity of terms and concepts needs problematizing
rather than glossing over. The ways in which *terceme* has been *de-problematized* or
explained away in Turkish is a case in point. I would argue that an awareness of this
can in fact lead the way, if we are prepared to follow it, to the heart of some of the
difficulties in the historical and current paradigms of Turkish research.

4. How *terceme* was de-problematized

Going back to Hermans' question (cf. 1995: 221) quoted above, it is worth emphasizing its relevance also in terms of the Ottoman Turkish context: if we
(modern scholars) are trying to figure out what *terceme* is, do we take "as our
basis" *çeviri*, our modern culture-bound concept connoting fidelity to the source
text, hence minimum tampering with its fullness, or something that seems to
function like a 'universal' as in Hermans' "*translation*₂"? In view of the analysis of Levend I have presented so far, I think the answer is clear. It is our (i.e.
the researchers') 'universal' concept. For it is *this* 'universal' notion that seems

to stand for an awareness, a recognition of the distinction between our modern, culture-specific concept of translation and what we expect to find as translation in Ottoman culture. If this distinction has so far been overlooked or remained unformulated, it is due to the fact that *terceme* as an ensemble of translational practices was de-problematized.

I think one of the most important reasons for this is that modern Turkish scholars, including Levend (who came close to some form of problematization but failed to clarify his terms), have followed a certain ideological paradigm in scholarship. This had been established over the years as a result of the widely influential studies of Mehmed Fuad Köprülü (1890-1966), a pioneering modern historian, literary cultural critic and a prolific scholar of exceptional erudition. Actively involved in the cultural movement underlying the Turkish nation-building process, Köprülü set up the Institute of Turcology (Türkiyat Enstitüsü) in the University of Istanbul in 1924, a year after the foundation of the Republic. The nationalist paradigm his work set for Ottoman literary scholarship in republican Turkey was adopted by following generations both in terms of ideology and methodology. Pre-Ottoman and Ottoman Turkish was examined in terms of gradual contamination by an increasing Perso-Arabic linguistic influence: an artificial literary language was thought to have been wrought for the élite (in the so-called *Divan* literature), as opposed to the Turkish discourse of folk poets such as that of the (13th-century) mystic Yunus Emre. The *Divan* poets, in adapting syllabic Turkish to the Perso-Arabic *aruz* metre, were considered instrumental in forging the 'artificial' Ottoman poetic discourse. American scholars in Ottoman literature, Walter Andrews (1985) and Victoria Holbrook (1994), have argued that such views were and still are motivated by the early ideology of the Turkish nation-state, reflected in 'narratives' (or in discourse) which reconstructed Ottoman culture in terms of a dichotomy, i.e. two mutually alienated, isolated entities (the people and the court) in order to justify dissociating the élitism of the Ottoman past from the populism of the Turkish republic.

In such a context, linguistic and poetic inventiveness or originality in Turkish became important elements for literary studies to seek, locate and foreground, while translations identified as *terceme* by their authors or by tradition were superficially evaluated in terms of the modern concept of fidelity. Reluctance to discuss in terms of *terceme* those works that were judged not faithful but something different, led to the de-problematization of the Ottoman *terceme* practice. Intertextual transfer from Persian and Arabic was examined mostly in terms of 'influence' emerging from a common Islamic heritage of linguistic, literary and cultural conventions, not in terms of translation.[15]

---

[15] This approach which conceals translations, is abundantly clear in Levend's (1984: 44-51) "Comparative Literature" section where the focus is on "imitation" and "influence", without any reference to *terceme*.

In her critical review of Köprülü's *Edebiyat Araştırmaları* (Literary Research, 1966), Ebru Diriker has observed that in this work Köprülü used the terms *terceme* and *taklid* (imitation), *mütercim* (translator) and *mukallid/taklitçi* (imitator) interchangeably; and that his tendency was to dismiss 'faithful' *terceme* and elevate those that were expanded or abridged in ways that enriched Turkish culture in fine Turkish (Diriker 1997: 97). Works rendered into Turkish with minimum Persian contamination, were, in Köprülü's view, of great merit. For instance, evaluating Gülşehri (14th century)'s translation of Attar's Persian *Mantıku't Tayr*, Köprülü wrote:

> This great poet, who seems to have produced not a casual translation (*gelişigüzel bir terceme*) but a work of his own, was well aware of the signifi-cance of what he was doing. He said that his work was no less worthy than the Persian *Mantıku't-Tayr* and that no one before him had produced as fine a work in Turkish (1966 I:274-275; 1993:239-241)

Köprülü accepted Gülşehri's self-assessment but ranked him not specifically as a translator but as a poet who made an important contribution to Turkish poetry, es-pecially by his inventive use of additional poetic sources *(ibid.)*. Thus, in Diriker's words, "the translator [in this case, Gülşehri] was made 'visible', but no longer considered a translator" by Köprülü (Diriker 1997: 97). This sums up what I mean by '*terceme* de-problematized'. Comparing Levend's comments (below) on the same poet and translation, we find that his last statement illustrates yet another attempt to de-problematize: "For example Gülşehri's translation of Attar's *Mantıku't Tayr* and [...] are not proper translations (*çeviri*). The authors have made many contributions of their own while translating (*çevirirken*). They have designated their works as *terceme* (or is it *tercüme*) out of deference to the author of the source text whom they considered a master" (Levend 1984: 81). Referring to such statements, Zehra Toska writes: "Even though Levend describes such works as 'expanded transla-tions', he also says that 'one cannot call them translations'. How then is it possible for us to distinguish them from original works?" (2002: 63). Similar questions that have been coming up repeatedly in our Boğaziçi University project seem to arise not only from such conceptual and terminological ambiguity as in the use of *terceme* and *çeviri* in Levend's discourse, but more importantly from a gen-eral literary-ideological thrust to "conceal" (cf. Toury 1995) *terceme* in order to highlight what was thought to be innovative and original and contributing to Turkish poetry and culture.

It cannot be said that Köprülü diverged from the Ottoman literary discourse in which there is criticism of imitative and plagiarizing practices in translation as well as tolerance for the interventions of competent, manipulative poet-translators. But the distinction Köprülü made between, on the one hand, *translators* as imitators and, on the other, *poets* who used their talent to make worthwhile individual

contributions to the source texts they worked on, was instrumental in (a) restrict-
ing the researchers' scope in examining Ottoman *terceme* practice and (b)
de-problematizing its diversity, thereby (c) erasing *terceme* from Turkish literary-
critical discourse as a functional concept for linguistic, literary and cultural
analysis.[16] In this context it is important that Zehra Toska, a scholar in Ottoman
literature who leads the second Boğaziçi University project, criticizes tendencies in
current research to gloss over the translational features of work by Ottoman poets
(2002: 59-61). It is equally important that she draws attention to a need for studying
the work of Ottoman biographers of poets to see if their terminology (such as *nazire*)
can be adopted in describing translations today (2002: 66).

5. Problematizing aspects of Ottoman translation practice in terms of *translation* (in English)

In this section, and in the following one, I shall focus on two recent essays, one by
Victoria Holbrook (2002), the other by Walter Andrews (2002). Both Andrews and
Holbrook ground their arguments in the notion of a shared Perso-Ottoman language
of poetry and culture. They also foreground poets as agents of translation and transmission. These points help in reinforcing the connection between poet-translators
and the notion of an 'Ottoman interculture' in my conceptual framework.

In her essay Victoria Holbrook reviews Ottoman literary translation practice in
terms of "outright" and "concealed" translation. The context for both is set in a
discussion about literature by the followers of the Persian mystic poet Mevlana
Celaleddin-i Rumi (d.1273) for the dissemination of his mystical precepts, that is,
in an intercultural domain shared by Turkish, Persian and Arabic. Holbrook's notion of "concealed" translation covers strategies of transfer in which the cultural
context that gave rise to them remains hidden. She defines "outright" translation as
"translation in the conventional sense" (2001: 13). Her subsequent reference to the
sixteenth-century chronicler Nergisi shows that "outright" corresponds to his description of literal translation. His words on free translation, on the other hand, are
interpreted as "reworkings of thematic material which exhibited the independence
of Ottoman style [...], praised for their originality"*(ibid.)*, that is, an activity akin to
the *nazire/imitatio* practice which will be discussed below. It will be remembered,
however, that Nergisi described each strategy specifically as a form of *terceme*. We
must bear this in mind while reading Holbrook's statements below, which follow
upon her contention that "outright" translation was no longer practiced by the sixteenth century, i.e. once Ottoman imperial authority had been firmly established:

---

[16] Amil Çelebioğlu's (1999) study of thirteenth- and fifteenth-century *mesnevi* narratives is the
most recent example of the restricted and de-problematized view of *terceme* practice.

> Once Arabic-Persian-Islamic literate culture had been absorbed by a suffi-
> ciently large Turkish-speaking but multilingual coterie, from which the ruling
> classes of a now vast empire were drawn, there was no reason to produce
> translations; they could read the originals, they were writing works in Ara-
> bic and Persian as well as Turkish, and Ottoman Turkish had achieved
> widespread authority as a literary language. The conditions favorable to
> cultural transfer from Persian had ceased to obtain; the culture which had
> been assimilated was no longer regarded as foreign, but rather as part of
> the 'organization of life' in Even-Zohar's phrase, and so did not need to be
> translated. (2002: 99)

It is difficult to see why there should be no need to translate, unless we connect
"cultural transfer" in the above context to Holbrook's view that "medieval translation [for purposes of acculturation] from Persian and Arabic into Turkish in general
ceased to be a significant activity among the Ottomans" by the middle or end of the
fifteenth century (2002: 97). At this point my main questions are: can we assume
that all translations in the early period were "outright" or literal translations? And,
even if we accept that "outright translation" came to an end by the sixteenth century, how do we account for so many texts identified as *terceme* in the Ottoman
tradition up to the early twentieth century? Since Holbrook does not refer to the
practice of translation as the Ottomans named it, one can only conclude from the
above quotation that Ottoman translation practice before the sixteenth century, is
judged not in terms of the culture-bound *terceme* but in terms of "translation in the
conventional sense"; and that the latter appears to stand for a concept covering both
English and Ottoman, involving not much more than literal interlingual transfer.
Intentional or not, *terceme* as a culture-bound practice and notion is erased from
Holbrook's discourse.

Holbrook's main concern, however, lies in certain forms of "concealed" translation, the most significant one of which, in my view, involves the politics of Ottoman
culture and language. In her discussion of the poetic transmission of Rumi's literary
mystical tradition, Holbrook leads us to consider some forms of "concealed translation". About the most significant of these she says:

> It may be true that texts assumed to be translations in their time also con-
> ceal – by not mentioning, not revealing – what may likely have been fierce
> contests [i.e. between Turkish and Persian] for power and identity intimately
> connected with language by way of the changing status of one language, and
> the form of political power associated with it, relative to another (2002: 94).

Holbrook's subsequent reference to "nationalist-teleologist judgements" *(ibid.)*
which have ignored the implications of such concealment, brings to mind certain
points which we could connect to the use of Persian and Arabic in Ottoman translations, and the way it has been interpreted by modern Turkish scholars.

Some comments by Cem Dilçin on the poet-translator Hoca Mesud (d. *ca*.1370), for instance, may serve to illustrate this point. Hoca Mesud in the formal ending ("*hatm şüden-i kitab ve özr averden*") or epilogue to his *Süheyl ü Nevbahar* [17] (Persian source-text unidentified), states that he "translated word for word" (*lafzen-be-lafz eyledüm tercüme*; Dilçin 1991: 575). Mesud also complains of the difficulties he encountered in translating poetry into Turkish and refers specifically to metric constraints: (literally) "when the Arabic or Persian wording is rendered in Turkish verse, sometimes it is in harmony with the original, sometimes it is not, because the metre does not accept it" (Dilçin 1991: 574, ll.5593-4). Cem Dilçin, in his excellent critical edition of *Süheyl ü Nevbahar*, attributes Hoca Mesud's complaints and certain flaws in his Turkish verse to the fact that the poet did not have accomplished mentors (like Persians) to follow in Turkish; he explains that if, in a period where Persian poets were so influential on Turkish literature, Hoca Mesud "had filled up his language with Persian and Arabic words, as did the poets in later centuries, that way of writing too would have been severely criticized today. Contrary to our expectation, it is significant that he produced works in plain Turkish" (Dilçin 1991: 19). Such an explanation seems to overlook in Hoca Mesud's words possible hints of a poetic-linguistic struggle between the pull of Persian and Turkish. At the same time it gives expression to a certain ideological anxiousness to emphasize the importance of plain Turkish against that 'contaminated' by Persian and Arabic.

Hoca Mesud is not the only one among the early poets and writers to complain about the constraints of Turkish on his work. Dilçin himself has drawn attention to several: Gülşehri, Şeyhoğlu, Aşık Paşa, Sarıca Kemal (1991: 6-7,19). Kadi-i Manyas is another (Özkan 1993: 10). We cannot ignore the fact that in the fourteenth and fifteenth centuries poets themselves found it a problem to express themselves in Turkish. Levend (1984: 83-87) quotes many examples, mostly from poets of the sixteenth century, who took pains to show that, in their verse, they shunned translating Persian poets. It is worth looking deeper into the context of such statements and their possible underlying reasons. Why indeed did those poets protest so much? Was it simply to draw attention to the difficulty of finding precise Turkish correspondences to Perso-Arabic lexical and metric elements, or were they also acknowledging certain pressures and tensions in a struggle for dominance between Turkish and Persian linguistic and cultural identities – tensions which remain hidden from view until we tease them out? This is what Holbrook may have been pointing to in her reference (above) to translations that conceal. However, the related question of Perso-Arabic preponderance in the Ottoman translations *after* the fifteenth century, which I shall illustrate below with

---

[17] In his statement of purpose, Hoca Mesud specifically identifies himself as a *terceman* (translator): "sebeb-ı nazm-ı terceman-ı in-kitab" (Dilçin 1991: 213). He also defines his activity in terms of (literally) "doing a commentary (şerh eyleyem Türkice)" (Dilçin 1991: 218).

some examples, is also relevant to Holbrook's argument for the end of "outright translation" in the sixteenth century.

Zehra Toska and Nedret Kuran-Burçoğlu point out that a random episode taken from Zaifi's (16th century) translation of Attar's *Mantıku't Tayr* kept unchanged up to *70 words out of 136* in the Persian source-text (1996: 259), i.e. more than half. But we have to bear in mind that Persian poetic source-texts already contained Arabic elements; that the number of *Arabic* lexical items syntactically incorporated in an episode in *Persian* prose (in Sadi's *Gülistan*, for example) could be as high as *fifty percent* or even higher (Apak 1999: 28, 31). So Ottoman translators working on Persian source-texts were dealing with an already hybrid poetic language. Another comparative study of a random episode taken from sixteen versions of the Persian prose-and-verse classic *Gülistan* by Sadi (d.1291), shows that *26 of the 28 Arabic* words as well as *17 of the 27 Persian* words in the source-text were kept in the translations ranging from the fifteenth to the twentieth centuries; that in the versions up to the twentieth century more correspondences were found in *Arabic* rather than Turkish to translate the Persian work, and that the overall number of Arabic elements reached *over* fifty percent of the total lexical items in the seventeenth and eighteenth-century versions (Apak 1999: 28, 31-32). In his comparative study on five translations of *Mantıku't-Tayr*, Cem Dilçin reminds us that while the earlier translators of the fourteenth and fifteenth centuries were largely concerned with translating "the meaning" into Turkish, the poets Kadizade Mehmed and Zaifi (16th century) and Fedai Dede (17th century) also tried to preserve the Perso-Arabic stylistic and narrative features of their source-texts (Dilçin 1993: 36).

In this context of obvious trilingual hybridity, it is perhaps easier to understand the reasons for Victoria Holbrook's contention that "outright", i.e. literal translation, had lost its importance by the sixteenth century.

6. Problematizing *nazire*

The erasure of *terceme* observed in Victoria Holbrook's discourse is also to be seen in Walter Andrews' arguments in "Starting Over Again: Some Suggestions for Rethinking Ottoman Divan Poetry in the Context of Translation and Transmission" (2002). Here we find a groundbreaking problematization of "*nazire (imitatio)*", in terms of its creative translational function in parallel and response poetry (2002: 19).[18] *Nazire* appears as *the* culture-bound concept of translation par excellence, in opposition to "substitutive translation", which I read as Andrews' English for *terceme* (and Holbrook's "outright translation").

Andrews begins by pointing to the problem he has "separating out what we usually think of as 'translation' from a spectrum of activities, some of which would

---

[18] Cf. Levend (1984: 70-80) on *nazire (imitatio)* and *cevap* (response) practices and Toska (2002: 65-6) on *nazire*, referred to above.

correspond to anybody's definition of 'translation' and some which would not"; he adds: "it is precisely the activities which seem the least like 'translation' that interest me the most as instances of translation" (2002: 15). Here I note the distinction Andrews makes between a modern concept of translation and a specific one, *nazire*. By drawing on Harold Bloom's notion of "inter-poem" and relating it to the wide range of "parallel or competitive or response poems", "additive poems" and "allusive poems" in the Ottoman poetic repertoire, Andrews urges an exploration of translation in terms of intertextuality. He concludes that "by recognizing relationships between poems that are 'primary' and 'creative' (as the now common notion of 'rewriting' already implies) in addition to those relationships that we think of as secondary and to some degree 'substitutive' we are induced to ask some quite unusual questions about translation" (2002: 16-17).

Andrews argues that *nazire* most commonly served as *the* means of translating other Ottoman lyrics as well as Persian lyric poetry, except in cases of "outright theft" (2002: 25). In his view, the *nazire* form is also important for "understanding how the development, transmission, and dissemination of the Perso-Ottoman episteme occurred from the early fifteenth century on" (2002: 19). It is important at this stage to see *nazire* as a metaphor in itself:

> It is in the nature of Ottoman *nazire* (and *nazire*-like gestures) to efface borders (or to elide 'difference' in a hegemonic way). Just as it is in the nature of 'translation' – in the most limited sense – to reinforce them [...] The similarity implicit in the notion of *nazire* reflects or tropes a sense of *essential* similarity at the level of poetic (or poeticised) language that extends across the languages of the epistemic domain. (2002: 33)

Because they are languages belonging to the same "epistemic domain", Andrews finds the Ottoman, Persian and Urdu poetic languages mutually "untranslatable" in the sense Walter Benjamin uses it with reference to "sacred" texts *(ibid.)*; it is implied, therefore, that we should not be thinking of Ottoman Turkish translations of Persian poetry. Instead, Andrews argues, we ought to be looking at how the Ottoman poetic language was transmitted or translated "into other sociolects of Turkish", e.g. from the idiom of the élite to that of the populace.

> [B]ecause the language of Ottoman literature is the central productive agent of the Ottoman cultural/epistemic universe, it is transmission and translation *from* this language that establishes the character of Western Turkish in the Ottoman period and becomes the primary ancestor of today's Turkish. (Andrews 2002: 28-29) (my italics, SP)

Andrews is thus pointing to an area of *intra-lingual* transfer[19] which has escaped

---

[19] Intra-lingual translation into modern Turkish still continues for post-republican generations so that they can understand texts in Ottoman Turkish.

critical notice due to adherance on the part of scholars to the notion of Turkish as a "national core language", whereby Ottoman Turkish is considered contaminated by Persian and Arabic. He assumes that "an intermediate class of poets and storytellers" who were instrumental in introducing Turkish into the courts of Persian-speaking princes in the thirteenth and fourteenth centuries "went on to mediate between the Persianized Turkish of the elites and the language of the populace, constantly recreating (through various kinds of "translation") the vocabulary and sentences of Turkish" (2002: 35).

This form of intralingual translation Andrews regards as a different kind of activity (and one more worthy of study in terms of 'translation') than what he calls "substitutive translation". He reminds us that the latter, close to "slavish imitation", was held in contempt by some Ottoman poets and literary biographers because they knew how thin the line was between Ottoman and Persian poetry (2002: 30). His examples from certain poets who express their contempt show, as expected, that they were actually referring to *terceme*, a term Andrews never actually uses. Clearly the reason is that he regards this term as an example of Borgesian *hrönir*, perpetuated by "our [i.e.Turkish] scholarly tradition [that] has insisted – based on the presumed lucidity of the present – that they [the poets] were indeed translating, and were indeed imitating" *(ibid.)*.Here I think Andrews is right in being critical of scholarship because it has failed to observe and to study certain cultural specificities like *nazire* in Ottoman translation. This is one of the main points of my argument. But in equating *terceme* (or any other term in Turkish to denote 'translation') with a modern concept of translation (in English) to which he refers at the beginning of his essay as "anybody's definition of translation", Andrews too seems to be overlooking a certain culture-specific practice

If we are to re-examine certain established assumptions in the light of what the Ottomans said about themselves and their works, first we have to bear in mind that what the Ottomans referred to so often as *terceme* seems to be an important activity which they continued to engage in and struggle with in their cultural life. Secondly, we also have to be aware of a certain ambiguity in modern Turkish literary-critical discourse. This discourse, which Andrews is critical of, depends heavily on *terceme* (or *tercüme*) as a *term* which is used to refer to and identify certain works in the Ottoman tradition, or to dismiss certain works and elevate others, but not on *terceme* as a culture-specific, functional *concept*. Scholarship has de-problematized the concept, taking as its basis, the modern notion of translation (i.e. what *çeviri* seems to stands for) not *terceme* as a culture-bound notion. Therefore, in my view, their insistence on "translation", to which Andrews refers above, remains inconsequential.

To sum up, the strength of Andrews' argument for *nazire* as a creative translation practice and a culture-bound concept makes it imperative to include it in a conceptual framework intended to expand the researchers' field of inquiry in Ottoman translation history. In problematizing *nazire* as creative translation, Andrews has foregrounded the active agency of Ottoman poets deeply involved in intertextual operations in an intercultural space. Within that same space he has also drawn attention to the role of intra-lingual translators as mediators between canonical and popular poetry. His arguments serve as an excellent introduction to the concept of 'interculture'.

7. Ottoman interculture

Anthony Pym, in his initial broad definition of "interculture", uses the concept "to refer to beliefs and practices found in intersections or overlaps of cultures, where people combine something of two or more cultures at once" (1998: 177). More recently, he has argued for "at least two definitional constraints": that "people" should be groups of a more or less professional status, and that the "intersections" should be considered hierarchically "secondary to a division of cultures" because "as soon as the line between cultures becomes non-operative, as soon as there is no functional barrier to overcome, interculturality loses its derivative status and becomes indistinguishable from general cultural practice" (2000: 5). Pym also points out that, however loose, these restrictions should warn us against "any universalist common base shared by different cultures" *(ibid.)* – such as 'a common Islamic culture'. Thus, an Ottoman interculture would have to be conceptualized in the intersection of three cultures (Persian, Arabic and Turkish), as the trilingual, tricultural site of operation of Ottoman poet-translators.[20] While 'interculture' seems to be a simple construct, the notion of an Ottoman interculture certainly is not. Its very simplicity, or flexibility, lends itself to a much wider range of studies on the work and the practices of the Ottoman poet-translators, allowing researchers to adopt, if they wish, within the frame of 'interculture', such postcolonial theoretical constructs as Mary Louise Pratt's "contact zone" (1992: 6-7) or Homi Bhabha's "hybridity"(1996: 58).[21]

Given the systemic foundations of the conceptual framework I have in mind, my interest at this point concerns the question whether an Ottoman interculture can also be conceived of as a system in its own right. Taking up Gideon Toury's reference to "intercultures" (Toury 1995: 172n), Pym criticizes Toury for failing to deal

---

[20] Rina Drory, in a most interesting article (on a Hebrew work modelled on an Arabic genre in the cultural climate of Christian Spain, by al-Harizi, a Jewish author of the twelfth century) draws attention to a point often forgotten: "very often we find cultural dynamics to be much more complex and elaborate, as literary contacts and relationships are often established among more than two literatures concurrently, and in ways more subtle and intricate than can be defined as the 'influence' of one literature over the other [...] At times a whole cultural context has to be reconstructed in order to understand the actual circumstances that made possible the writing or production of a particular text" (1994: 66).

[21] In fact, in view of the arguments below, I think studies on "the hybrid strategy [e.g. in the Ottoman *nazire* or *terceme*] or discourse [which] opens up a space of negotiation where power is unequal but its articulation is equivocal", would be of primary significance (Bhabha 1996: 58).

with this concept effectively, arguing that thinking the concept through would have "upset numerous other parts of his theory" (1998: 180). In his discussion Pym draws attention to a point which is rather important from our perspective: "[...] Toury naturally finds substantial interculturality 'totally unthinkable', declaring that 'as long as a (hypothetical) interculture has not crystallized into an autonomous (target!) systemic entity [...] it is necessarily part of an existing (target!) system'" *(ibid.)*. However, Toury's actual statement contains two crucial points (underlined below) which Pym has omitted from his quotation. Toury writes:

> What is totally unthinkable is that a translation may hover in between cul-
> tures, so to speak: as long as an (hypothetical) interculture has not crystallized
> into an autonomous (target!) systemic entity, e.g., in processes analogous to
> pidginization and creolization, it is necessarily part of an *existing* (target!)
> system. (1995: 28)

Would it be possible to argue that Ottoman literature and culture *had* in fact "crystallized into an autonomous systemic entity" through a process similar to that delineated by Walter Andrews? Here is Andrews, who in this instance takes his cue from Richard Rorty:

> New usages, new meanings, new words come about, he [Rorty] argues, as
> metaphors gradually become concrete. Thus literary and especially poetic
> usage, in which words are constantly thrust into new relations, are primary
> generators of the language that makes new conditions of knowledge possi-
> ble. [...][I]t seems indisputable that new literary languages arise at times of
> major change and share certain salient characteristics. For example, the new
> language is a major departure from the old literary language (i.e. it is not
> explicable solely as a development of the old language), it is chock-a-block
> full of foreign elements, it is often the product of a multi-lingual élite, it is
> contaminated by 'translation', it is ungrammatical (in that its features are not
> fixed by a formal exposition). The language of Ottoman poetry is certainly
> like this, but so too are New Persian, the Arabic, Hebrew, and Spanish of al-
> Andalus, Provençal, Middle English [...]
>   If we take the position that the Ottoman literary language developed (much
> as New Persian developed) as the lingua franca of a new cultural, territorial,
> linguistic, and epistemic domain, then it is precisely 'its nature' to do the
> things it does, to write the poems it writes in the rhythms and words it uses.
> The vocabulary it shares with Persian, and Arabic or Perso-Arabic (not to
> mention with Greek and Italian) are its own vocabulary and not something
> 'borrowed' from somewhere else. (Andrews 2002: 27)

In view of Toury's and Andrews' arguments, the answer is yes: we can think of the Ottoman literary-epistemic domain as an interculture that had evolved through hybridization by the sixteenth century.

Would it then also be possible to hypothesize, insofar as Ottoman interculture-as-a-system is concerned, that Persian and Arabic literatures and cultures served as sources for Ottoman, while Perso-Ottoman literature and culture functioned primarily as target for Arabic and Persian? If we accept the following argument by Andrews, our answer is again positive:

> The scope of 'Ottoman Turkish' and 'Ottoman culture' includes and subsumes Persian (and later Urdu) culture, just as Persian (and Urdu) culture includes and subsumes Ottoman. (And it is important to suggest, without elaboration, that this reciprocity does not appear to extend to Arabic literature, which is subsumed in the Perso-Ottoman-Urdu universe of discourse but does not include it or participate in it). (Andrews 2002: 33)[22]

Thus we can conceptualize Ottoman interculture as a literary and cultural system in itself, where Ottoman translators received and processed Persian and Arabic sources. In view of the arguments offered by Andrews, we can conceive of Ottoman poet-translators as operating in Toury's "in between cultures" (or in Bhabha's "culture's in-between"), producing works, creative or substitutive, that conformed to norms of hybridization they negotiated in the intercultural space in which, we assume, they were situated. From this perspective the concept of Ottoman interculture-as-a-system could also serve as an excellent context for the study of literary-critical encyclopedic biographies of Ottoman poets, generally written by poets who had important things to say about translation and translators in their critical evaluations (cf. Toska 2002: 64-65)[23] and whose views reflected changing perceptions of translation practices.

8. Conclusion

In the preceding pages I have outlined a conceptual framework based on a problematization of Ottoman literary translation practices in terms of *terceme* and

---

[22] This explanation brings greater clarity and precision to the view expressed by Zehra Toska in the following statement: "Although each reflects its own particular linguistic and cultural characteristics, it would not be wrong to claim that Arabic, Persian and Turkish literatures form, in a network of relationships, a common cultural system based on Islam" (2002: 72)

[23] Harun Tolasa (1983: 322), in his study of three pioneering Ottoman critic-biographers of the sixteenth century, states that they were careful to indicate not only the language (Arabic, Persian or Turkish) in which the poet had chosen to write, but also if it was "original" or "translated". Although their remarks were generally brief, the biographers took noticeable care to point this out. Tolasa comments that his three critic biographer "do not essentially object to translating. On the contrary, they offer appreciative remarks on successful interventions and additions to the content of the work, and on the personal stylistic features of the translator. However, they also expose, or severely criticize those who pretended or professed to be original, but were detected to have produced translations, imitations or examples of theft" *(ibid.)*.

nazire in an intercultural systemic context. From the general research perspective, the arguments leading up to and centring on interculturality are intended to call for a broader critical outlook on the diverse practices of poet-translators, from the literal/substitutive to creative forms such as parallel and competitive poetry, subsumed in this paper under the concept of *nazire/imitatio*. The distinction drawn by Walter Andrews between creative and substitutive translation is taken not as a binary opposition between *nazire* and *terceme* but as indicating a spectrum of Ottoman literary translational activities. The conceptual framework is suggested to help define the field of inquiry as much as to question established approaches to Ottoman translations. The arguments for the problematization of *terceme* and *nazire* call for special attention to these concepts in scholarly discourse, be it in Turkish or English. An understanding of their cultural specificity, and their revival as functional terms to be used in the modern scholarly discourse on literary translation history, will bring conceptual and terminological clarity to research.

Examination of *terceme* and *nazire* practice necessarily involves the study of poet-translators and their strategies deriving from their linguistic, literary and cultural interaction with Persian and/or Arabic source texts (assumed or clearly identified) and their authors, as well as with the work of previous and contemporary Ottoman poet-translators; such interaction can involve both rivalry and deference. In this context, the concept of Ottoman interculture as a tri-cultural (Turkish, Persian, Arabic) site for the activity of poet-translators and their work gains major importance. A critical ability to observe the implications of the notion of an Ottoman interculture continuing well into the twentieth century can be effective in decentring the established nationalist paradigm of research in literary history. Intertextuality and linguistic hybridization can be examined more objectively in the framework of an Ottoman interculture that is conceived as gradually gaining systemic autonomy. The framework can accommodate not only canonical poets and their translational work on Persian and Arabic sources but also non-canonical ones who may be assumed to have translated from Perso-Ottoman into popular Turkish.

Seeking and finding answers to such questions as what linguistic and literary strategies poet-translators used, how they responded to the work of other poets, Ottoman or Persian, how their works were described, evaluated and interpreted by the literary biographers (cf. Toska 2002: 64-65) will no doubt illuminate how translation in its many forms was practised at specific times over many centuries. Close inspection and description will reveal to what extent the basic distinction between substitutive and creative translation can be useful in interpreting the translational aspects of individual works, and in observing changes in the concept of *terceme* (for example, hinted at by the literary biographers) in the course of time. The findings would serve as reminder that the practice and notion of *terceme* should not be regarded as unchanging over several hundred years, not even in a single century. Though certain generalizations about (e.g. linguistic) differences between, say, early and later translations may sometimes be useful, they blind us to undercurrents of cultural change. The systemic aspect of Ottoman interculture is important in reminding us of change. Studied in the context of an interculture that evolved into a system with centre-periphery relations which could not have remained static for long, *terceme* and *nazire* will be seen to answer more questions than we as researchers have so far put into words.[24]

References

Andrews, Walter G. (1985) *Poetry's Voice, Society's Song, Ottoman Lyric Poetry*, Seattle & London: University of Washington Press.

----- (1997) 'Ottoman Lyrics: Introductory Essay', in Walter G. Andrews, Najaat Black, Mehmet Kalpakli (ed. & trans.) *Ottoman Lyric Poetry. An Anthology*, Austin: University of Texas Press, 3-23.

----- (2002) 'Starting Over Again: Some Suggestions for Rethinking Ottoman Divan Poetry in the Context of Translation and Transmission', in Paker (2002:15-40).

Apak, Fundagül (1999) *Gülistan'ın "Gemideki Köle" Hikayesi: Tercümelerdeki Bağlaçlar* (The tale of 'The slave on the boat" in *Gülistan*: conjunctions in the translations), unpublished M.A. thesis, Boğaziçi University, Istanbul.

Berk, Özlem (1999) *Translation and Westernisation in Turkey (from the 1840s to the 1980s)*, unpublished Ph.D. thesis, Centre for British and Comparative Cultural Studies, University of Warwick.

Bhabha, Homi K. (1996) 'Culture, In-Between', in Stuart Hall and Paul Du Gay (eds) *Questions of Cultural Identity*, Sage Publications, 53-60.

Bloom, Harold (1983) *Kabbalah and Criticism*, New York: Continuum.

Çelebioğlu, Amil (1999) *Türk Edebiyatında Mesnevi – XV. yüzyila kadar* (The *Mesnevi* in Turkish Literature – to the fifteenth century), İstanbul: Kitabevi.

Dilçin, Cem (1991) *Mes'ud bin Ahmed, Süheyl ü Nev-bahar, İnceleme-Metin-Sözlük*, (Critical edition of Mes'ud bin Ahmed's *Süheyl ü Nev-bahar*) Ankara: Atatürk Kültür Merkezi Yayınları.

----- (1993) '*Mantıku't-Tayr*'ın Manzum Çevirileri Üzerine Bir Karşılaştırma' (A comparison of the verse translations of *Mantıku't-Tayr*), *Fakülte Dergisi* Sayı 369, Ankara: Ankara Üniversitesi, Dil ve Tarih-Coğrafya Fakültesi.

Diriker, Ebru (1997) 'Mehmed Fuad Köprülü: Tarih Boyunca Çeviri ve Çeviri Eserlere bir Bakış' (Mehmed Fuad Köprülü's views on translation and translated literature), in Hasan Anamur (ed) *Hommage a Hasan Ali Yücel / Anma Kitabı*, İstanbul: Yıldız Teknik Üniversitesi, 89-98.

Drory, Rina (1994) 'Al-Harizi's *Maqamat*: A Tricultural Literary Product?' in Roger Ellis and Ruth Evans (eds) *The Medieval Translator 4*, Exeter: University of Exeter Press, 66-85.

---

[24] All translations in this paper are my own except where indicated otherwise. My thanks to Zehra Toska and Cem Dilçin for their help with the translation of quotations from Nergisi and Hoca Mesud.

Hermans, Theo (1995) 'Toury's Empiricism Version One', *The Translator* 1(2): 215-23.

Holbrook, Victoria R. (1994), *The Unreadable Shores of Love, Turkish Modernity and Mystic Romance*, Austin: University of Texas Press.

----- (2002) 'Concealed Facts, Translation and the Turkish Literary Past', in Paker (2002:77-107).

Kafadar, Cemal (1995) *Between Two Worlds, The Construction of the Ottoman State*, Berkeley & Los Angeles & London: University of California Press.

Kayaoğlu, Taceddin (1998) *Türkiye'de Tercüme Müesseseleri* (Translation Institutions in Turkey), İstanbul: Kitabevi.

Köprülü, Mehmed Fuad (1966) *Edebiyat Araştırmaları* (Studies in Literature) Vols. I-II, İstanbul: Ötüken.

----- (1993) *Türk Edebiyatında İlk Mutasavvıflar* (The first mystics in Turkish literature) Ankara: Diyanet İşleri Başkanlığı. (first published 1934).

Lefevere, André (1990) 'Translation: Its Genealogy in the West', in Susan Bassnett and Andre Lefevere (eds) *Translation, History and Culture*, London & New York: Cassell, 14-28.

Levend, Agah Sirri (1984) *Türk Edebiyatı Tarihi* (History of Turkish literature) Vol.I (Introduction), Ankara: Türk Tarih Kurumu (first published 1971).

Özkan, Mustafa (1993) *Mahmud b. Kadi-i Manyas, Gülistan Tercümesi* (Critical edition of Mahmud b. Kadi-i Manyas' translation of *Gülistan*) Ankara: Türk Dil Kurumu Yayınları.

Paker, Saliha (2002) (ed) *Translations: (re)shaping of literature and culture*, Istanbul: Boğaziçi University Press.

----- and Zehra Toska (1997) 'A Call for descriptive Translation Studies on the Turkish Tradition of Rewrites', in Mary Snell-Hornby, Zuzana Jettmarova and Klaus Kaindl (eds) *Translation as Intercultural Communication*, Amsterdam and Philadelphia: John Benjamins, 79-88.

Pratt, Mary Louise (1992) *Imperial Eyes: Travel Writing and Transculturation*, London & New York: Routledge.

Pym, Anthony (1998) *Method in Translation History*, Manchester: St. Jerome.

----- (2000) *Negotiating the Frontier. Translators and Intercultures in Hispanic History*, Manchester: St.Jerome.

Rorty, Richard (1989) *Contingency, Irony and Solidarity*, Cambridge, Cambridge University Press.

Susam-Sarajeva, Şebnem (2002) *Translation and Travelling Theory. The Role of Translation in the Migration of Literary Theories Across Culture and Power Differentials*, Doctoral thesis in Comparative Literature, University College London.

Tahir-Gürçağlar, Şehnaz (2001) *The Politics and Poetics of Translation in Turkey: 1923-1960*, Doctoral thesis in Translation Studies, Boğaziçi University, Istanbul.

Timurtaş, Faruk K. (1980) *Şeyhi ve Hüsrev ü Şirin, İnceleme – Metin* (Critical edition of Şeyhi's *Hüsrev ü Şirin*), İstanbul: İstanbul Üniversitesi Yayınları No.2670.

Tolasa, Harun (1983) *Sehi, Latifi, Aşık Çelebi Tezkirelerine göre 16.yy'da Edebiyat Araştırma ve Eleştirisi I*, (Literary enquiry and criticism in the 16th century according to the critical biographies of Sehi, Latifi and Aşık Çelebi), İzmir: Ege Üniversitesi Edebiyat Fakültesi Yayınları No.4.

Toska, Zehra (2002) 'Evaluative Approaches to Translated Ottoman Turkish Literature in Future Research', in Paker (2002:58-76).

----- and Kuran-Burçoğlu, Nedret (1996) *'Ferideddin-i Attar' ın Mantıku't-Tayr' ının* 14., 16., 17., 20. Yüzyıllarda Yapılmış Türkçe Yeniden Yazımları' (14th, 16th, 17th and 20th century rewrites of Ferideddin-i Attar's *Mantıku't Tayr*), *Journal of Turkish Studies= Türklük Bilgisi Araştırmaları:* Abdülbaki Gölpınarlı Hatıra Sayısı 20(2), 251-65.

Toury, Gideon (1995) *Descriptive Translation Studies and beyond*, Amsterdam & Philadelphia: John Benjamins.

Power and Ideology in Translation Research in Twentieth-Century China
An Analysis of Three Seminal Works

MARTHA P. Y. CHEUNG

Abstract: *The essay is concerned with assertions of difference and resistance to dominant ideology in translation research. It argues that the emphasis on historicization and contextualization that has characterized recent work in translation history, can be applied to the relation between translation studies and prevailing sociopolitical and ideological structures. I consider three twentieth-century Chinese essays on Chinese translation history. Hu Shi's 'The Translated Literature of Buddhism' (Parts 1 and 2) of 1928 championed translations into the vernacular at a time when neither translations nor literature in the vernacular (baihua) formed part of the canon. Qian Zhongshu's 'The Translations of Lin Shu' (1964), with its emphasis on Lin Shu's creativity as a translator, challenged the prescriptive insistence on accuracy which was the orthodoxy of the day. Luo Xinzhang's 'A System of its Own – Our Country's Translation Theories' (1983) emphasizes the uniqueness of the Chinese translation tradition and is thus an exercise in identity construction, but an identity markedly different from that propagated by the state at the time. In all these cases it is the agency of the translation researcher as a political subject which is at stake.* **

A friend of mine recently said to me, "Ideology is a totalizing fiction". She is right. Whether we like it or not, whether we are aware of it or not, ideology acts on us all the time – as norms, constraints, regulations, prohibitions, dogmas or orthodoxies. Its aim is to exert power over the individual through the fashioning of a particular mind set. Subservience is what it seeks, or, short of that, identification, conformity, or compliance.[1] In this sense, ideology is totalizing. But resistance is possible. And resistance can adopt a multiplicity of forms – dissent, intervention, disruption, subversion, opposition, revolution, and even compliance. In this sense, ideology is a totalizing fiction. There really is no way to determine exactly how ideology will

---

* This is the revised and expanded version of a paper first presented at the international conference on "Research Models in Translation Studies" held at Manchester in April 2000. I am grateful to the Hong Kong Baptist University for providing me with a Faculty Research Grant (FRG/97-98/II-49) to conduct research on this topic. I am also grateful to Professor Jane Lai, Dr. Stuart Christie and Dr. Tan Zaixi for their comments and suggestions.
[1] For an illuminating treatment of ideology as a concept the theorizing of which requires a multidisciplinary framework combining the insights of cognitive science, sociology and discourse analysis, see Teun A. Van Dijk (1998).

work on the individual. I find this indeterminacy fascinating, for it affirms the possibility of difference. It affirms my belief in the individual as capable of thought and critique, and thus also of choice and action. In this paper, I shall study how assertion of difference and resistance to the dominant ideology is achieved in one particular area of human endeavour – translation research.

In the last few decades, translation research has in fact been practising assertion of difference and resistance to dominant ideology. The ideology of subservience, which for decades (mis)placed translation within the confines of disciplines such as linguistics and comparative literature, and which (mis)led translators into believing that fidelity to the source text exists in the commonsense scheme of things and is natural and unproblematic, has been contested from different angles. In his programmatic essay, 'The Name and Nature of Translation Studies' of 1972, James Holmes argued eloquently for the study of translation as an academic discipline in its own right. His initiative received a boost from scholars of the polysystem school, whose research into the roles played by translated literature in the target culture in different historical periods provided strong support for the legitimacy of the discipline's claim for independence (Even-Zohar 1978). Scholars of the influential 'manipulation school' focused research efforts on revealing how, instead of being faithful copies of the original, "all translation implies a degree of manipulation of the source text for a certain purpose" (Hermans 1985: 11), a purpose which, more often than not, is linked to the operation of ideology, patronage and poetics (Lefevere 1992). Others, such as Lawrence Venuti, have argued that translations done in a fluent and transparent style are ideologically suspect because what is involved in the process is the repression of difference (Venuti 1995, 1998). Assertion of difference and resistance to dominant ideology is also the purpose behind translation research that theorizes how translation, in different historical periods and in different cultures, has been pressed into the service of different ideologies such as imperialism (Cheyfitz 1991), colonialism (Niranjana 1992) and gender inequality (Simon 1996; Flotow 1997). A similar agenda lies behind translation research that studies translations for their power of mediation, subversion and opposition to dominant ideology (Tymoczko 1999; Bassnett and Trivedi 1999).

Significantly, no such attention has been directed to translation research itself, even though Peter Fawcett has queried the hidden ideology of those who write about ideology and translation (Fawcett 1998: 106-7). But as I hope to show in this paper, translation studies, as a discipline, can be substantially enriched by the inclusion of translation research into its purview of study. Moreover, existing methodologies and approaches, in particular, the emphasis on historicization and contextualization, can be fruitfully applied to the investigation of the relationship between the ideology of difference and translation research.

Such an investigation can be conducted on the translation research carried out in any country and at any historical period. I shall focus on three pieces of work published in China in the twentieth-century:

- "*Fojiao de Fanyi Wenxue*" (*Shangjuan, Xiajuan*) [The translated literature of Buddhism (Parts 1 & 2)], by Hu Shi (in Hu Shi 1928);
- "*Lin Shu de Fanyi*" [The translations of Lin Shu], by Qian Zhongshu (1964); and
- "*Woguo Zichengtixi de Fanyi Lilun*" [A system of its own – our country's translation theories], by Luo Xinzhang (1983).

The reasons are twofold. First, China in the twentieth century underwent a series of cataclysmic ideological upheavals. It thus provides fertile ground for observing how ideological battles are fought – in translation research as much as in other discursive practices and other human activities. Second, being an academic in Hong Kong in the post-1997 era, it is important I avail myself of strategies of resistance and of assertion of difference rather than rely on the guarantee of 'one country two systems' provided by China upon Hong Kong's return to Chinese sovereignty.[2] The strategies practised by translator scholars in China therefore impressed me with a special sense of relevance. These two factors notwithstanding, I hope that the study carried out in this paper will carry a validity that goes beyond the Chinese context. For the paper aims to bring to light the importance of two issues for translation studies in general – the ideology of translation research and the translation (i.e. the carrying across) of ideology in translation research.[3]

1. Hu Shi, 'The Translated Literature of Buddhism' (Parts 1 & 2) (1928)

Hu Shi (1891-1962) was a scholar, educator, writer, critic, translator, theorist and thinker.[4] He was credited with having launched the '*xinwenxue yundong*' [New

---

[2] Hong Kong, a British colony since 1842, was returned in 1997 to China, a communist country. To allay the fears of Hong Kong people, China gave Hong Kong the guarantee that for fifty years, Hong Kong would remain a capitalist society and its inhabitants would continue to enjoy the freedoms and the way of life they had been used to under the British rule. Hence the term 'one country, two systems'.

[3] The inspiration for these two expressions is drawn from the expressions used by Basil Hatim and Ian Mason in their discussion of ideology and discourse – "the ideology of translating" and "the translation of ideology" (Hatim and Mason 1997: 145, 146).

[4] Because Hu had great influence on the intellectuals and writers of his time, first in China, then in Taiwan as well as abroad – as can be attested by the thirty-five honorary doctorates he received in his life time (Yi 1987:104) – and because of his anti-Communist stance, the story of his life is a sharply contested site for biographers of different ideological and political convictions. For a short biographical account of Hu, see "Hu Shi" (1968). For a biography that strives, with varying degrees of success, to give a portrait of Hu that is relatively free from the prejudices of Communist politics, see Yi (1987). Jerome B. Grieder's *Hu Shih and the Chinese Renaissance: Liberalism in the Chinese Revolution, 1917-1937* (1970) shows a different ideological slant. It belongs to the category of intellectual biography and the study it offers, of "the ideas of Hu and of his efforts to shape China's intellectual response to the modern world", is implicitly

Literary Movement] in China in 1917. This was a movement aimed at bringing about a literary revolution in China as part of an overall effort to modernize the nation, and Hu's article '*Wenxue Gailiang Chuyi*' [Tentative suggestions for literary reform] (1917)[5] was the catalyst of this movement and its earliest manifesto. The work I shall focus on – 'The Translated Literature of Buddhism' (Parts 1 & 2) – featured as two chapters in Hu's 1928 publication, *Baihua Wenxue Shi* [A History of *Baihua* [vernacular] Literature] – a book based on a series of lectures the Ministry of Education commissioned Hu to give in 1921. These lectures enjoyed great impact since Hu had become an influential literary figure after 1917 and many writers had responded to his call to reform literature by writing in the vernacular. 'The Translated Literature of Buddhism' (Parts 1 & 2) was not part of the original set of lectures but written for inclusion in *A History of* Baihua *[vernacular] Literature.*[6] The two chapters provide ample illustration of how translation research can be used as a weapon for ideological resistance.

Hu's moves in 'The Translated Literature of Buddhism' (Parts 1 & 2) deserve careful study. He presented the translations of Buddhist sutras as literary works and analyzed them in terms of form and style, generic features, tropes, rhetoric and other composition techniques. In particular, he stressed the literary appeal of these translations and their impact on art and literature in China. Some of the fables contained in the translations were the "most beautiful fables in world literature" and had "considerable influence" on Chinese literature (Hu 1928/1998: 239). The sutra

---

anti-communist in stance (ix). There are also autobiographical accounts. See, for example, *Sishi Zishu* [A Self-account at Forty] (Hu 1939/1993). See also *Hu Shi Koushu Zizhuan* [Dr. Hu Shi's Personal Reminiscences] (1983), or the English original, preserved in typescript in the archive of the Oral History Project, Columbia University.

[5] The article was first published in China's leading journal of radical opinions, *Xin Qingnian* [New Youth] in January 1917, see Hu (1917/1991). A partial English translation of this article was published in de Barry (1960: 820-4).

[6] In the "Introduction" Hu wrote for *A History of* Baihua *[vernacular] Literature* (1928/1998: 141-8), Hu told the remarkable history of its publication. He revised the lectures every time he delivered them after 1921 and had plans for a more thorough revision, but he had not been able to find the time to do it. Then in 1927, when he was in Japan, he learned from his family that these lectures had been put together as a book and published, with a long introduction written by his friend, Li Shaoxi. He further learnt that the publishing house was run by Li's students and that they had published only 1000 copies of the book, primarily to provide reference material for students attending classes on the history of Chinese literature. Embarrassed that some of the views expressed in these lectures were "immature" (1928/1998: 144), and encouraged by the discovery of historical documents and new materials that supported the interpretation of literary history he presented in his lectures, Hu allowed himself no more delay in revising his lectures. He also prepared 'The translated literature of Buddhism' (Parts 1 & 2) for inclusion in this revised version. A comparison of *Guoyu Wenxue Shi* [A history of *Guoyu* [national language] literature] (title of the 1927 version prepared by Li) and *A History of* Baihua *[vernacular] Literature* (title of the 1928 version prepared by Hu himself) shows that Hu at first had not included translation for consideration in his mapping of literary history.

Vimalakirtinirdesah was "half novel half play" (1928/1998: 238) and told a compelling story that fascinated generations of Chinese writers and painters, who either used episodes from this story as subject matter for the mural paintings in temples, or made allusions to this story in their own literary works. Many Buddhist texts, rich in supernatural elements and descriptions strung together by a freewheeling imagination, had a "truly liberating effect" on the Chinese mind. Its influence was perceptible in popular Chinese literary works such as *Xi You Ji* [Journey to the West] and *Feng Shen Zhuan* [Creation of the Gods] (1928/1998: 251). *Buddhacarita* [Acts of the Buddha], the crowning achievement of the Buddhist poet Asvaghosa, was translated into Chinese by the monk Dharmaraksha in 420 CE and, with a total of about 46,000 characters in unrhymed verse, was the first long poem in Chinese literature at the time (1928/1998: 246). These new forms and genres, imported into China through the translations, contributed to the evolution and development of literature in China. The juxtaposition of prose and verse, a characteristic style in Indian oral literature and Buddhist sutras, was a legacy with an "unexpected influence" (1928/1998: 241): the same style was used in *tanci* – a type of performance whereby stories are told (usually in various southern dialects) to the accompaniment of stringed instruments.

Not only did Hu present translations of Buddhist works as literature, he placed them in the *baihua* [vernacular] tradition of literary writing in China, which he claimed had a history that could be traced back to the earliest times. To Hu Shi, the special strength of the translations of Buddhist sutras lay in their vernacular flavour, their closeness to the way people talked and spoke. Citing the comments made by Buddhist monks over the centuries, Hu argued that the translations which enjoyed acclaim and could stand the test of time were all characterized by a simplicity of style and a plainness of language that made them accessible to ordinary people. These translations did not fit into mainstream literary writing, which was at the time steeped in a rigid and highly adorned formalism. The translations, by their sheer number, acquired a place of their own and became a new type of literature (1928/ 1998: 252). The respect and dignity enjoyed by religious texts raised the status of this type of vernacular literature, and of vernacular literature as a whole. Although these translations had no immediate impact on home literature, not even when Buddhism was at the height of its popularity (300-500 CE) in China, Hu argued that they were like seeds which germinated and came to fruition in subsequent centuries (1928/1998: 253). As illustrations of his argument, he pointed to Buddhist temples and Zen monasteries as important "birthplaces" of vernacular poetry and vernacular writings (1928/1998: 252).

Taking works of translation not in isolation but as a constituent part of one's home literature, focussing discussion on how translations interact with, and impact on, the literary developments of one's home country – this is an approach advocated by theorists of the polysystem school. It should be noted, however, that Hu Shi carried out his research in the 1920s. Moreover, although Hu Shi did his doctoral studies in philosophy at Columbia University, he did not situate his discussion of the translations of Buddhist sutras within the discourse of philosophy or religion, or of intellectual history, but within that of literary history – the history of *baihua* literature, to be exact.

There is little doubt that Hu was engaged in a reconfiguration of literary tradition and a systematic act of subversion. He was pursuing an ideological rebellion through the assertion of difference. Literature that for centuries had been regarded by the literati as canonical (i.e. literature done in classical Chinese and governed by a strict and elevated formalism – a reflection of the rigid power structure of feudalistic China) was dethroned. A different kind of literature, *baihua* literature, was accordingly privileged. The term *baihua* is usually translated as 'the vernacular' and used to refer to the vernacular. But Hu, in the introduction to *A History of* Baihua *Literature*, attributes three meanings to this term. (1) The character *bai*, in collocation with the character *nian* [read aloud], refers to the spoken parts of a Chinese opera and *baihua* [*hua* (meaning 'language')] therefore means 'the spoken language', or the vernacular. (2) The character *bai* takes on the meaning of another character it collocates with – *qing* [clear] – and *baihua* accordingly means language that is unadorned. (3) *Ba*i also collocates with the character *ming* [light] and *baihua* can also mean language that is easy to understand (1928/1998: 147).

Within this broad construction of the term *baihua*, Hu argued that *baihua* literature was living literature, i.e. literature which had vitality and was the most creative and representative of its time.[7] Moreover, he could point to the use of *baihua* in ancient classics of the highest literary status such as *Shi Ji* [Records of the Historians] and *Zuo Zhuan* [Zuo's Commentary], in the folksongs and ballads composed in the Han dynasty (206 BCE-220 CE), and in the *"jueju"*[8] of the Tang dynasty (618-907 CE) (1928/1998: 147). In addition, he could point to the use of *baihua* in translations of Buddhist texts and discuss these translations as an integral part of the *baihua* tradition of literary writing. With this new way of charting literary tradition, with this new emphasis on a living literature, Hu was able to make the radical claim that "the history of *baihua* literature lies at the very heart of the history of Chinese literature" (1928/1998: 146).

Clearly, Hu was engaged in an elaborate manoeuvre at re-alignment of power. It was a manoeuvre involving complex moves such as the incorporation of religious translations into the domain of *baihua* literature, formation of a counter-canon, re-interpretation of literary tradition, and re-writing of literary history. What was Hu's agenda?

---

[7] It should be noted that the English title Hu himself used for *A History of* Baihua *[vernacular]* Literature *is* History of the Living Chinese Literature *(Hu 1983: iii). The ideological significance of this rendering cannot be overemphasized.*

[8] *Jueju* is the name of a poetic form. It refers to a poem of four lines, each containing five or seven characters, with a strict tonal pattern and rhyme scheme.

Earlier on, I remarked that Hu was credited for being one of the instigators of the New Literary Movement in China. This movement was spearheaded by theories and manifestoes. Slogans calling for the use of *baihua* and for the production of literary works in *baihua* preceded the actual appearance of *baihua* works.[9] Even when the movement was in full swing, *baihua* literary works of quality were meagre in output[10] and the movement was largely sustained through translations. Translations, however, were open to the charge of being subservient to the original source. The literary reform envisaged by Hu Shi and others was intended as part of a bigger and more ambitious programme of national revitalization of culture. If the New Literary Movement continued to be reliant on, or dominated by, translations, it would be vulnerable to the charge of being stagnant or parasitic. What good then would the translations do to literature? Would the dominance of translations not lead to the eventual erosion or even destruction of the identity of one's home literature? What right did a literature heavily dependent on translations have to replace traditional literature – the pride of a country with over a thousand years of glorious civilization? How could such a literature contribute to the national revitalization of culture?

Obviously Hu's challenge was not simply to promote the use of *baihua* for literary writing by broadening the definition of *baihua* literature so that it could be shown to have had a long tradition in history. Such had been the strategy Hu used in his 1921 lectures but such a strategy provided justification for the movement at its initial stage only. The actual course of development taken by that movement, and the disproportion in output between *baihua* translations and *baihua* literary works (especially from 1917-25) made it possible for the skeptics to voice doubts concerning the sustainability of that long tradition. But if it could be proved that translation was a central component of that tradition, the picture would be different. Translation would then acquire meaning as a cultural act with full ideological legitimacy in

---

[9] In a powerful and thought-provoking critique of the New Literary Movement, Wang Xiaoming, a Mainland critic, commented on "the main difference" between the birth of modern literature in China and that in Europe. In the case of China, theory preceded practice (Wang 1993: 171), theory shaped literary practice. The literary works thus produced were like products of a rational, pre-set programme – Wang was "tempted to say" (1993: 172).

[10] Hu's own literary oeuvre is a case in point. While he was strong in academic and manifesto writing, he was weak in literary composition and his literary output was meagre, as he himself freely admitted (Yi 1987:180; Grieder 1970: 86). Lu Xun and Mao Dun, also leading figures of the New Literary Movement, had also commented on the "loneliness" of the *baihua* writers, especially during the first five years of the Movement (Mao 1935/1980: 4; Lu 1935/1980: 8). Even in as late as 1925, Xu Zhimo, a famous *baihua* poet, was moved by the success of the relaunching of *Jia Yin* [The Tiger], a weekly magazine in classical Chinese and the mouthpiece of critics of the New Literary Movement, to comment that *The Tiger* was doing much better, in sales figures at least, than other *baihua* magazines of a similar orientation in contents (Xu 1935/1980: 230-1).

history. Moreover, the vernacular used as the language of translation would also acquire ideological legitimacy. Consequently, the past would justify the present. The continual pursuit of translation would not pose a threat to the identity of the nation's literature; rather, it would sow the seeds for future literary development. More importantly, such an evolutionary view of *baihua* literature would help to consolidate the new power structure resulting from the dethronement of traditional literature by the rise of the New Literary Movement. Hu had long declared that he wanted to bring about a Chinese Renaissance.[11] As early as 1917 he had made the point that during the Renaissance in Europe, translation was used as means to raise the vernacular to the same status as Latin, the language of power, and to hone the vernacular for the production of national literature (1917/1991: 12). The situation of China in the early 1920s, however, was vastly different from that of Europe. Hu could not simply predict that translation could help to hone the vernacular for the production of national literature, especially since classical Chinese [*wenyan wen*] had also been used for translation and many of these translations were extremely popular. Hu would be obliged to provide an argumentative basis for his prediction.

Hu's need to find an argumentative basis for his prediction is the key to understanding why 'The Translated Literature of Buddhism' (Parts 1 & 2) was not part of Hu's 1921 set of lectures and only featured in the revised version of 1928. These two chapters were a strategic addition. Hu had used translation research for a purpose: the ideological empowerment of translation. With his reading of the behaviour of translated literature in the literary polysystem of China, and specifically of the central role played by the translations of Buddhist sutras in the development of *baihua* literature in China, Hu sought to provide justification for his conviction that sooner or later translation would accomplish its mission – expansion of literary horizons, cultivation of the mind, and, ultimately, cultural revitalization and literary regeneration. His was an elaborate attempt at legitimization through historicization.

2. Qian Zhongshu, 'The Translations of Lin Shu' (1964)

Qian Zhongshu (1910-98) was a writer, an essayist, and a man of great learning – at once an acknowledged master in the study of Chinese classics as well as an

---

[11] "Renaissance" was initially translated in China as "*xin chao*" [new trends] or "*xin sichao*" [new trends of thought]. What Hu meant by "Chinese Renaissance" was spelt out in his essay, "Xinsichao de Yiyi" [The meanings of *xin sichao*] (Hu 1919/1953). Hu had also given a number of lectures, in English, on this topic. See Hu (1926/1995) and Hu (1934). The reason – largely ideological – as to why Hu preferred to describe what he wanted to bring about in China with the term "Chinese Renaissance" rather than other descriptions current at the time such as "*xin wenhua yundong*" [New Culture Movement], "*wenxue geming*" [Literary Revolution] was explained in "Zhongguo Wenyifuxing de Sizhong yiyi" [Chinese Renaissance: four dimensions of significance] (Hu 1983: 175-6).

accomplished scholar in Western literature.[12] 'The Translations of Lin Shu',[13] one of the most important essays on translation to have appeared in twentieth-century China, provides another illustration of how ideological resistance can be achieved through the deployment of translation research.

The very title of Qian's work alerts one to the need to think ideologically about translation research. Lin Shu (1852–1924) was a monolingual who had to rely heavily upon his collaborators in his work of translation. And yet he turned out to be a prolific and highly influential translator of Western literary works into Chinese. His translations were enormously popular in his day. During the last two decades of his life, however, Lin was severely attacked for his conservative politics (i.e. his loyalty to the Qing dynasty), his stubborn defence of classical Chinese against the campaign to promote the use of *baihua* [the vernacular] in writing, and his mistake-ridden translations. After the establishment of the People's Republic of China in 1949, the orthodox view was that Lin had contributed substantially to the introduction of western literary works to the Chinese populace, but he was lax in his selection of texts to be translated, and in his later years, he lacked seriousness in his attitude and his translations were slipshod.[14]

Why did Qian Zhongshu research the translations of Lin Shu when such a consensus had already been established? The question becomes more urgent when the political context is taken into consideration. The 1950s were a time of great political upheaval. The influence of Marxism and Leninism was paramount. Mao Zedong's views on the need for art and literature to serve social and political functions rather than abide by the principle of art for art's sake or that of self-expression, delivered

---

[12] It should be noted that for decades, Qian's fictional achievements remained unacknowledged by critics on the Mainland, largely because Qian did not place literature at the service of social and political causes. In fact, Qian's talents as a fiction writer were "discovered" by a Chinese living in the States, Professor C.T. Hsia, who rated Qian's novel, *Weicheng* [Fortress Besieged], first published in 1946, as "perhaps" modern China's "greatest novel" in his authoritative *A History of Modern Chinese Fiction 1917-1957* (1961: 441). It was not until 1979, when Qian's monumental four-volume work, *Guan Zhui Bian* [Limited Views: Essays on Ideas and Letters] was published that critics on the Mainland began to pay serious attention to his achievements and Qian became a canonized figure. For a detailed biographical account of Qian in Chinese, see Kong (1992). For a summary account in English, see "Translators' preface", *Fortress Besieged* (Kelly and Mao 1979).

[13] "The translations of Lin Shu" was first published in *Wenxue Yanjiu Jikan* [Anthology of Literary Studies], Vol. 1, in 1964. George Kao has translated a large part of this article into English, entitled "Lin Ch'in-nan Revisited" (Ch'in-nan, or Qinnan – according to the Pinyin system used in this article – is the courtesy name of Lin Shu) (Qian 1975). I am using the 1964 version rather than later versions (slightly revised by Qian) for discussion because of the importance of reading the text in the historical, political and ideological context of the time.

[14] This was the assessment of Lin Shu given by Mao Dun in the Report he presented, in his capacity as the Minister of Culture, at the National Conference on Literary Translation held in August 1954 (Mao 1954/1984: 2).

at *Talks at the Yenan Forum on Art and Literature*[15] in 1942, had hardened into dogma. In 1954, Yu Pingbo, Qian's colleague at the Institute of Chinese Literature, the Academy of Social Sciences, was openly criticized for not employing the Marxist view of literary criticism in his analysis of *Dream of the Red Chamber*, a famous Chinese classic, and for having fallen prey to the idealism of the capitalist class (Mao 1979: xv). The Anti-Rightist Struggle (a counter-attack against the bourgeois Rightists) commenced in 1957 (Kong 1992: 16), and Qian's father was branded a Rightist in 1957. A year later, Qian himself was severely criticized for a work he edited, *Song Shi Xuan Zhu* [An Annotated Selection of Song Poetry] (1958), and was saved from the fate of his father only by the intervention of influential figures in the central government (Kong 1992: 162).

With this context in mind, let us now look at 'The Translations of Lin Shu'. Qian begins by dipping into etymology. Citing the authority of Xu Shen, the Han dynasty philologist, Qian states that the character *yi* [translate] has etymological connections and semantic associations with the characters *you* [entice, mislead, lead], *mei* [mediate, match-make] *e* [errors, misrepresentations] and *hua* [transform] (Qian 1964: 1). Then, he uses these characters to thematize his views on the functions of translation, the pitfalls that are hard to avoid, and the highest state to which translation aspires. He starts with the character *hua* ('transform' in a total sense), which for him represents the highest standard to be reached by literary translation (*ibid.*). A literary work in one language could be said to have been "transformed" into a literary work in another language if no trace was left of the strain and awkwardness caused by the differences between the two languages, and if the flavour and feel of the original was fully preserved. Such a translation would then be said to have reached *"huajing"* – the highest, the most natural, and most marvelous state, transformation in a total sense. Such a translation would not read like a translation, for the original would not read like a translation in the first place. He notes that in seventeenth-century Europe, George Savile, First Marquess of Halifax, had advanced a similar notion of translation with the metaphor of the "transmigration of the soul" (*ibid.*). The outer form of the text has been replaced, the body is different, but the spirit, the inner charm, remains the same.

Qian, however, admits that this state of transformation is not easy to attain (1964: 2). In his view, errors and misrepresentations (*e*) are inevitable, due to all sorts of reasons. There are, however, different types of "mistakes". Some may well be deliberate liberties the translator takes with the source text. In the case of Lin Shu's translations, the "errors" could be divided into two types – those due to Lin's own carelessness and those which, upon careful analysis, would be seen as additions, compensations and embellishments (1964: 6-9). The "errors" of the second type were Lin's own "contributions" to the text he was translating because they

---

[15] This is the title of the English translation of these talks published by the Foreign Languages Press in 1956.

added colour, verve, drama and humour to the translation (1964:8), making it as good as, if not better than, the original. Strictly speaking, these interventions should not be encouraged in works of translation, yet they often have provided inspiration for anyone interested in rhetoric and the art of composition. Qian even says that a translator who is also a writer, or fancies himself as one, could hardly resist the urge to act as the original author's "best friend and severest critic" when he comes across passages which in his view are weak and need improvement (1964: 10). Further-more, Qian argues that the history of translation (especially its early stages) of any country shows that Lin Shu was in good company.[16] Translation history also abounds with examples of translators whose command of the target language was superior to the author's command of the source language[17] – as was Lin Shu when compared with a writer like Rider Haggard (1964: 25).

In Qian's view, because the transformation brought about by the act of transla-tion is not always thorough and complete but can take many different forms, the appeal of translation also takes different forms. When transformation is complete and total, the reader will find the translation so enticing (*you*) he will fall in love with the original. The translation will then have brought about a "literary romance" between nations. In terms of cultural exchange, the translation will then have func-tioned like a match-maker (*mei*). When transformation is incomplete and partial, some readers will realize that the translation is misleading (*you*) and their curiosity to know what the original is really like will lead them (*you*) to learn the foreign language so that they can read the original for themselves (1964: 3).

It seems quite clear that Qian's article is as much about Lin Shu's translations as it is about Qian's own view of translation. Qian was actually using his research on Lin and on the history of translation in the countries in the west to provide examples to illustrate his own view of translation. It is a view of translation that is realistic rather than prescriptive, for Qian shows no insistence on translation being what it should ideally be (transformation in a total sense), and simply accepts translation for what it is in reality – misrepresentation, distortion, disguised composition of a parasitic nature, or enhanced performance. It is a view of translation that enter-tains the possibility of translation as transgression, as re-writing and as betrayal –

---

[16] In a footnote, Qian cited Sir Thomas North and John Florio (discussed in F. O. Matthiessen's *Translation: An Elizabethan Art*) as examples of free prose translation. As for examples from poetry translation, Qian cited the two classic translations of the Homeric epics by Alexander Pope and Vincenzo Monti as something in between translation and creative poetry-writing (1964: 10). He also mentioned Edward FitzGerald's *The Rubáiyát of Omar Khayyam*, which was popu-lar in China at one time.

[17] Qian gave the following examples: Walter Horatio Pater's preference for Charles Baudelaire's French translation of Edgar Allan Poe's short stories to Poe's own work in English, Johann Wolfgang von Goethe's alleged preference for Gérard de Nerval's French translation of his *Faust* to his own work, and Walt Whitman's admission that F. Freiligrath's German translation of his *Leaves of Grass* could well be better than the English original (1964: 25).

reference is made to the Italian saying *traduttore, traditore* (1964: 2). It is a view that embraces translation in all its contradictions and paradoxes: translation leads as well as misleads; it can be "worse" or "better" than the original but it is seldom what people think it should be (i.e. as good as the original); translation should not read like a translation. The implicit point is that the subservience of the translator, and the concomitant notion of faithfulness, are not absolute or axiomatic. The translator can betray, excel, manipulate the source, play with it, display traces of his own creativity, be highly visible, and can receive praise for it. Lest it should be said that Lin Shu's case is an aberration, Qian takes a broad sweep of translation history and cites examples of translations produced in the west that had been praised for being better than the original. While Qian is still critical of the mistakes made by Lin Shu, he shows genuine appreciation of Lin's more inspired treatment of the source text and he does not disguise his envy in talking about the "bold abandon" with which Lin Shu translated Dickens (1964: 10).

Read in isolation, Qian's view of translation may be fascinating because of the dazzling use he makes of the play of signifiers to convey his arguments, and because of his impressive display of scholarship. Qian's view of translation may be fascinating, too, because he embodies radical and provocative ideas – translation as transgression, for example. But because Qian privileges "*huajing*" (transformation in a total sense) and upholds it as the highest standard for literary translation, because he remains source-text oriented in his evaluation of Lin Shu's translations and in his evaluative stance as a whole, the radical energy of these ideas is contained, if not dissipated. The ideas may even be thought of as clever rather than radical.

However, when 'The Translations of Lin Shu' is measured against the discourse about translation at the time and when the historical political context is taken into consideration, a different scenario emerges. In the 1960s, discourse about translation, under the "direct leadership of the Party", was dominated by the notion of faithfulness advocated by Lu Xun, an extremely influential leftist writer, especially since Mao Zedong had spoken openly in favour of Lu Xun's strategy of rigid translation and personally championed the importance of "accuracy" in translation (Chen 1992: 383). Qian's remarks concerning the mistakes of translation, however discriminating and judicious, would likely be construed as militating against the orthodoxy of accuracy. In particular, Qian's view of translation as betrayal, though expressed in terms of disapproval, would be construed as militating against the ideology of loyalty, upon which the notion of faithfulness was founded as the first principle of translation. Such a position would be dangerous, loyalty being crucial to the maintenance of the democratic dictatorship of the Communist Party.

The 1960s discourse about translation also attributed to translation certain social and political functions. Qian's article on Lin Shu made no mention of them. Instead Qian talked blithely about how translations could play the role of matchmaker, bring about a literary romance between nations and entice people to learn foreign languages. This was deviant thinking and would make him vulnerable to attack.

Qian cannot have been unaware of the dangers to which he was exposing himself. And because the stakes were so high, his attempt to present a view of translation that deviated from the dominant view without seeking to overthrow it, must be taken as a stubborn, if also foolhardy assertion of positionality. In any case, his was a daring plea for the acceptance of differences, whether they were political, ideological or simply academic. Qian's translation research, therefore, was deeply inscribed with the power politics of the time. Indeed the full significance of Qian's translation research will only emerge when his article is interpreted not simply as a self-contained, disinterested and innocent disquisition on translation but as an act of political engagement. However compliant he might have seemed on the surface, Qian was in fact using translation research for the purpose of staging a quiet protest against orthodoxy and dogmatism. The attempt was heavily camouflaged, carefully veiled, hidden behind ambivalences, and therefore compromised. But it is a forceful testimony of the individual as a thinking agent. It shows that even compliance can be a form of resistance.

3. Luo Xinzhang, 'A System of its Own – Our Country's Translation Theories' (1983)

Luo Xinzhang (1936-) is a distinguished translator of French literature into Chinese and a highly respected translation scholar in China.[18] 'A System of its Own – Our Country's Translation Theories' (literal translation of "*Woguo Zichengtixi de Fanyi Lilun*") was first published in 1983 in *Fanyi Tongxun* [*Translators' Notes*]. Launched on 15 February 1980, this was the first journal on the Mainland to be devoted specially to translation (Wu 1980; Chen 1992: 464) and hence the primary national forum for discussion and debate on translation issues. Luo's choice of this journal – a locus of disciplinary power – for the publication of his article therefore deserves attention. Equally significant is the fact that in 1984 Luo used this same piece of work as the introductory essay of *Fanyi Lunji* [*An Anthology of Essays on Translation*], which he edited and compiled. Being the most comprehensive collection of essays on translation at the time, and the first one of its kind to include essays on the translation of Buddhist texts, this anthology had great impact when it first appeared and remains an authoritative collection today.

In addition to these two contextual points, the very title of Luo's article also bursts with ideological significance. In fact, of the three pieces of work studied in this paper, Luo's is the most explicit in terms of ideology where the title is concerned: 'A System of its Own – Our Country's Translation Theories'. Here, "Our

---

[18] For further biographical information on Luo, see "Luo Xinzhang" (1988) and Wu (1997).

country" is read as a rallying call. 'A System of its Own' is an assertion of unique-ness and of distinct tradition. What Luo does in his essay is to signpost the development of Chinese translation theory with key conceptual terms and present Chinese discussions about translation, selected from different historical periods, in a way that stresses conscious inheritance, relatedness, consolidation and elabora-tion so that the whole would emerge as a perceptible system of its own.

According to Luo, this "system" is composed of four major strands:

- "Follow the source" [*anben*]. This was the dictum left to posterity by the Buddhist monk Dao An (314-85 CE) and upheld by many translators of the Buddhist sutras. According to Luo, while there had been arguments about the validity of this dictum, the authority of the source was firmly established during this first major wave of translation activities in China, which lasted throughout the first ten centuries of the Christian era. Subsequent Chinese theories on translation, especially those that constitute the other major strands of the system (discussed below), can also be traced, through verbal echoes and conceptual reverberations, to this notion of "*anben*". In Luo's scheme of things, therefore, "*anben*" becomes the source for Chinese theories on trans-lation (Luo 1983/1984: 19).

- "Aim at faithfulness" [*qiuxin*]. *Xin* [faithfulness], *da* [comprehensibility] and *ya* [elegance] are the "three major difficulties" of translation discussed by Yan Fu in his preface to his translation of T. H. Huxley's *Evolution and Ethics* (1898).[19] According to Luo, for much of the twentieth century on the Mainland, *xin, da, ya* formed the main conceptual grid for theorizations about translation. Luo further explains that *xin, da, ya* gain paradigmatic impor-tance because these notions are especially useful for assessing translations, and criteria for evaluation lie at the very "heart" of translation theory (1983/ 1984: 5). In the fifty years after the appearance of Yan's preface, discussions about criteria for translation criticism have all been predicated upon this para-digm. There have been attempts to redefine these terms and to discuss their order of importance; there have also been attempts to challenge their valid-ity. But there has not been any alternative paradigm strong enough to overthrow it (1983/1984: 10). And "the sole explanation" for the position of supremacy enjoyed by this paradigm (1983/1984: 9), according to Luo, is that *xin, da, ya* can, to a certain extent, sum up succinctly the main features of translation and bring out a certain regulative pattern that lies behind trans-lation" (*ibid.*). With a note of pride, Luo remarks that "even in other countries, it is probably not often that a standard set for translation in the last years of the nineteenth century can, eighty years later, still retain its vitality and is

---

[19] C. Y. Hsu's English translation of this preface, entitled "General Remarks on Translation", was published in 1973. See Yan (1973).

still readily used as a criteria for evaluation" (1983/1984: 16). Yan Fu's theory
therefore "deserves a place" in the "world history of translation theory" (*ibid.*).
In Luo's panoramic view of Chinese translation theories over the centuries,
Yan Fu's three notions are also important because they form a direct link
with the thoughts on translation left by the translators of Buddhist sutras.
Citing the exegetical work on ancient texts carried out by Qian Zhongshu,
Luo points to Qian's observation that *xin, da, ya* already feature as concepts
of translation in *"Fa Ju Jing Xu"* [Preface to the *Dharmapada*] (224 CE),
generally considered to be the first piece of writing in China addressing problems of translation (1983/1984: 2). In addition, Luo cites the authority of Lu
Xun's research on Yan Fu to make the point that Yan, in preparing himself
for his work of translation, had studied the translations of Buddhist sutras for
reference and ideas (1983/1984: 6). Yan himself actually makes no reference
to the prefaces of Buddhist sutras in the preface he wrote for his translation
of *Evolution and Ethics*. Instead Yan uses quotations from Confucius and
The Book of Changes to show that *xin, da, ya* are not idiosyncratic values of
his own but have a long and illustrious history, being values much stressed in
classical writing. Whilst Luo admits there is no direct evidence to show Yan
had "inherited" the notions of *xin, da, ya* from the translators of Buddhist
sutras, he nevertheless invests Yan's *xin, da, ya* with historical and genealogical significance. He presents Yan's essay as the summation of what had
been produced earlier in theoretical discussions about translation of Buddhist sutras as well as a programmatic preparation for subsequent
theorizations about translation (1983/1984: 6). The equally valid point that
Yan Fu may have drawn inspiration from the three general laws of translation proposed by Alexander Fraser Tytler (1747-1814) was not mentioned,
even though Luo included in his anthology the essay by Wu Lifu, who made
this assertion (1983/1984: 461). When Luo mentions Tytler in his introductory essay, it is to point out that Tytler's work was introduced into China
in the 1920s and that Tytler's three general laws, although similar to Yan's
xin, da, ya, did not catch on (1983/1984: 15-16).[20]

---

[20] In "Qian Zhongshu de Yiyitan" [Qian Zhongshu's art of translation], an article published in
1990, Luo revealed that Qian had written to tell him that Yan Fu's three notions, *"xin", "da",
"ya"* were derived from Tytler's *Essay on the Principles of Translation* (1791) and that Qian had
even given him the source for this piece of information (1990/1996: 147). Luo did not mention
the exact date of Qian's letter. He simply said he received it four years after the publication of
Qian's *Limited views: Essays on Ideas and Letters*. The first edition of this work (in four
volumes) was published between August to October in 1979. 'A System of its Own – Our
Country's Translation Theories' was first published in *Translators' Notes* in 15 July 1983 and
15 August 1983. This same essay features as the introduction of *An Anthology of Essays on
Translation*, which was published in May 1984. These dates suggest that Qian might have sent
the letter to Luo after having read Luo's essay in 1983. It should be noted, therefore, that Luo
has remained silent on this point until 1990, when he brought up the question of the genesis of
of Yan Fu's *"xin", "da", "ya"* for discussion again in "Qian Zhongshu's art of translation".

- "Likeness in spirit" [*shensi*]. It was Fu Lei (1908–66) who, in 1951, argued for the importance of achieving "likeness in spirit":[21] "Speaking of effects, translation should be like copying a painting. The aim is not to produce likeness in form but likeness in spirit" (quoted in Luo 1983/1984: 10, my translation). The importance of transmitting the spirit [*chuanshen*], first propounded by the painter Gu Kaizhi (*ca.* 348-409) as a principle for doing portraits, had grown into a key concept in traditional aesthetics, and Fu Lei had transposed it into a translation principle (1983/1984: 15). In so doing, Fu Lei elevated translation to the status of art and set for translation an aim higher than that of the mere transmission of ideas (1983/1984:13). ("Ideas transmitted" [*dazhi*] was how Yan Fu labelled his translation of Huxley's work.) In the "system" delineated by Luo, "likeness in spirit" is an important signpost, an indication of the "progress" made by half a century of critical thinking about Yan Fu's three notions (1983/1984: 13). The pattern of such thinking, according to Luo, is one of increasing discrimination and depth. During the initial period, the three notions were embraced as the golden rules of translation. Then the validity of *ya* [elegance] as a principle of translation was questioned. After that, the relationship between *xin* [faithfulness] and *da* [comprehensibility] was looked at dialectically, and *xin* emerged as primary, *da* and *ya* as secondary. A further deepening of such thinking resulted in the conclusion that absolute faithfulness is only an ideal, and translation can, at best, attain "likeness" to the original (1983/1984: 9) – "likeness in spirit", to be exact.
- "State of total transformation" [*huajing*]. As discussed in the previous section, this credo was put forth by Qian Zhongshu in 1964 as the highest standard attainable in literary translation. In Luo's argument, when compared to "likeness in spirit", the "state of total transformation" marks "yet another step forward" and reaches "an even deeper level" in terms of the demand it makes on the translator and the degree of difficulty involved (1983/1984: 14). Even though total and complete transformation is an unattainable ideal, the setting of such a standard has the effect of encouraging the pursuit of excellence in literary translation.

It is clear that Luo, in his mapping of the tradition of Chinese theoretical thinking about translation, has employed a number of strategies. They include locating of the

---

Even then, he chose to present this question as a yet unresolved case in the history of Chinese translation (1990/1996: 147). Such a presentation is significant since Luo, in his writings, has shown great respect for Qian and has seldom, if ever, cast doubts on Qian's research findings. In fact, it was the authority of Qian's work that Luo relied on most frequently in "A system of its own – our country's translation theories".

[21] Fu Lei was a highly acclaimed translator of French literature into Chinese and the mentor of Luo Xinzhang. He first reflected on "likeness in spirit" as the effect to be aimed at in translation in his preface to his second rendition of Honoré de Balzac's *Le Père Goriot* [*Gao Lao Tou* Chongyiben xu].

source, unveiling of the close relation between translation poetics and the poetics of classical writing and of art, forging of genealogical links, and plotting of developments to a course marked by progress. Locating of the source of Chinese translation theories in the words of Dao An rather than those of Zhi Qian (a non-Chinese monk who had also commented on the importance of "following the source") allows Luo to preserve, as it were, the "purity" of the Chinese tradition.[22] Depicting Chinese translation theories as offshoots from the discourse on literary composition, painting and other cultural pursuits enables him to press his point that the Chinese tradition is separate and independent from other traditions of translation theory. The emphasis on relatedness through the tracing of genealogical links – even if they pertain more to ghostly resemblance, dormant memories, verbal echoes and conceptual reverberations rather than solid empirical proof – allows Luo to highlight the continuity and internal coherence of this long tradition. The careful charting of progress enables Luo to conclude that "we" have inherited a rich legacy of translation theories and that the way forward is to "carefully work out the interrelations between these theories" (1983/1984: 5) and build up "a system with unique characteristics of our own" (1983/1984: 19). Such a remark is at once a call for action and Luo's attempt to seek validation for what he has done with his translation research.

Luo's essay is an attempt at identity construction. It should be noted, however, that it is an identity distinctly different from that envisaged by the propaganda machine of the state in the early 1980s, as the essay is remarkably free from party rhetoric and jargon. A further look at the background reveals that Luo's attempt at identity construction and the manipulation strategies he employs for his mapping of translation tradition are really the effort of an intellectual responding to the situation of his time – a situation best described with Yeats' lines "Things fall apart, the centre cannot hold". The early 1980s was a traumatic time for the intellectuals. In the immediate aftermath of the Cultural Revolution, there was a prevailing sense of devastation and of spiritual bankruptcy. With the policy of 'opening up' and economic reform, there was a sudden influx of new ideas, new values, new ventures, new excitements, new temptations and new threats. Luo's essay attempted to invoke a new cohesive force. He located this force in tradition, heritage and culture. He was using translation research for the ideological invention of a new spiritual order. Hence his emphasis on building "a system of our own".

---

[22] Zhi Qian, a native of Yueshi who lived in the third century of the Christian era, had discussed the pros and cons of following the source as the supreme principle of translation in the Preface to the *Dharmapada* in 224 C.E., more than one hundred and fifty years before Dao An commented on the same topic (Chen 1992: 15). Luo has also included Zhi Qian's Preface to the *Dharmapada* in *An Anthology of Essays on Translation* (Zhi 224/1984). His privileging of Dao An's words is therefore deliberate.

4. Conclusion

As can be seen from this discussion, translation research can be used by individual researchers for ideological purposes different from those endorsed by the dominant ideology and as a way of intervening in the power politics and/or cultural politics of the time. Although not many people today have to conduct research in situations as starkly ideological as those just analyzed, there is no cause for complacency. Our entry into the age of the information superhighway, which renders the boundaries of nation and culture superfluous to the travel of ideas and ideologies alike, makes the prospect of the totalizing power of ideology more daunting than ever. But such a prospect also means that more and more individuals will confront competing ideologies and will be forced to recognize this as a fact of their consciousness. It is of crucial importance, therefore, that we know how assertion of difference and resistance to dominant ideology can be achieved – not as an end in itself, but as a means of self-empowerment, of ensuring that we remain thinking subjects capable of engaging critically with competing ideologies.

Whilst I am not advocating that translation research should be explicitly ideological, and whilst I am aware that the cases studied in this paper are too few in number to support generalizations, I am encouraged by the findings to call for the transgression of a boundary – the boundary between the object-level and meta-level of translation studies. Rather than keeping translation research – in its usual form of discourse about translation – to the meta-level, translation research could well be taken as a legitimate object of study. This will focus attention on what Theo Hermans as recently as 1999 considered to be "a problem" with descriptive translation studies, pointing out that debates about the untenability of a disinterested, value-free point of view in research and discourse about translation had "hardly begun" (Hermans 1999: 146). Debates will begin, or will be rendered unnecessary, when there is serious engagement with the two issues which this paper, itself steeped in ideology, attempts to bring to light – the ideology of translation research and the translation (carrying across) of ideology in translation research.

References

(1968) 'Hu Shi', in Howard L. Boorman (ed) *Biographical Dictionary of Republican China*, New York: Columbia University Press, Vol. II, 167-74.

(1988) 'Luo Xinzhang', in Lin Hui (ed) *Zhongguo Fanyijia Cidian* [Dictionary of Chinese Translators], Beijing: China Translation and Publishing Corporation, 420-1.

Baker, Mona (ed) (1998) *Routledge Encyclopedia of Translation Studies*, London & New York: Routledge.

Bassnett, Susan and Harish Trivedi (eds) (1999) *Post-Colonial Translation: Theory and Practice,* London & New York: Routledge.

Chen, Fukang (1992) *Zhongguo Yixue Lilun Shigao* [Draft History of Chinese Transla-
    tion Theory], Shanghai: Shanghai Foreign Language Education Press.
Cheyfitz, Eric (1991) *The Poetics of Imperialism: Translation and Colonization from*
    The Tempest *to* Tarzan, New York: Oxford University Press.
de Barry, William Theodore (ed) (1960) *Sources of Chinese Tradition*, New York: Co-
    lumbia University Press.
Even-Zohar, Itamar (1978) 'The position of translated literature within the literary
    polysystem', in his *Papers in Historical Poetics*, Tel Aviv: Porter Institute for Poet-
    ics and Semiotics.
Fawcett, Peter (1998) 'Ideology and Translation', in Baker (ed), 106-7.
Flotow, Luise von (1997) *Translation and Gender: Translation in the 'Era of Femi-
    nism',* Manchester: St. Jerome.
Grieder, Jerome B. (1970) *Hu Shih and the Chinese Renaissance: Liberalism in the
    Chinese Revolution, 1917-1937*, Cambridge: Harvard University Press.
Hatim, Basil and Ian Mason (1997) *The Translator as Communicator*, London & New
    York: Routledge.
Hermans, Theo (1985) 'Introduction. Translation Studies and a New Paradigm', in T.
    Hermans (ed) *The Manipulation of Literature, Studies in Literary Translation,* Lon-
    don & Sydney: Croom Helm, 7-15.
----- (1999) *Translation in Systems. Descriptive and Systemic Approaches Explained*,
    Manchester: St Jerome.
Holmes, James S. (1988) 'The Name and Nature of Translation Studies' [1972], in *Trans-
    lated! Papers on Literary Translation and Translation Studies* (ed. R. van den Broeck),
    Amsterdam: Rodopi, 67-80.
Hsia, C. T. (1961) *A History of Modern Chinese Fiction 1917-1957*, New Haven &
    London: Yale University Press.
Hu, Shi (1917/1991) 'Wenxue Gailiang Chuyi' [Tentative suggestions for literary re-
    form], in Yang Li (ed) *Hu Shi Wencui* [A Selection of Hu Shi's Writings], Beijing:
    Zuojia Chubanshe, 3-13.
----- (1919/1953) 'Xinsichao de Yiyi' [The meanings of x*in sichao*], in *Hu Shi Wencun*
    [Collected Essays of Hu Shi], Vol.1, Taipei: Yuandong Tushu Gongsi, 727-36.
----- (1926/1995) 'The Renaissance in China', in Zhou Zhiping (ed) *A Collection of Hu
    Shih's English Writings*, Taipei: Yuanliu Chuban, 197-217.
----- (1927/1998) *Guoyu Wenxue Shi* [A History of *Guoyu* [national language] Litera-
    ture], in Ou-yang Zhesheng (ed), Vol. 8, 3-137.
----- (1928/1998) *Baihua Wenxue Shi* [A History of *Baihua* [vernacular] Literature], in
    Ou-yang Zhesheng (ed), Vol. 8, 139-390.
----- (1934) *The Chinese Renaissance: the Haskell Lectures*, Chicago: The University of
    Chicago Press.
----- (1939/1993) *Sishi Zishu* [A Self-account at Forty], Beijing: Zhongguo Wenlian
    Chubanshe.
----- (1983) *Hu Shi Koushu Zizhuan* [Dr. Hu Shi's Personal Reminiscences] (Interviews,
    compiled, edited and translated, with a translator's preface, by Tang Degang), Taipei:
    Zhuanji Wenxue Chubanshe.
Kelly, Jeanne and Nathan K. Mao (1979) 'Translators' preface', in Qian Zhongshu *For-*

tress Besieged, trans. Jeanne Kelly and Nathan K. Mao, Bloomington/London: Indiana University Press, xi.

Kong, Qingmao (1992) *Qian Zhongshu Zhuan* [Biography of Qian Zhongshu], Nanjing: Jiangsu Wenyi.

Lefevere, André (1992) *Translation, Rewriting and the Manipulation of Literary Fame*, London & New York: Routledge.

Lu, Xun (1935/1980) 'Introduction', in Zhao Jiabi (ed), Vol. 4, 1-17.

Luo, Xinzhang (1983/1984) 'Woguo Zichengtixi de Fanyi Lilun' [A system of its own – our country's translation theories], in Luo Xinzhang (ed), 1-19.

----- (ed) (1984) *Fanyi Lunji* [An Anthology of Essays on Translation], Beijing: Commercial Press.

----- (1990/1996) 'Qian Zhongshu de Yiyitan' [Qian Zhongshu's art of translation], in Fan Xulun and Li Hongyan (eds) *Ch'ien Chung-shu Survey 1996*, Beijing: Social Sciences Documents Publishing House, 144-68.

Mao, Dun (1935/1980) 'Introduction', in Zhao Jiabi (ed), Vol. 3, 1-32.

----- (1954/1984) 'Wei Fazhan Wenxue Fanyi Shiye he Tigao Fanyi Zhiliang er Fendou' [Let us work hard for the development of literary translation and for the improvement of quality and increase in output], in *Translators' Notes*, Editorial Department (ed), 1-16.

Mao, Nathan K. (1979) 'Introduction', in Qian Zhongshu *Fortress Besieged*, trans. Jeanne Kelly and Nathan K. Mao, Bloomington/London: Indiana University Press, xiii-xxix.

Mao, Zedong (1956) *Talks at the Yenan Forum on Art and Literature*, trans. Editorial Department of Foreign Languages Press, Beijing: Foreign Languages Press.

Niranjana, Tejaswini (1992) *Siting Translation. History, Post-Structuralism and the Colonial Context*, Berkeley: University of California Press.

Ou-yang, Zhesheng (ed) (1998) *Hu Shi Wenji* [Collected Works of Hu Shi], Beijing: Peking University Press.

Qian, Zhongshu (1964) 'Lin Shu de Fanyi' [The Translations of Lin Shu], in *Wenxue Yanjiu Jikan* [Anthology of Literary Studies], Vol. 1, Renmin Wenxue Chubanshe, 267-295.

----- (1975) 'Lin Ch'in-nan Revisited', trans. George Kao, *Renditions* 5 (Autumn 1975): 8-21.

Simon, Sherry (1996) *Gender in Translation: Cultural Identity and the Politics of Transmission*, London & New York: Routledge.

Translators' Notes, Editorial Department (ed) *Fanyi Yanjiu Lunwenji: 1949-1983* [Selected Papers in Translation Studies: 1949-1983], Beijing: Foreign Language Teaching and Research Press.

Tymoczko, Maria (1999) *Translation in a Postcolonial Context. Early Irish Literature in English Translation,* Manchester: St Jerome.

van Dijk, Teun A. (1998) *Ideology: A Multidisciplinary Approach*, London: Sage Publications Ltd.

Venuti, Lawrence (1995) *The Translator's Invisibility. A History of Translation,* London & New York: Routledge.

----- (1998) *The Scandals of Translation: Towards an ethics of difference,* London & New York: Routledge.

Wang, Xiaoming (1993) 'Yifen Zazhi he Yige "Shetuan" – Lun "Wusi" Wenxue chuantong' [A magazine and an 'organization' – on the 'May Fourth' literary tradition], in Chen Guoqiu (ed) *Zhongguo Wenxueshi de Xingsi* [Reflections on Chinese Literary History], Hong Kong: Joint Publishing, 149-85.

Wu, Lianghuan (1980) 'Letter to the Editors', *Fanyi Tongxun* [Translators' Notes] 1980(2): 25.

Wu, Ming (1997) 'Luo Xinzhang', in Lin Huangtian (ed) *Zhongguo Fanyi Cidian* [A Companion for Chinese Translators], Wuhan: Hubei Jiaoyu Chubanshe, 452.

Xu, Zhimo (1935/1980) 'Shoujiu yu "Wan" Jiu' [Abiding by tradition and flirting with tradition], in Zhao Jiabi (ed), Vol. 2, 227-33.

Yan, Fu (1973) 'General Remarks on Translation', trans. C. Y. Hsu, *Renditions* 1 (Autumn 1973): 4-6.

Yi, Zhuxian (1987) *Hu Shi Zhuan* [Biography of Hu Shi], Hubei: Renmin Chubanshe.

Zhao, Jiabi (ed) *Zhongguo Xinwenxue Daxi* [Anthology of Modern Chinese Literature], 10 Vols., Shanghai: Liangyou Tushu Gongsi.

Zhi, Qian (224/1984) 'Fa Ju Jing Xu' [Preface to the *Dharmapada*], in Luo Xinzhang (ed), 22.

Tlaloc Roars
Native America, the West and Literary Translation

GORDON BROTHERSTON

Abstract: *The confrontation with native American texts challenges received models of translation studies. Western translators who approach native texts are faced with questions not just of radically different language structures, but of little-known or even deliberately obscured literary traditions. These in turn may involve processes of transcription not just from oral enactments and performance but from prior systems of visual language of which western philosophy has shown painfully limited understanding.*

The order of difference is well exemplified by the Mesoamerican screenfold books, which use a system of representation called tlacuilolli *in Nahuatl. Non-phonetic,* tlacuilolli *may register sound-concepts when required; highly flexible, it may conform by turns to a narrative, an icon or map, or a mathematical table. Integrating into one holistic statement what for us are the separate concepts of letter, picture and arithmetic, it flouts received western notions of writing and literature. Reading and translating these and comparable American texts involves a radical re-think of what otherwise would seem to be the most solid and reliable of western categories, a philosophical adventure which in its turn may reveal new constants and suggest new models for translation studies.*

On the eve of America's quincentenary, five hundred years on from the conquest/ encounter/invasion initiated by Columbus, UNESCO thought to promote fuller understanding of that continent's original inhabitants by publishing a piece on Mexico in the *Courier*. Written in Spanish, it is the work of the eminent authority Miguel León-Portilla, and deals with the idea of Mexico's deeper culture, of the long and rich histories of its peoples, a history knowable in part thanks to native records that go back for millennia. So that it would be absurd to think that somehow Mexican history began only after Columbus and Cortés. Alongside León-Portilla's piece is an accompanying English version; in it, certain key terms are modified – *memoria* for example, which in Spanish can mean either memory or memoir-like document. But the main argument remains palpably the same.

How curious, then, to discover that this apparently well-intentioned attempt by UNESCO to promote cultural understanding of the native New World should have fallen foul of one of today's better-known commentators on translation. Basing himself on a prior workmanlike analysis by Ian Mason (1994), Lawrence Venuti went off in a direction of his own, to find the English translation of the Mexican piece lamentable, highlighting it in the opening pages of his recent *The Scandals of Translation* (1998). This is not the place to go into the detail of Venuti's objections or to

quibble with his understanding of Mexican Spanish. What matters here is the sociolinguistic premise on which Venuti's comments rest. For, establishing a clear
binary between the invasive and the resident cultures of Mexico in terms of written and oral, Venuti chides the English-speaking translator for insidiously favouring
the former at the expense of the latter, for doing down "the pre-Columbian Mexi-
cans whose oral culture is represented as inferior, especially as a reporting of the
past" (1998:3).

This sort of reading, of how non-oral western imperialism has intruded on
America, will of course be familiar enough. It is there already in Montaigne's *Essays*, in his declared sympathy for the denizen of "a New World so infantine that
he has yet to learn his ABC" (Brotherston 1992: 41).[1] Via Rousseau and de
Saussure, it came massively to underpin Lévi-Strauss's structuralism, with its intense and exclusive focus on what is claimed to be oral America; I refer to the
four copious volumes of Lévi-Strauss's *Mythologiques* (1967-74). In all, such a
reading rightly alerts us to the role of the alphabet itself as a weapon in the historical spread of imperialism.

Yet what it ignores is Derrida's deconstruction of all that, his careful demonstration of how 'script' may be encoded in the most various modes and media, ultimately
including speech itself, much fraying the supposedly clean edge between written
and oral. For Derrida (1967) and the poststructuralists, appealing so unqualifiedly
to the written-oral binary must of itself be suspect, indicative of a certain
'phonocentrism' that in practice may prove ideologically even more sinister than
the propagation of an alphabet.

In our own domain of translation, to judge from the announced focus of work
that has appeared over the last decades, it would appear that such a phonocentrism
is quite the norm. Where, o where, may we find close examinations of the immensely
rich question of script and translation – from the history of transcriptions between
various writing systems to the kind of concern with visible language typified by,
say, Apollinaire's *Calligrammes* or Concrete Poetry (Herrick 1975; Campos 1975).
When the *Assises de la traduction littéraire* decided boldy to introduce an *Atelier
d'écriture* in 1996, it turned out to be entirely drawn to the differences between
spoken and written French, with no concern, to date, for the issue of visible language as such (Volkovitch 1997).

At any event, in the present case of Mexico's native cultures, Lawrence Venuti's
critique of the UNESCO translation must seem at best misplaced. The very phrases

---

[1] The question of orality and America is explored at length in this source (chapter 2), as are
details of native American texts that are otherwise unspecified below. The present piece owes
much to approaches developed in the Department of Literature, University of Essex, in teaching
the M.A. course 'Theory and Practice of Literary Translation' (1965-), among whose more influential products was counted André Lefevere. I should also like to thank Ian Mason and Theo
Hermans for their help.

he quotes as "badly translated" into English carry over from the Spanish a series of direct references to the wealth of Mexico's *written* past – to the corpus of native inscriptions and histories. Yet he somehow fails to notice what the quotes actually say, so strong for him is the written/oral binary.

For in planetary history, Mexico or Mesoamerica was unquestionably one of the lands of books, *amoxtli* in Nahuatl, *uoh* in Maya, the paginated texts of skin and paper commonly known as 'codices' (Marcus 1992; Boone and Mignolo 1994; Brotherston 1995). Long before the European invasion, consciousness of being literate was integral to local experience. Miguel León-Portilla enjoys repeating the story of how a sixteenthth-century Nicaraguan, at the east end of Mesoamerica, came upon a Spaniard reading a volume and with surprise and delight said: "Ah, so you too have books". In rejecting the Franciscan mission sent to convert them in 1524, the Aztec priests appealed to the fact that scripture in itself was not necessarily grounds for single authority, since they had their own sacred books (León-Portilla 1986; 1989). Writing in Nahuatl a century later, the historian Chimalpahin drew on this same tradition when attempting to correlate the early Christian story with the Aztec calendar – for example Vespasian's razing of Jerusalem in the year 70 CE or 1 Rabbit (Brotherston 2000: 244). The authors of the Mexicanus Codex chose the moment of the Gregorian Reform of 1582 – which endeavoured somewhat belatedly to make good the strikingly inept calendrics of Rome – to embark on a comprehensive comparison between the imported and local chronological systems, at the same time as critically assessing – ever within Mexican iconic script – the Aristotelean model of the four 'elements'. Cumulatively, the sheer number of such cases cannot but raise the question: 'In 1492, who entered whose history?'.

This brings me to my first main point: in the general story of relations between the west and what Eric Wolf called the "people without history" (1984), between Europe and its others, the kind of model that came to prominence out of concern with subsequent French and British penetration of Africa – the original *tiers monde* or Third World – may be not so much inappropriate as actually misleading when applied to native America. Commonwealth norms can be shown, for example, to be getting in the way of Jack Goody's insight when he comes to talk about literacy in traditional societies such as the Maya ("It is not clear who ever was literate in that language", 1968: 6). Again, though the line of vision is reversed, much of the Goody approach effectively survives in Gordon Collier's, *Us/Them. Translation, Transcription and Identity in Post-Colonial Literary Cultures* (1992), insofar as the 'transcribing' referred to proves in practice always to be from spoken sources (Caribbean, Native American) to the imported Roman alphabet. This, aside from the yet larger and more urgent question of exactly what 'post-colonial' can be expected to mean in a world in fact more thoroughly dominated by empire than it ever has been. In a context usefully established by Tejaswini Niranjana (1992), Delisle and Woodsworth (1995), Bassnett and Trivedi (1999) and others, this point has been well made, with specific reference to Native America, by the Brazilian Else Vieira ('New Registers for Translation in Latin America', 1998), and Frances Karttunen (1994).

In other words, in the case of Native America, translation really can and should be had 'both ways', within Bourdieu's understanding (1988) of literary 'field'. For while the west undoubtedly has taken and takes as it chooses, through the roaming acquisitiveness of a conquistador or a modern compiler of anthologies, there is the other side to the story, of constant native response. Salient examples include the Quechua reworking of Faust, according to the norms and logic inherent in the Inca quipu recording system; Cinderella adapted to the month calendar of the Mapuche in the Southern Cone, and to the Navajo philosophy of domestication and turkey breeding; the Aztec Aesop and the Aztec Calderón; and the Maya versions of the Arabian Nights (Brotherston 1992: 311-40). In native America, translation was as well conceptualized in theory as it was widespread in practice, long before Columbus arrived, notably at the courts of Tenochtitlan and Cuzco. Going back to the inscriptions of the Classic Maya, we find such suggestive statements as the parallel texts, in Maya hieroglyphs and Mexican iconic script, engraved in eighth-century Copan.

In the 'writing culture' debate, James Clifford (1988) has pointed out the problem of interference, of how what are commonly referred to as ethnographic texts will always somehow be distorted by the premises and agendas of the (western) observer or compiler. In these terms, texts composed in the visible languages and scripts of the New World serve by contrast as a direct window. Considered in their own right and duly correlated – as in practice they very rarely have been –, these American texts constitute an invaluable authority, of major theoretical interest to the student of translation.

With Mesoamerica, reliant as it was on a script functionally comparable with that of invading Europe, it is possible and desirable to think rather in terms of equivalent systems, and to be constantly on guard against that easy western assumption of intellectual superiority, not just now, which is bad enough, but projected back into the past, which is absurd yet far too often the norm. In the sixteenth century, when compiling his encyclopaedic *Historia de las cosas de Nueva España*, the Franciscan friar Bernardino de Sahagún adopted the format of the parallel text, Nahuatl to the left and Spanish translation to the right. It is not hard to see how much the latter in fact reduces and traduces the former, but what is more noteworthy is how seldom such reduction has been understood to correspond not so much to the deliberate strategy of demeaning the native as to the sheer intellectual limitation of Renaissance Europe, certainly of Counter-Reformation Spain, in such basic matters as agronomy (most of the world's best food was genetically developed millenia ago in the American tropics), astronomy (the Maya calendar had an unrivalled capacity to integrate celestial and terrestrial rhythms), the evolution of the human species (the story of which is told in the *Popol vuh*, three centuries before Darwin), the age of the earth's rock formation (put at millions of years in the codices), and so on.

To see what sense there might be in this approach, I now turn to two specific examples, each a page from a pre-Cortesian book, to see how each has been and might possibly be translated. All this, of course, in the context suggested so far, and with a view to seeing what happens to the norms and categories we most often take for granted in translation, even in what would otherwise be considered to be the radical reworking of a text. Salient here are deictics, the articulation of time and space, and the whole question of proper names, of people and places.

Each of the two pages uses the kind of iconic script known as *tlacuilolli* in Nahuatl, which is closely related to the phonetic scripts developed early in Mesoamerica by speakers of Zapotec, Maya and other languages (Nowotny 1961). Going against what is normally understood to be the necessary 'progress' towards phonetic script, *tlacuilolli* is not bound to the sounds of any single Mesoamerican language, being in principle legible in all. In given contexts, *tlacuilolli* may however appeal to phonetics. It also may make semantic use of colour, a dimension lost in the pages quoted here, whose original colour has had to be reduced to black and white (for colour reproductions see Brotherston 1992, plates 4 and 16a).

Both pages are from screenfold books of skin, read from right to left, and represent the two known genres to which those books belong (*Figures 1* and *2* below). The first, from Vindobonensis (p.21; p.32, corrected pagination), exemplifies the genre of annals, for which the Nahuatl term is *xiuhtlapoualli*. In this genre, the reading sequence always moves forward through time, guided by a succession of year dates. The second page is the penultimate in Laud (p.45, corrected pagination), one of the few surviving books of the kind known as 'ritual', or 'dream' books; here by contrast the reading sequence proceeds within self-contained thematic chapters, and from one chapter to the next.

Now housed in Vienna (hence its name), Vindobonensis records, on its obverse, annals which cover the longest span extant in the genre, formally several millennia. In the broader process of transcription and translation of the codices, the annals genre has been more favoured than any other, thanks basically to the fact that its reading sequence, moving forward from date to date, corresponds so closely in principle to that of Old World annals. In this way, native-script texts from all over Mexico became the antecedent of a whole corpus of histories in native languages as well as Spanish and Latin.

The Vienna text tells the longer history of an area in south-central Mexico centred on the town Tepexic, now in the Estado de Puebla. It has been the subject of many commentaries (Jansen 1992), which from the start alert us to the immense amount of information contained in the text and to the difficulty of rendering it into prose narrative. Recent editions of these and closely related annals by the Netherlands scholar Martin Jansen include both a diagram of each page, and a translation into Mixtec, the language supposedly spoken by the authors. Like other Mesoamerican languages still spoken today, Mixtec has the advantage of being able to render directly calendrical and other technical terms constantly used in the original for which it is often hard to find equivalents in European speech. An example is the seventeenth of the Twenty Signs, *Ollin* in Nahuatl (visible to the left of Tlaloc's forward-thrusting hand in *Figure 2*), which means at one and the same time rubber (unknown in Europe before Columbus), earthquake, and the movement of a celestial body through the sky.

The main event reported on the Vindobonensis page illustrated is a New Fire ceremony (see *Figure 1*). Reading in boustrophedon from lower right on the previous page (p.31), preparations are made for a fire-drilling to be conducted by a character named Five Lizard under the auspices of Two Dog (middle of right margin). The smoke and flame from the new fire issue in volutes that can also denote speech. The date (just to the left of the fire drill) is the year 5 House, day 5 Snake (probably sometime early in the ninth century CE), the year being marked by an 'A'-shaped solar ray (centre-right, below the base of the mountain). The place is the 'split-mountain' Tepexic and nearby towns (middle register), grouped in three pairs of toponyms that have characteristic 'mountain' profiles (*tepetl* in Nahuatl) found already in inscriptions from the first millennium BCE. Reading from the right, Tepexic itself is paired with the chequerboard place Tliltepexic; next comes Huehuetlan, the twin towns of the 'old ones', male and female; finally, come the places of the gourd and the maguey plant. The motifs of the first and last of the three pairs are reflected in the row of houses or palaces depicted above. For its part, the cipher three numbers the stones of hearth and home.

A highly political statement, the New Fire ceremony entails the delivery of commodity tribute – the previous page shows such items as chocolate, maize dough and elaborate textiles –, as well as labour tribute, specified in the construction of pyramids and temples (lower left), for which material was quarried and brought in from other places (note the human feet conveying the block of multicoloured stone at lower left). At the same time, calendrical adjustments are made, to ensure a precise measurement of the year, as with a stretched rope (middle of lower margin).

This is the baldest statement of action, that avoids most of the significant detail. Such detail is encoded in features like the toponyms. For example, the seven disks inset into Tepexic's mountain recall a specific history, that of the Chichimecs who, having emerged from Seven Caves (the seven disks) far to the northwest two centuries previously, were then having a powerful local impact in the Tepexic area. Intimating the seven orifices of the head, the caves are coloured red as if inset into the skin of the mountain. At the same time, in the geological register of the codices that is also visible in the multicoloured strata of the quarried stone, red may indicate *tezontli*, a kind of volcanic rock.

The hand gestures, clothing, insignia and, above all, calendrical names of the characters involved, carry a similar semantic load. The names Dog and Wind belong to the same set of Twenty Signs as those that name the year and day of the event (House and Snake). Each carries a complex set of associations which may then be further elaborated in the course of any one text, associations so strong between

Figure 1: New Fire at Tepexic, *Vienna Codex p. 32 [21] (Brotherston 1995: 81)*

themselves that they may occlude or elude those Cartesian obsessions with individual identity that have played so major a role in western understandings of narrative.
The Two Dog seen here reappears over large spans of time, yet differently attired
on each occasion, differences that a western translator would presumably feel obliged
to endow with essence, or at least correlate with a succession of people who happened to have the same 'proper' names.

Paginated like European books, Mesoamerican screenfolds may additionally be
opened out over part of or all their length. This enables comparisons to be made
simultaneously between two or more passages of a narrative, in a fashion impossible in a spine-bound European volume. The Tepexic text was written with such
flexibility in mind, much of the meaning conveyed on any one page depending on
its structural and other relationship to other like pages. This New Fire scene is very
much a case in point, since it is the second in ten such ceremonies reported over the
narrative as a whole, and the first of five (within the ten) to be given a precise
geographical location. Only by looking simultaneously at these other fire-drillings,
especially the four others that are also located by toponyms, can we fully appreciate
the specificity of this one.

The five geographical locations shown, at New Fire ceremonies 2 (this one), 4,
6, 9 and 10, are registered as here by conjoint toponyms, with particular place-signs
rising from a common mountain profile; and all in principle are locatable on today's
maps. Directionality, to east, south, north and west, is indicated by the detail of the
place-signs (e.g. a rising sun in the east), and the amount of page height they occupy, being low in the south (also the underworld Mictlan) and high in the north
(also the home of the rain deity Tlaloc). As such the sequence adheres to the
paradigm of the quatrefoil map of tribute quarters, defined already in Olmec culture, which appears as such in the dream books and, along with the New Fire
ceremony, is the subject of a theme chapter. The first of the five conjoint toponyms,
that of Tepexic at the metropolitan centre, is seen to precede and dominate the
succeeding four by the fact that it is unique in having a raised base. The other
four, in the quarters, all rest on the lower edge of the page. To be at all adequate,
any prose narrative translation of these annals would somehow have to find a
means of signalling this precedence from the start, since, on the page, local
preeminence appears to have been a, if not the, major concern of the authors of
these Tepexic-centred annals.

Like other screenfold annals, this Tepexic text is thoroughly concerned with the
passage of time and the material history of a particular place. Yet the very elements
through which this story is told of themselves are allowed to induce a logic of their
own. This is true of the complex lexicon of attire, gesture, toponymy and, above all,
the calendar. For example, the cycle to which the New Fire year 5 House belongs
consists of fifty-two years, and this is also the total of the number of pages in the
screenfold text. Similarly, the Sign within the set of twenty which denotes the character Two Dog is the tenth, and this is the number of times a character with that

calendar name appears over the text as a whole. In other words, while remaining diachronic, such history acquires a ritualized and poetic feel that demands attention in its own right.

Many of the concepts relating to the limits of transcription and translation that emerge when we consider the Tepexic page reappear, much intensified, in the page from Laud (see *Figure 2*). Named after Charles I's archbishop, Laud is one of five Mexican books first accessioned to the Bodleian Library of Oxford University (another of them, screenfold Mixtec annals like Vindobonensis, actually bears Thomas Bodley's name). As a 'ritual' or 'dream' text, it is highly sophisticated in its layout of chapters and in the way it organizes its argument. In general, per page and chapter, this genre is semantically yet denser, and constantly appeals to a principle of multiple reading or significance.

The page quoted is the first of a pair, devoted to the powers of rain and sun, which rounds off the text, at the end of the reverse side of the screenfold (pp.45-6). Chronologically they allude not just to yearly weather cycles but, at a far deeper time level, to the pair of catastrophes, Flood and Eclipse, that punctuate the American story of creation and world ages. Kneeling between the waters above and the waters below (the horizontal bands at top and bottom), the Rain deity Tlaloc endeavours to bring them together: under his influence, and to amphibian delight, clouds pour down and the water surface froths up. He holds a sinuous sceptre in his right hand and, in his left, a flaming axe in which copper streaks are intercalated with a blue steel then known only in meteorites. The axe blade with its volutes may be double-read as the tongue of the head into which it is inset. Tlaloc's emblem colour, blue, is celebrated in several subtly distinguished hues. The jade blue of the caiman below is confirmed by the round jade sign inset into its body.

Tlaloc's powers in this role are spelled out through the Twenty Signs that are disposed around his body (Brotherston 1979: 102-3). The first of them is the Caiman (Sign 1), which as a very ancient vertebrate conventionally signifies the earth: here, it is not beneath Tlaloc's foot, but somehow hangs beside it (it seems to extend from Tlaloc's forward-thrusting foot), as if floating like the caiman in the water below. The second Sign is Wind (Sign 2), shown as the open jaws of the mask worn by such figures as Eecatl and Quetzalcoatl; here, it is trapped before Tlaloc's nose, as in the sultry prelude to a storm. The third Sign is House (Sign 3), seen in profile and placed up in the clouds (top band, left of centre) where Tlaloc belongs. And so on. In comparable icons of other deities, for example the war-like Tezcatlipoca (Borgia codex p.17), the same Twenty Signs are differently disposed so as to produce other definitions. There, the Caiman earth trembles directly beneath Tezcatlipoca's foot; Wind indicates the speed of the thought and power streaming behind him; and his body shields the House of the community. Clues to the meanings that the sets of Signs construct, with respect to the 'identity' of these and yet other gods, can be found in the Nahuatl manuscript known as the Twenty Sacred Hymns, comprising songs once sung in their honour. Fearing their demonic power, the Franciscan friar

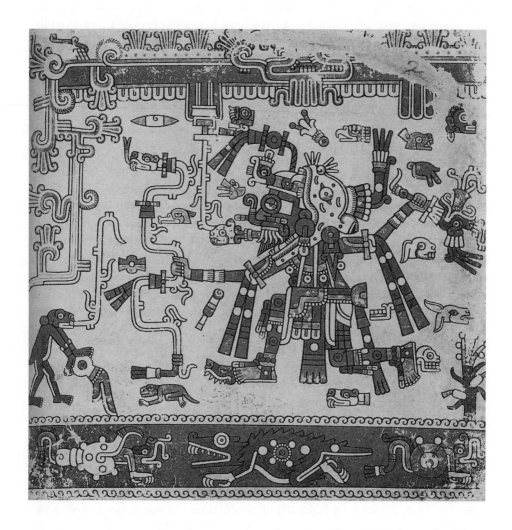

Figure 2: Tlaloc, *Laud Codex p. 45 (Brotherston 1995: 135)*

Sahagún who collected and transcribed them, left them in Nahuatl, untranslated, in an appendix to Book 2 of his *Historia*.

In Tlaloc's attire, three of the Twenty Signs disposed around him are replicated in much magnified form. Snake (Sign 5, below his lower knee) also heads the long sinuous sceptre he holds in his right hand, and in that position represents the lightning he hurls from the sky. Specifying as roaring thunder the sound that issues from his mouth in two volutes, Jaguar (Sign 14) reappears as his huge headdress. Rain (Sign 19, to the right of the house in the clouds) is also his mask, goggle-eyed and long-toothed, his literal persona. The scribes in Tepepulco who worked with Sahagún on the first version of his *Historia* defined Tlaloc through just these three concepts: *quiaui, tlatlatzinia, tlauitequi* (he rains, he thunders, he strikes [with lightning] (Sahagún 1997:121).

The point of formally replicating the three corresponding Signs here in Laud becomes clearer when we refer to the Twenty Sacred Hymns manuscript, where, as the maker of rain (*quiauhtl*), Tlaloc is further referred to as *ocelo-coatl*, which in Nahuatl literally means 'jaguar-snake'. In other words, the phenomenon of rain is announced by lightning (snake lightning) and thunder (jaguar roar). Finally, because each of the Twenty Signs always carries an inherent number value, this definition of Tlaloc in image (Laud) and word (Sacred Hymn) involves not just phenomenology but numeracy. For, according to the kabbala-like logic of *tlacuilolli*, rain (Sign 19) may likewise be the arithmetical result and sum of thunder (Jaguar, Sign 14) and lightning (Snake, Sign 5).

Pages like this one bring out the degree to which 'deities' in the codices are deliberately constructed from precise and limited sets of elements and factors. Shown here as rain-maker and paired with the sun (on the following page), Tlaloc is one of the Thirteen Heroes who regulate agriculture, amongst other activities. In other contexts, he is cast as the ninth of the nine Night Lords (*Youallitecutin*) who supervise human gestation and birth: the aqueous element is still there (in the amniotic waters), yet the function and to this extent the identity is not the same. In yet other contexts Tlaloc may actually switch sex.

Hence, in the corpus of the dream books, we are far from classical European notions of a pantheon of gods, each with its own ontology and autonomy; and we are still further from absolute distinctions between good and bad. It is more a question of alliances and oppositions that shift according to situation and purpose. The maize plant shown with Tlaloc (bottom right) may depend on his thunder and rain but can also be easily destroyed by an excess of it, by a weakness in Sun or Wind. The theme chapter in the dream books devoted to maize planting shows such a plant drowning in Tlaloc's flood, arms thrust up as if in human supplication.

From a translator's point of view, this situation may at first pose huge problems of adjustment and demand, at times, quite new ways of thinking. Yet once the system and its mechanisms are entered to some degree, then the process of translation may actually become more feasible, even into a European language, precisely because of native resistance to notions of quiddity and essence.

In the general history of script, *tlacuilolli* has most often been ignored or dismissed as mere 'picture writing'. Even this brief look at pages written in it must be enough to indicate how much information and argument may in fact be embedded in single images and sets of images. 'Picture' it may be, but one which appeals intricately to formal mechanisms of sign and figure sets, and to numerical and symbolic logic.

In this sense, the term 'picture writing' may here be ransomed from the implicit charge of being unsophisticated or underdeveloped. So that the genius of *tlacuilolli* may rather be understood to reside precisely in the ingenuity with which is defines and disposes non-phonetic images on the page. In Book 6 of his *Historia,* Sahagún shows how conscious and elaborate these procedures can be, by recording examples of 'riddle' language which reflects the multiple meanings of *tlacuilolli* images. One such we saw above: the axe blade that is also a tongue.

In the line that stretches from the Middle East to Greece and Rome, script was progressively neutralized and reified. In the corresponding 'field' of literature (to use Bourdieu's term), the order of formal vigour inherent in *tlacuilolli* has perhaps for this reason excited little theoretical interest, and has certainly escaped the purview of semiotics and Saussurean linguistics alike, with respect to image and word. The nearest available corollary would sooner be in the work of certain twentieth-century poet-critics who have confronted those officious 'scientific' accounts of language that insist on separating metaphor from norm. With stupendous insight, Ezra Pound perceived how Western discourse could be renewed and enlivened through reference to the non-phonetic logic of scripts like Chinese (Pound 1969; Oseki-Dépré 1999). The Brazilian Haroldo de Campos has worked along similar lines in creating and discussing Concrete Poetry (1975).

In the case of the pages from Mesoamerican books quoted here, translations into English can by these means acquire the lift of poetry and in so doing gain rather than lose in accuracy. The Tepexic page might suggest phrases like:

- raised before their quatrefoil, the capital towns of Tepexic stand pre-eminent;
- the drill-block utters the New Fire of hearth and home;
- the year spans its length in taut cord.

Besides the play with jaguar roar and snake lightning, the Laud page encodes such possible readings as:

- curling as steam and featherdown rain gushes from clouds;
- the tongue of the meteoric axe pronounces meteorology;
- the jade-blue caiman bathes in azure water.

Taking our cue from León-Portilla's piece on the cumulative history of America, we have suggested that that continent's recorded experience is often obscured by an effortless assumption of cultural superiority on the part of the West. In part, that assumption is rooted in the all-pervasive written/oral binary, one which could usefully be deconstructed, more than it apparently has been, in the particular field of translation studies. Considering the tradition of books native to Mexico or Mesoamerica can lead to further insights of a theoretical as well as a cultural order, given the properties of the *tlacuilolli* script in which they are written. These include the construction of identity – the proper names of people and places – through transferable component elements, and the definition of meaning through such factors as colour, disposition on the page, and playing with created expectation.

No less important are concepts inherent in the codices which have *not* been even touched on here, for the obvious reason of space. For there is the whole question of layout, and the rigorous interplay between designs in profile (like these pages) and those in plan (like the quatrefoil map, for instance); and the strongly reflexive tendency of *tlacuilolli,* which will, for example, depict the act of writing itself, on a deerskin page that is painted on the deerskin page of the actual book.

Having its roots in inscriptions that date back well into the first millennium BCE, this script continuously adapted itself to new historical circumstances, including the European invasion. From the translation point of view, the corpus of post-Cortesian texts written in *tlacuilolli*, which number over four hundred, are remarkable for the way they incorporate and adapt to local norms. After 1519, horseshoes imprint roads previously marked only by the human foot; on being introduced into the economy in 1536, copper coinage is quoted according to the existing exchange rates of cloth and cacao; the steel of invading weapons is rendered in a hard metallic blue previously reserved for Tlaloc's meteorite axe. And so on. Even the strange phonetics of proper names are caught as needed: Gallegos becomes house (*calli*) and bean (*e-tl*), and Cortés quite aptly is snake (*coatl*); and in the Tlatelolco Annals, 'Peru' is ingeniously translated by a hybrid glyph consisting of a Spanish dog (*perro*) and a Nahuatl rubber ball (*ollin*).

At the same time, in terms of cultural geography, these Mesoamerican texts stand as a central reference for much of the continent. The genre of annals represented by the Tepexic page stretches far north, successively modified, to the Year and Winter Counts of the Pima, the Kiowa and the Sioux. The quatrefoil map on which the Tepexic tribute system was based recurs more or less verbatim in the dry-painting tradition of Anasazi. Looking in the other direction, the close integration of writing with numeracy can likewise be found in the quipu script of the Inca, while the imagery of tropical America as a whole ceaselessly surfaces on the codex page, not least in the thunder that is the jaguar's roar.

References

Bassnett, Susan and Harish Trivedi (eds) (1999) *Post-colonial Translation: Theory and Practice*, London & New York: Routledge.

Boone, E. and W. Mignolo (1994) *Writing without Words: Alternative Literacies in Mesoamerica and the Andes*, Durham: Duke University Press.

Bourdieu, Pierre (1996) *The Rules of Art: Genesis and Structure of the Literary Field*, Cambridge: Polity.

Brotherston, Gordon (1979) *Image of the New World: The American Continent Portrayed in Native Texts*, London: Thames & Hudson.

----- (1992) *Book of the Fourth World: Reading the Native Americas through their Literature*, Cambridge: Cambridge University Press.

----- (1995) *Painted Books from Mexico*, London: British Museum Press.

----- (2000) 'Indigenous Intelligence in Spain's American Colony', *Forum for Modern Language Studies* xxxvi: 241-253

Campos, Haroldo de (1975) *A arte no horizonte do provável*, São Paulo: Perspectiva, 3rd ed.

Clifford, James (1988) *The Predicament of Culture: 20th-Century Ethnography, Literature and Art*, Cambridge (MA): Harvard University Press.

Collier, Gordon (1992) *Us/Them: Translation, Transcription and Identity in Post-Colonial Literary Culture,* Amsterdam: Rodopi.

Delisle, Jean and Judith Woodsworth (eds) (1995) *Translators Through History*, Amsterdam: John Benjamins.

Derrida, Jacques (1967) *De la Grammatologie*, Paris: Minuit.

Goody, Jack (1968) *Literacy in Traditional Societies*, Cambridge: Cambridge University Press.

Herrick, E. M. (1975) 'A Taxonomy of Alphabets and Scripts', *Visible Language* 8: 5-32.

Jansen, Martin (1992) *Origen e historia de los reyes mixtecos* [Vienna Codex], Mexico: FCE.

Karttunen, Frances (1994) *Between Worlds: Interpreters, Guides and Survivors,* New Brunswick: Rutgers University Press.

León-Portilla, Miguel (1986) *Coloquios y Doctrina Cristiana*, Mexico: UNAM.

----- (1989) 'Have we really Translated the Mesoamerican "Ancient Word"?', in Swann (ed), 313-338.

Lévi-Strauss, Claude (1967-74) *Mythologiques*, 4 vols. Paris: Plon.

Marcus, J. (1992) *Mesoamerican Writing Systems: Propaganda, History and Myth in Four Ancient Civilizations*, Princeton: Princeton University Press.

Mason, Ian (1994) 'Discourse, Ideology and Translation', in R. de Beaugrande, A. Shunaq and M. H. Heliel (eds) *Language, Discourse and Translation in the West and Middle East*, Amsterdam & Philadelphia: John Benjamns, 23-34.

Niranjana, Tejaswini (1992) *Siting Translation: History, Post-Structuralism and the Colonial Context*, Berkeley: University of California Press.

Nowotny, K. A. (1961) *Tlacuilolli: Die mexikanischen Bilderhandschriften, Stil und Inhalt,* Berlin: Gebr. Mann.

Oseki-Dépré, I. (1999) *Théories et pratiques de la traduction littéraire*, Paris: Colin.

Pound, Ezra (ed) (1969) *Fenollosa. The Chinese Written Character as a Medium for Poetry* [1936], San Francisco: City Lights.

Sahagún, Bernardino de (1997) *Primeros memoriales,* ed. by T. Sullivan, H.B.Nicholson, A.J.O. Anderson, C.E. Dibble, E. Quiñones K., W. Ruwet, Norman: University of Oklahoma Press.

Swann, B. (ed) (1992) *On the Translation of Native American Literatures,* Washington: Smithsonian Institution.

Venuti, Lawrence (1998) *The Scandals of Translation. Towards an Ethics of Difference,* London: Routledge.

Vieira, Else (1998) 'New Registers for Translation in Latin America', in P. Bush and K. Malmkjaer (eds) *Rimbaud's Rainbow. Literary Translation in Higher Education*, Amsterdam: John Benjamins, 171-95.

Volkovitch, M. (1997) 'Atelier d'écriture', *Assises de la traduction littéraire XIV.*

Wolf, E. (1984) *Europe and the People without History*, Berkeley & Los Angeles: University of California Press.

Culture as Translation – and Beyond Ethnographic Models of Representation in Translation Studies

MICHAELA WOLF

Abstract: *In ethnographies as well as in translation in the traditional sense of the word, the cultural Other is not verbalized directly but indirectly, filtered and arranged through the consciousness of the ethnographer or translator. The recognition of the problematic connection between the textualization and conceptualization of culture has provoked a 'crisis of representation' in literary studies, historiography and ethnography. Recent ethnographic approaches have tried to transcend binary oppositions like that between observer and observed, and focus instead on a view of culture marked by pluralism. I argue that cultural representation through translation can obtain significant impulses from cultural studies. The paper discusses some of these approaches to translation, assesses their relation to other approaches dealing with cultural representation as well as current translation studies, and explores the applicability of such models in the study of translation. The discussion shows that this heuristically oriented translation model yields insight into power relations between the cultures involved and helps to identify interrelations between various cultural levels.*

1. Introduction

Concepts of alterity as originally conceived in cultural studies can be seen as constitutive for translation studies once we view translation as a linguistic and cultural practice which in fact produces the 'Other'. The notion of the cultural Other, which includes the issue of the translatability of cultures, has only recently been extensively dealt with in translation studies. It will be good to remember, however, that since in Western societies the "acceptance of difference has become a foremost ethical claim" (Assmann 1996: 99), "the transvaluation of values that is commonly associated with postmodernism [...] is characterized by the fundamentalization of plurality" (*ibid*.). Thus the Other, as one of the central values of postmodern culture, is in danger of being mystified as another fundamentalism and may be labelled a 'uniformitarian' tool (see Budick 1996: 2). This might be one of the reasons why the concept was questioned in other disciplines, such as ethnography or literary studies, before its consideration was regarded as leading to a valuable approach in translation. Ever since the rise of deconstructionist thinking, any sort of textual criticism based on binary oppositions has been confronted with the accusation of ideological bias. In addition, the creation of stable boundaries between Self and

Other implies the essentialization of cultural difference. Approaches like Kristeva's 'strangers to ourselves' (*Etrangers à nous-mêmes*, Kristeva 1988) embody this crisis and help to transcend the dichotomy by focusing on the phenomenon of estrangement as a psychoanalytic category through which Otherness is explored within the Self. This exploration implies that the Self is not a self-contained, authored whole, but the product of reflections, absorptions and transformations. The concept of intertextuality is intrinsic to this approach and, in the context of translation, can be interpreted as the result of the transaction between cultures which are already marked by pluralism.

Against this background the question arises as to what methodology could cope with the problem of dichotomies in the context of Self and Other. Once we admit that binary oppositions can never be totally abandoned (take, for example, the dichotomy male/female), one option could be a more accurate focus on the functional mechanisms of antithetical images. A lively discussion about this issue has been going on in ethnography during the last few years. In ethnographies as well as in translation in the traditional sense of the word, the cultural Other is not verbalized directly but only indirectly, and filtered and arranged through the ethnographer's or the translator's consciousness. For a long time, the connection between 'conceptualizing' culture and 'textualizing' it was taken for granted and seen as unproblematic. This provoked the so-called 'crisis of representation' in such disciplines as literary studies, historiography and ethnography. The 'writing culture' debate (Clifford and Marcus 1986), which followed the rise of the 'culture as text' concept as developed in interpretive anthropology, attempted to view ethnographic representation not as the reconstruction of some pre-existing reality, but as a literary construct. Such a view of cultural representation helps to focus on the aspects of process and production of translation.[1]

Cultural representation through translation can obtain important impulses from ethnographic insights. In the following pages I will discuss various ethnographic approaches to translation and establish their relations to other approaches dealing with cultural representation as well as current translation studies. In addition, I will explore the applicability of ethnographic models in translation studies. The discussion will show that this heuristically oriented translation model yields insight into power relations between cultures and helps to identify the interrelations between various cultural levels in an intercultural context. The approach stands for a view which tries to transcend the analysis of specific cultural items (i.e. the lexical level) and is geared instead to an analysis that operates on the level of discourse and social context.

---

[1] This concept can be traced also in New Historicist criticism, where both the historicity of texts and the textuality of history are emphasized; see Montrose (1986).

2. Ethnographic approaches in translation studies

If translating between cultures, in ethnography as well as in translation, means intercultural interaction, it is of paramount importance to identify the agencies that are active behind this interaction, in historical as well as in contemporary contexts. Back in the 1950s Godfrey Lienhardt depicted the task of anthropology as one of translation:

> The problem of describing to others how members of a remote tribe think then begins to appear largely as one of translation, of making the coherence primitive thought has in the language it really lives in, as clear as possible in our own. (Lienhardt 1954:97, quoted in Asad 1986: 142)

Lienhardt's use of the term "translation" here refers not only to the question of language, but primarily to "modes of thought" in a translational context and across power relations. In Talal Asad's list of anthropological statements on translation another scholar worth citing is Edmund Leach, who claimed in the early 1970s that "for practical purposes a tolerably satisfactory translation is always possible" and that "social anthropologists are engaged in establishing a methodology for the translation of cultural language" (Leach quoted in Asad 1986: 142). The engagement with the question of translation, which already goes beyond a metaphoric view of the transfer between cultures, is obvious enough here, although its methodological claims seem somewhat over-optimistic. It must be equally obvious, however, that the concept of translation as used by anthropologists like Lienhardt, Leach and others (see Asad 1986:142ff) amounts, in Tejaswini Niranjana's words, to "the desire to *construct* the primitive world, to *represent* it and to *speak on its behalf*" (Niranjana 1992: 70; her emphasis). Niranjana's footnote highlighting parallels with Edward Said's *Orientalism* (*ibid.*) points to the lack of awareness among these anthropologists regarding the asymmetrical power relations between the cultures involved.

The metaphor of the 'translation of culture' suggests that in principle it is actually possible to translate cultures. This claim is problematic not only because it presupposes the existence of stable cultural units which can be transferred between an 'original' and a 'target' culture, but also because in the final analysis such a translation turns out to be an ethnocentric operation. Ethnographers (viz. translators) cannot help using the categories of their own language and culture to represent what they observe (viz. to translate the foreign text). As this is a problem that cannot be fully resolved, Clifford Geertz has suggested that ethnography cannot be equated with the 'translation of cultures', since this would mean the transfer of a foreign culture into analogue concepts. That, in turn, runs counter to the anthropological endeavour to understand and describe foreign cultures from the perspective of its members (Geertz 1997: 290). Do we find ourselves in a cul-de-sac here?

As far as the overlap between ethnography and translation is concerned, it seems worth pointing out that, as first readers of the other culture, translators and ethnographers have to represent the Other in a primary process (Valero-Garcés 1995: 556). Both can be called interpreters of the 'culture' in question. While the ethnographer interprets experiences, notes and observations, the translator interprets a pre-given text. For their translations, both have at their disposal a wide range of answers or solutions to their respective interpretations, in their own language. The ethnographer engages in 'participant observation' and direct communication, and is thus confronted with cultural expectations. Here the process of translation is two-fold. In a first step, the ethnographer has to interpret the social discourse of his or her informants. In a second step this interpretation is systematized and textualized for the benefit of the target audience in the 'First World' and their expectations. In order to represent his or her observations in the target language and culture, the ethnographer has to comply with the (Western) academic discourse strategies of the intended audience. The ethnographer produces a new text to be integrated into the (Western) target cultural repertoire (Wolf 1997a).

The translator, on the other hand, is typically faced with a pre-existing written text, which she or he transposes in a complex process for her or his target audience. The question whether the translator, too, creates a new text through translation has been widely discussed also in postmodern approaches to translation (see, for example, Wolf 1997b) and is necessarily linked with that of the production of meaning. It should be stressed in this context that ethnography as well as translation are inevitably positioned between systems of meaning which are marked by power relations. 'Translating between cultures' consequently means that 'other' meanings are transferred to cultural practices which are themselves embedded in and shaped by institutions and traditions, i.e. by history. In Niranjana's view, general translation studies have so far failed to make a constructive contribution to a postcolonial history of translation precisely because they have been too preoccupied with the notion of "pure meaning" (Niranjana 1992: 55). As Kate Sturge has reminded us, Niranjana's work claims to "look precisely at the (unequal) relationship between source-language and target-language culture and the ways in which practices of representation reinforce or subvert these relationships" (Sturge 1997: 23-24). When we realize, in addition, that translation as well as ethnographic writing means that the Other's voice is always filtered through the translator's or the ethnographer's consciousness, it is not hard to see that the translational and ethnographic representation of the Other is bound to be seen as highly problematic. The traditional view of translation and ethnography as attempts to integrate the Other in an objectifying way is no longer tenable; in fact, each representation can be seen as an act of political oppression (Tyler 1993: 288).[2]

---

[2] Tyler goes even further: "Because the text can eliminate neither ambiguity nor the subjectivity of its authors and readers, it is bound to be misread, so much so that we might conclude [...] that the meaning of the text is the sum of its misreadings" (Tyler 1986: 135). The metaphor of translation is also criticized by Hans Peter Duerr, who views ethnographic translation as a process

Among the first attempts to tackle this 'crisis of representation' was the so-called 'writing culture' debate initiated in 1986 by James Clifford and George E. Marcus, who proposed to view cultural representations as literary constructs. At the end of the 1970s some influential anthropologists, Claude Lévi-Strauss, Mary Douglas and Clifford Geertz among them, showed a keen interest in literary theory and practice. The 'literary turn' in ethnography, which also became popular in historiography (White 1978), revealed that literary forms like metaphor, figuration or narrative affect the ways in which cultural phenomena are registered. As a result, ethnographic texts could not avoid expressive tropes, figures and allegories: "Power and history work through [the ethnographic texts], in ways their authors cannot fully control" (Clifford 1986: 7). Seeing ethnographies as fictions therefore suggests the partiality of cultural and historical truths.[3] It also transcends the self-image of the ethnographer who casts himself not only as the translator but also as the chronicler of and spokesman for the culture observed (see Malinowski 1979: 25 and *passim*).

The crisis of representation as conceived by scholars like Clifford and Marcus (1986) or Edward Said (1989) goes to the heart of the problem of the textual objectivation of the Other as it is still practised by some ethnographers and ultimately also by translators in the traditional sense of the word. The observation that "[t]o talk about others means talking about oneself" (Berg and Fuchs 1993: 11, my translation, MW) may serve as a reminder that the construction of the Other implies the simultaneous construction of the Self, thus stressing the relational character of both Self and Other. These relations are asymmetrical by their very nature. As Michael Werner argues, symmetrical relations between cultures and societies are never possible, for they would presume the existence of homologous "developments" of cultures. The comparison of cultures and societies is always faced with asymmetrical constellations which "elude uniform tools of description" (Werner 1997: 89, my translation, MW).

Given the asymmetrical character of relations between cultures, the cultural appropriation of the Other is caught up in political and economic dependencies recognizable mainly in present-day postcolonial realities. Edward Said's doubts about some terms related to this postcolonial situation such as 'representation' or 'anthropology' speak a clear language in that these terms are affected by limitations and pressures which spring from their being "embedded in settings that no amount of ideological violence can dismiss" (Said 1989: 212). "Anthropological representations" bear as much on the represeter's world as on who or what is represented. The terms therefore vacillate between various possibilities of meaning according to the perspectives under which they are considered; they cannot be assigned essential

---

during which the Other is usurped and appropriated by the target culture and therefore neutralized (Duerr 1985: 152).
[3] Not entirely without reason, Vincent Crapanzano portrays ethnographers as "tricksters" (1986: 52ff).

or fixed significations. As a consequence, Said observes,"there is also some (justified) fear that today's anthropologists can no longer go to the post-colonial field
with quite the same ease as in former times" (*ibid.*: 209). The point applies with
equal force to translators in the postcolonial context, where sensitivity to political
or ideological implications is badly needed.

In contemporary ethnography the act of writing itself, the actual production of
the text, is no longer assumed to be a marginal activity but, in Clifford's words, one
that is "central to what anthropologists do both in the field and thereafter" (1986: 2).
The fact that it has only recently been portrayed and seriously discussed reflects, for
Clifford, "the persistence of an ideology claiming transparency of representation
and immediacy of experience" (*ibid.*). In ethnography as well as in translation studies that ideology has largely crumbled. Meanings are no longer perceived as being
roughly the same across different cultures, but as something to be represented in
codes and symbols linked to the translator's and the ethnographer's subjectivity and
background. In translation studies this altered outlook has shed new light on the
issue of the translator's invisibility and raised questions about the translator's authority (Sturge 1997: 34). Translation is no longer understood exclusively in terms
of transfer between a cultural 'Self' and an 'Other', but also – and even primarily –
in terms of its regulative effect, as for instance in the case of the deployment of
translation in the context of colonial domination.

3. The implications of 'cultural' approaches in translation studies

In translation studies, the repercussions of the anthropological 'writing culture' debate, which have been explored mainly by Doris Bachmann-Medick (see e.g.
Bachmann-Medick 1997), can be considered to form part of the cluster of developments subsumed under the 'cultural turn' (Bassnett and Lefevere 1990, 1998), even
though to my knowledge they have never been explicitly brought under this label.
Towards the end of the 1980s, translation studies began to take issues of context,
history and convention into consideration, and the emphasis in the reflection on
translation shifted from matters of language and linguistics to matters of culture.
Of course, culture had repeatedly received attention in the study of translation,
from as early as Eugene Nida's work on Bible translation (beginning with Nida
1945), but most of these approaches were still informed by an ethnocentrically
biased anthropology. Following the discipline's opening up to the broader cultural contexts of translation, the notion of cultural pluralism as understood
especially in gender-based and postcolonial translation studies (see e.g. Simon
1996) finally paved the way to a process-oriented and dynamic concept of culture
informing the reflection on translation.

The 'cultural turn' has shown us, among other things, that culture is best conceived, not as a stable unit, but as a dynamic process which implies difference and
incompleteness. As translators and translation researchers we are becoming increasingly aware that translation is not only a matter of transfer 'between cultures'
but that it is also a place where cultures merge and create new spaces. In the context
of the interaction between asymmetrical cultures translation does not confirm borders and inscribe the dichotomy of centre versus periphery; rather, it identifies
'pluricentres' where cultural differences are constantly being negotiated. In such a
view, cultures themselves do not appear as "original lifeworlds" but as translations in
the sense that they are already the results of translation activities (Bachmann-Medick
1997: 14). The concept of 'culture as translation' thus projects culture as the site of
interaction of the components of translational processes and as the space where
translation is conceived as the reciprocal interpenetration of Self and Other. When
this perspective is adopted it becomes clear that postcolonial communities such as
the 'mixed cultures' and syncretic societies of Latin America are dependent on translation not only in terms of texts but also in terms of intracultural traditions, cultural
practices and conventions.

How can these considerations benefit our insight into the interrelations between
the cultures involved in translation? What is their impact on translation research
models? And who are the agents and agencies behind the cultural representation
performed through translation? In the following paragraphs these questions will be
discussed on the basis of the hypothesis that the notion of cultural pluricentres represents a paradigmatic turn in the discussion of the translatability of cultures.

4.   The 'in-between'

The function of translation is paramount in the context of a view of cultural
pluricentres which seeks to deconstruct the idea of stable cultures bridged with the
help of cultural mediators such as translators or ethnographers. The shift away from
ethnocentric modes of cultural interpretation in terms of the patterns of perception
and behaviour prevalent in the ethnographer's or translator's own culture, and towards a concept of culture which emphasizes the symbolic articulation of social
discourses,[4] necessarily implies a writing practice which questions the production
of knowledge of the Other. Some models of representation which focus on a so-
called 'in-between space' highlight this change of paradigm. Fifty years ago Margaret
Mead already argued in favour of an anthropological representation that would

---

[4] Social discourse is understood here as "everything which is and can be said, written and shown
in a given society at a given moment, which can be narrated and discussed, according to a vari-
able set of norms" (Robyns 1992: 214).

emerge from a space located somewhere between her own observations and the subsequent statement thereof, and the reader's consideration:

> I should like to be able to interpose between my statement and the reader's consideration of that statement a pause, a realization not of what authoritative right I have to make the statement I make, but instead of how it was arrived at, of what the anthropological process is. (Mead 1974: 53f)

The encounter between, on the one hand, the culture being observed and to be represented through the anthropologist's textualization, and, on the other, the (academic) reader's reception of that textualized representation, is perceived by Mead as a means of reflecting the process of cultural representation at the very point where the perspectives of the observer and the observed merge, thus transcending the dichotomy of the agents involved (see also Wolf 2000: 136).

In her introduction to the collection *Between Languages and Cultures* (1995) Anuradha Dingwaney goes several steps further. In the context of postcolonial translation she defines the 'between' as "that space from within which the (colonized) native deliberately (mis)translates the colonial script, alienating and undermining its authority", proceeding from an "awareness of the 'other's' agency and own forms of subjectivity, which 'returns' the 'other' to a history from which she or he was violently wrenched" (Dingwaney 1995: 9). In viewing the in-between space as a fertile and at the same time disquieting space where the dynamic interaction of at least two cultures takes place, Dingwaney's approach not only represents another important contribution to the concept of cultural pluricentres mentioned above, but also reveals another feature peculiar to 'translation between cultures': it uncovers the relations of power inherent in any process of translation.

The consideration of the implications of power in the translational process have become an essential part of most 'cultural turn' approaches. The asymmetrical relations between cultures intimate that power is constantly operating in any transfer process between cultures, be it in social, political or economic power manifestations. If we see power in line with Michel Foucault as a means of control, subjection and repression which in modern societies comes to surface as a network of practices internalized by human beings as part of the socialization process and which becomes particularly vital in the interaction with other people (Foucault 1975: 43), then the various kinds of power relations at work in the process of translation are all too clear. Power actually operates at different levels, in the performance of translation, i.e. in all agencies responsible for translational production, as well as in the function of translation in the cultures involved.

What in addition is relevant here is its epistemological contribution to the discussion. In the colonial context, power relations are particularly visible: the discourses of Western institutions, for instance, are perpetuated in the discourses of societies of the 'Third World' and thus perpetuate colonial structures (see

Niranjana 1992: 3). Equally, it can hardly be denied that today's economic and communicational globalization brings about both a displacement of the Other and the levelling out of cultural differences. In situations like these the role of translation is crucial. Translation can be interpreted as a strategy to consolidate the cultural Other, a process which implies not only the fixation of prevailing ideologies and of cultural filters but also the blocking of any autonomous dynamics of cultural representation. This phenomenon can be observed, for instance, at different levels of the production of translations, from the selection of texts to be translated to the modes of distribution, all marked by power relations, including the translation strategies adopted.

This brings us to another point which seems central to the discussion: the role of the agents involved in the process of translation, i.e. individuals and/or institutions located in different cultural contexts. Of particular interest are the power relations inherent in the production and reception of translation which are explicitly reflected in the agents' activities. In such a context, several questions arise. Who is responsible for the selection of the text to be translated? Who is responsible for their publication? Who selects the translator? What are the relations between these factors and the corresponding factors in the so-called source culture? What are the criteria for 'marking' the translated text, for instance the inclusion of a book in a certain series or the addition of a paratext to the translation?

These brief considerations of some sociological aspects of translation seem to have diverted us from our initial discussion of ethnographic approaches in translation studies. However, if we take a closer look at the processes sketched above, we realize that power relations inherent in the encounter of cultures mark not only the control over modes of representation, but they also affect the interaction between the different agents. In other words, by focussing on the different agencies involved in the translation process we have already moved towards the attempt to transcend the one-way transfer model between a source and a target culture or 'text'. In the next step we will try to move beyond this by highlighting the potential of the space between the different agencies.

5.   Interference from the *Third Space*

The in-between space as the site of the encounter between different cultures becomes particularly relevant in the context of postcolonialism and migration. For Homi Bhabha, cultures are never unitary in themselves, nor simply dualistic as in the relation between Self and Other. Rather, there is a Third Space, which can be reduced neither to the Self nor to the Other, neither to the 'original' nor to the 'target text'. In this hybrid view of culture, translation is not only seen as a crucial activity, but, according to Bhabha, the Third Space is the potential location and starting-point for (postcolonial) translation strategies:

> It is that Third Space, though unrepresentable in itself, which constitutes
> the discursive conditions of enunciation that ensure that the meaning and
> symbols of culture have no primordial unity or fixity; that even the same
> signs can be appropriated, translated, rehistoricized and read anew.
> (Bhabha 1994: 37)

When exploring this Third Space, polarity can be avoided and the Self can be
experienced as the Other (Bhabha 1994: 39), thus foregrounding communication
forms such as translation and stressing its pluricentric character. As a consequence,
negotiation is required to debate the differences in culture and identity. This negotiation – the "only means for fostering the translatability of cultures" (Ziegler
1999:18) – has been interpreted as a synonym for translation, inasmuch as the effort
to translate demands the negotiation of cultural contradictions and misapprehen-
sions (see Bachmann-Medick 1997: 15ff). Of course, the Third Space, the locus
where this negotiation alias translation takes place, should not be thought of as a
space where we can witness the harmonious encounter of cultures to be translated
or the limitless productivity and abundance of inventive inspirations (Bachmann-
Medick 1999: 525). Nevertheless, the concept makes it possible to view
translational activity as an interactive process, a meeting ground where conflicts
are acted out and margins of collaboration explored. In a closer translational context, negotiation in the Third Space can be seen as the place where translators as
cultural mediators and other agents involved in the translation process discuss
and arrange a translation for its reception, including all imaginable means such as
reviews, critiques or anthologies.

A research model which takes on board the various aspects discussed so far in
this paper will be based on the assumption that culture is not only to be seen as a
dynamic process which suggests difference and incompleteness, but also and primarily as a point of convergence where translation is envisioned as the reciprocal
interpenetration of Self and Other. In this view of culture as the locus of translation,
any sort of cultural transfer, including ethnographic processes, can be conceived as
translation between cultures. As such, any translational process is constitutive of
any form of cultural transfer. An argument in favour of this assumption is the fact that
translation is never a one-dimensional transfer – *qua* importation, for instance – but
rather a multi-layered process of action and communication taking place within complex cultural and social networks.

Under such conditions, several factors can be taken into account within the concept of cultural transfer seen as translation between already hybrid cultures. Each of
these factors is again embedded in processes which are regarded as translation processes. First, the criteria for the selection of texts to be translated have to be
considered: what degree of legitimization is attributed to the cultural product that is
translation, and what are the results of operations regarding (e.g. literary) sanc-
tions? The motivation for the acceptance of cultural goods as translations is closely

related with selection and can be conceived as a reaction to the insight that cultures have structural gaps which translations then go on to fill (see also Toury 1995: 70ff and passim). Another important factor is norms, which are effective in each single phase of the translation process. Norms determine the selection as well as the character of the transfer; they presuppose an institutionalization process and thus determine the mechanisms for the acceptance of cultural products; and they determine the criteria governing the process of identity formation through translation as well as the nature of the relations between the cultures involved.[5] Consequently, norms affect all sorts of decision processes as agents negotiate these various factors. It is of paramount importance however to recognize that all these agents, whether individuals or institutions, can be thought of as operating at cultural borderlines and as symbolically acting, as mentioned above, in a Third Space where conflicts arising from cultural difference and the different social discourses involved in these conflicts are negotiated. Seen as a potential form of intercultural and social interaction, this Space constitutes a heuristic means to visualize transfer processes and the inherent changes of context that come with them, as well as the relational conditions underlying these transfers.

The adoption of a Third Space based on the concept of 'culture as translation' can thus bring important insights into the evolvement of the translation process. When Susan Bassnett calls for "more investigation of the acculturation process that takes place between cultures" and for "greater investigation of what Venuti has called 'the ethnocentric violence of translation'" (Bassnett 1998: 138), we realize that a huge step has been taken in the ontological discussion of how 'translation between cultures' can be dealt with. If translation is more than a transfer between linguistic systems and is viewed instead as the "representation of representations" (Bachmann-Medick 1997: 7) in that the representation of cultures itself is based on translation, the dynamics underlying this concept of translation give way to a research model of 'cultural translation' which tries to escape from the essentialist bias. This approach not only yields insight into the power relations between the cultures involved and their respective agents, it also sharpens the eye for cultural pluralism, not least through the inclusion of interdisciplinary discussions. Finally, it meets the requirements of emerging pluricentric societies and hybrid identities, where translators are called upon to be aware of their ambiguous situation between political processes fostering uniformity – witness 'globalization' – and the need for transcultural flexibility. As a result, translation is challenged to contribute to a (critical) reconciliation and at the same time a recognition of cultural difference in a world where the very act of translation has become a constitutive feature.

---

[5] Within this rather rough sketch of a research model the concept of norms cannot be dealt with in detail. For further reading see especially Toury (1998) and Hermans (1999: 72-90).

References

Asad, Talal (1986) 'The Concept of Cultural Translation in British Social Anthropology', in Clifford and Marcus (eds), 141-64.

Assmann, Aleida (1996) 'The Curse and Blessing of Babel; or, Looking Back on Universalisms', in Budick and Iser (eds), 85-100.

Bachmann-Medick, Doris (1999) '1 + 1 = 3? Interkulturelle Beziehungen als "dritter Raum"', *Weimarer Beiträge* 45(4): 518-31.

----- (ed) (1997) *Übersetzung als Repräsentation fremder Kulturen*, Berlin: Schmidt.

Bassnett, Susan (1998) 'The Translation Turn in Cultural Studies', in Bassnett and Lefevere (eds), 123-40.

----- and A. Lefevere (eds) (1990) *Translation, History and Culture*, London & New York: Pinter.

----- and A. Lefevere (eds) (1998) *Constructing Cultures: Essays on Literary Translation,* Clevedon etc.: Multilingual Matters.

Berg, Eberhard and M. Fuchs (1993) 'Phänomenologie der Differenz. Reflexionsstufen ethnographischer Repräsentation', in Berg and Fuchs (eds), 11-108.

----- (eds) (1993) *Kultur, soziale Praxis, Text: Die Krise der ethnographischen Repräsentation*, Frankfurt/M.: Suhrkamp.

Bhabha, Homi K. (1994) *The Location of Culture,* London & New York: Routledge.

Budick, Sanford (1996) 'Crises of Alterity: Cultural Untranslatability and the Experience of Secondary Otherness', in Budick and Iser (eds), 1-22.

----- and W. Iser (eds) (1996) *The Translatability of Cultures: Figurations of the Space Between*, Stanford: Stanford University Press.

Clifford, James (1986) 'Introduction: Partial Truths', in Clifford and Marcus (eds), 1-26.

----- and G. E. Marcus (eds) (1986) *Writing Culture. The Poetics and Politics of Ethnography*, Berkeley etc.: University of California Press.

Crapanzano, Vincent (1986) 'Hermes' Dilemma: The Masking of Subversion in Ethnographic Description', in Clifford and Marcus (eds), 51-76.

Dingwaney, Anuradha (1995) 'Introduction: Translating ,Third World ,Cultures', in A. Dingwaney and C. Maier (eds) *Between Languages and Cultures. Translation and Cross-Cultural Texts,* Pittsburgh and London: University of Pittsburgh Press, 3-15.

Duerr, Hans Peter (1985) *Traumzeit. Über die Grenze zwischen Wildnis und Zivilisation*, Frankfurt/M.: Suhrkamp.

Foucault, Michel (1975) *Surveiller et punir. La naissance de la prison*, Paris: Gallimard.

Geertz, Clifford (1997) 'Aus der Perspektive des Eingeborenen'. Zum Problem des ethnologischen Verstehens', in Geertz, Clifford: *Dichte Beschreibung. Beiträge zum Verstehen kultureller Systeme*, übersetzt von Brigitte Luchesi und Rolf Bindemann, Frankfurt/M.: Suhrkamp, 289-309.

Hermans, Theo (1999) *Translation in Systems. Descriptive and Systemic Approaches Explained*, Manchester: St. Jerome.

Kristeva, Julia (1988) *Etrangers à nous-mêmes,* Paris: Fayard. *Strangers to Ourselves*, translated by Leon Roudiez, New York: Columbia University Press, 1991.

Malinowski, Bronislaw (1979) *Argonauten des westlichen Pazifik. Ein Bericht über Unternehmungen und Abenteuer der Eingeborenen in den Inselwelten von*

Melanesisch-Neuguinea, hg. von Fritz Kramer, Schriften, Bd.1, Frankfurt/M.: Syndikat.

Mead, Margaret (1974) *Male and Female. A Study of the Sexes in a Changing World,* Harmondsworth: Penguin Books. [first publ. 1950].

Montrose, Louis (1986) 'Renaissance literary studies and the subject of history', *English Literary Renaissance* 11(1): 5-12.

Nida, Eugene (1945) 'Linguistics and ethnology in translation problems', *Word* 1: 194-208.

Niranjana, Tejaswini (1992) *Siting Translation: History, Post-structuralism, and the Colonial Context,* Berkeley etc.: University of California Press.

Robyns, Clem (1992) 'Towards a Sociosemiotics of Translation', *Romanistische Zeitschrift für Literaturgeschichte. Cahiers d'Histoire des Littératures Romanes* 16: 211-226.

Said, Edward W. (1989) 'Representing the Colonized: Anthropology's Interlocutors', *Critical Inquiry* 15: 205-25.

Simon, Sherry (1996) *Gender in Translation. Cultural Identity and the Politics of Transmission*, London & New York: Routledge.

Sturge, Kate (1997) 'Translation Strategies in Ethnography', *The Translator* 3(1): 21-38.

Toury, Gideon (1995) *Descriptive Translation Studies and Beyond*, Amsterdam & Philadelphia: Benjamins.

----- (1998) 'A Handful of Paragraphs on 'Translation' and 'Norms'', in C. Schäffner (ed) *Translation and Norms*, Clevedon etc.: Multilingual Matters, 9-31.

Tyler, Stephen (1986) 'Post-Modern Ethnography: From Document of the Occult to Occult Document', in Clifford and Marcus (eds), 122-40.

----- (1993) 'Zum, "Be-/Abschreiben" als "Sprechen für". Ein Kommentar', übersetzt von Ulrike Bischoff, in Berg and Fuchs (eds), 288-296.

Valero-Garcés, Carmen (1995) 'Modes of Translating Culture: Ethnography and Translation', *Meta* XL: 556-63.

Werner, Michael (1997) 'Dissymmetrien und symmetrische Modellbildungen in der Forschung zum Kulturtransfer', in H.-J. Lüsebrink and R. Reichardt (eds) *Kulturtransfer im Epochenumbruch. Frankreich-Deutschland 1770-1815,* Leipzig: Leipziger Universitätsverlag, 87-101.

White, Hayden (1978) *Tropics of Discourse,* Baltimore: Johns Hopkins University Press.

Wolf, Michaela (1997a) 'Translation as a Process of Power: Aspects of Cultural Anthropology in Translation', in M. Snell-Hornby, Z. Jettmarová and K. Kaindl (eds) *Translation as intercultural communication: selected papers from the EST Congress, Prague 1995,* Amsterdam & Philadelphia: Benjamins, 123-33.

----- (ed) (1997b) *Übersetzungswissenschaft in Brasilien. Beiträge zum Status von ,Original' und ,Übersetzung',* Tübingen: Stauffenburg.

----- (2000)'The *Third Space* in Postcolonial Representation', in S. Simon and P. St-Pierre (eds) *Changing the Terms: Translating in the Postcolonial Era,* Ottawa: University of Ottawa Press, 127-45.

Ziegler, Heide (1999) 'Introduction. The Translatability of Cultures', in Stuttgart Seminar in Cultural Studies: *The Translatability of Cultures. Proceedings of the Fifth Stuttgart Seminar in Cultural Studies 03.08.-14.08.1998,* Stuttgart & Weimar: Metzler, 7-19.

A 'Multilingual' and 'International' Translation Studies?

ŞEBNEM SUSAM-SARAJEVA

Abstract: *The paper questions certain import/export relations between the centre and the periphery of translation studies. It focuses on the common expectation about the role of researchers based in the periphery as providers of 'raw materials' in the form of translated texts, paratexts, translational behaviour and histories of translation. It contends that if theory continues to be seen as something that is supplied by the centre and consumed by the periphery, then the theories offered by the centre cannot be truly challenged just by testing them out on data provided by the periphery. The paper asks whether we should prolong the illusion that we are all offering equal contributions to a common goal, the progress of translation studies as a scholarly discipline. Would we not benefit from reflecting more critically on our own working methods and our relationship to the theories, models, tools and materials we use and develop?*

This essay started its life as a paper presented at the 'Research Models in Translation Studies' conference held in Manchester in April 2000. One of the aims and objectives put forward for this conference was to see "how Western models fare when faced with non-Western modes of thought and expression". Accordingly, among the suggested topics for papers was "Western research models and non-Western cultures". The juxtaposition or confrontation implied in this conference blurb also brings to mind the prevalent import/export pattern found within many contemporary disciplines, including translation studies, as well as a certain relationship of power which is often too much taken for granted and hence rather unspoken of.

It is, in fact, rather difficult to work with the terms 'Western' and 'non-Western'. Any adjective describing its subject as a negation, as a 'non-x', is derived from the vantage point of the 'x'. With the term 'non-Western', the majority of the world is being defined as a totality of 'non-x', although this majority does not define itself in opposition to the 'West' necessarily or exclusively. Being 'non-Western' has apparently become the only common denominator behind otherwise vastly different languages and cultures, spreading from Japan to India, from the Middle East to China, from Russia to Africa. "It is merely in the night of our ignorance that all alien shapes take on the same hue", says Perry Anderson (in his *Lineages of the Absolutist State*, quoted in Spivak 1999: 89). On the other hand, the same dichotomy renders 'the West' more homogeneous than it actually is (Cronin 1995: 85-6). It does not take into account the different positions of Irish, Dutch, Slovak or Finnish languages and cultures, to name but a few. These terms are also not helpful for the researcher who works on contemporary data, where borders are very much blurred and tracing 'influences' is often beyond one's grasp.

Nevertheless, one should be able to talk about the power differentials found *within* the discipline, and if these two terms are rather deceptive, others can be introduced. In my paper, I will use the rather more abstract dichotomy of 'centre' and 'periphery', except for a few occasions. The singular form used should not mislead the reader. There is not one centre in translation studies, neither is there a monolithic periphery. In any case, there is no way of measuring centrality or peripherality. Yet, in order to be able to discuss certain topics, one needs to start with certain terms, despite all the unease that goes with them. As we shall see below, the terms 'centre' and 'periphery' have the advantage of avoiding monolithic constructions such as those suggested by the 'Western/non-Western' dichotomy, since they allow the construction of a centre/periphery opposition also within both the periphery and the centre.

1.   Centre-periphery relations within translation studies

The centre and periphery of translation studies do not exactly correspond to those of the world's geopolitical situation today. As a consequence of the subject matter of the discipline, they are rather language-bound. Having a native proficiency in one or more of the dominant languages (English, French, German, and nowadays occasionally Spanish), choosing one's research material from these languages and/ or *publishing* one's research in them are frequently key factors in making one's voice heard. Working on and/or writing in 'exotic' languages, on the other hand, seems to indicate a rather peripheral position, and those who do so have to fight their way through in order to achieve international acknowledgement. The socio-economic power of the country of origin or residence often comes secondary to the might of the language the researcher writes in and works on.

There may also be central figures within peripheries, and peripheral figures in central locations. Certain scholars working in rather less famous countries can still be considered central thanks to their mother tongues or the dominant languages they write in. However, once a scholar based in a socio-economically powerful country starts working on data obtained from 'less common' languages, s/he might soon start feeling rather peripheral. Nevertheless the actual physical location of the researcher remains as a determining factor, since the issue of research outlet is closely related to this physical location. Institutional aspects and patronage play a major role in the dissemination of knowledge among the members of a scholarly community. Where one publishes one's work, in which journals or books (local/international, local but well-known or easily accessible, etc.) and with which publishing houses, is a crucial factor, as is one's proximity to central research institutions.

If the points I have made so far merely sound like 'common sense' or 'common knowledge', it is still worth being reminded of them, since one frequently hears the claim that the centre could be *anywhere* that produces interesting and useful hypotheses, models and theories. Such an approach underestimates the canonization process that goes with linguistic, cultural and economic imperialism.

2. Universality

One of the main characteristics of the centre is its actual will to act as *the* centre, and often claim universality or all-inclusiveness. Since its development stage in the 1970s and 1980s, translation studies was envisaged as such a comprehensive discipline. In his much-quoted article 'The Name and Nature of Translation Studies' (1972) James Holmes presented "the ultimate goal of the translation theorist" as being "to develop a full, inclusive theory accommodating so many elements that it can serve to explain and predict all phenomena falling within the terrain of translating and translation, to the exclusion of all phenomena falling outside it" (1988: 73). "Partial translation theories" were then seen as "little more than prolegomena to such a general translation theory" (*ibid.*). This will to exhaustiveness leads to the present increasing efforts to define rules and laws accounting for translational phenomena as diverse as possible. Calls for joint endeavours towards a coherent set of concepts and models, which can be applied across the board to all possible text types written in all possible languages at any time in human history are not infrequent.

Admirable though these ventures can be, they risk certain drawbacks. As has often been argued, models and tools originating from the centre and created initially by using central data, do not necessarily prove useful when they are taken out of their contexts and put to use on peripheral data (see for instance Dharwadker 1999: 125-30, 134-5; Cronin 1998: 147). Examples are not hard to find. It has been pointed out that central thinking on translation is based on a monolingual perspective and therefore cannot account for multilingual situations such as those in India (Devy 1999: 185; Viswanatha and Simon 1999: 164). Central translation theories owe too much to studies on Bible translation and many of the presuppositions of the latter do not work for non-Christian cultures, since different religions and metaphysics have different influences on the production and reception of translation (for a brief comparison of Western and Indian metaphysics and their impact on the understanding of translation, see Devy 1999). As for the work of individual scholars from the centre, Lawrence Venuti's views on the relationship between fluency and imperialism, for instance, have frequently been criticized as inapplicable outside the Anglo-American context (e.g. Tymoczko 2000: 39 and other references provided there; Paloposki and Oittinen 2000). In short, there can be a thin line between the usefulness of imported theories, tools and models, and their limiting or inappropriate nature for the material at hand.

3.   Testing out

This drawback is precisely the reason why many of today's prominent models and hypotheses, quite rightly and in an entirely scientific vein, ask for being tested out on material derived from diverse cultures and languages, so that their scholarly relevance and efficiency can be assessed. In fact, one of the underlying motives behind the will to comprehensiveness or exhaustiveness mentioned above was a similar concern to establish a *scientific* discipline. It was argued that theories and generalizations, in order to deserve the title, should be applicable to any arbitrary case, and if a theory "cannot stand up to such a test, it must be modified and reworked" (Tymoczko 1999b: 32). Accordingly, theories based and applied only on a limited number of texts, genres, periods, languages or systems, representing – as had been the case in the past – mostly modern, Western, written and/or high cultures would simply not be valid (*ibid.*). When a theory could not be fully generalized in this way, "its domain must be clearly stated […]" (Tymoczko 1999b: 33).

It was necessary, therefore, to increase the variety of material available for scrutiny, and peripheral systems were the obvious sources. Attention was drawn to translational phenomena in 'less common' languages and cultures (see, e.g. Bassnett 1993; Cronin 1998; Lefevere 1998). On the other hand, scholars from the periphery had already started using central models and theories in their own research on indigenous data, such as translated texts, paratexts, translational behaviour and translation history, and their publications in dominant languages consequently enhanced 'international' translation studies. As a result, we hear glad tidings today that the discipline is expanding its horizons. However, this expansion has an eerie resemblance to the enthusiastic "information-retrieval approach to 'Third World' […] literature" which Gayatri Spivak talks about (1999: 114, 118). There is a prevalent mechanism today in which central models and theories are expected to feed on periphery cultures and the data they offer.

Those who can do this testing-out are of course those who *have* the proficiency in peripheral languages, and who *choose* to work on them – hence, according to our definition given above, they are the periphery researchers. The generally expected course of action from these researchers is to apply theories supplied by the centre to peripheral 'raw material', with the twin objectives of elucidating local translation practices and testing the strength and comprehensiveness of the imported theories. The new generation of researchers from the periphery often start their career by absorbing whatever has been written on translation in and by the centre. If any original contribution is expected from them, it can only *follow* the wholesale internalization of central translation theories as the only conceivable and legitimate provider of models in contemporary translation studies. Consequently any transformation of the dominant paradigms can come only from within, from the application *of* the particular models *on* peripheral traditions. The tools, models and theories

intended to be at the service of these researchers thus shift to a position of authoritative overseers.

This is a widespread pattern, of course, and not confined to translation studies
only. It is usually taken to be just a part of the standard 'initiation and socialization
process into an academic community'. It is no wonder that 'testing out' is the type
of research most strongly advocated for postgraduate degrees (see e.g. Phillips and
Pugh 1995: 49). This type of research tries "to find the limits of previously proposed generalizations" and therefore, it provides "an established framework" and
an environment which gives "some degree of protection by the established nature
of much of the ideas, arguments, [...] etc." (Phillips and Pugh 1995: 51). In their
popular handbook on postgraduate research, which made two revised editions and
eleven reprints in less than a decade, Phillips and Pugh warn the newcomers:

> Of course, you will have to make your original contribution – merely repli-
> cating what others have done is not adequate. So, for example, you will have
> to use a methodology on a new topic where it has not been applied before
> and therefore make manifest its strengths in giving new knowledge and theo-
> retical insights. Or you will have to apply two competing theories to a new
> situation to see which is more powerful, or design a crucial experiment to
> produce evidence to choose between them. As a result you may produce your
> own innovative variant of the methodology or theory. [...] Testing out is the
> basic ongoing professional task of academic research, and doctoral work done
> well in this framework is much more likely to be *useful* and thus publishable
> and quotable. (Phillips and Pugh 1995: 51)

The keywords here are obviously 'useful', 'publishable' and 'quotable', but one
more thing is worth noting: 'testing out' is presented as "the basic ongoing professional task" of all academic research, not just of the postgraduate type. The
contribution expected from the researcher is, then, to consolidate, criticize and/or
reshape *existing* and *well-known* models, tools and theories, since only they will
provide the 'established framework' and the 'protection' necessary for successful
research. Through the itinerary that leads from background theory via the 'literature
survey' to the 'present state of the art' with which each and every researcher should
ideally be familiar, the discipline's self-generating and self-perpetuating mechanism is set in motion.

4.   What about the other knowledges, then?

Models from dominant systems are "to be imitated and reproduced" by weaker systems if the latter wish to be part of the global community, says Talal Asad (1986:
158). Quite often, knowledge of these models becomes "a precondition for the production of more knowledge" (*ibid.*). In cases where the flow of knowledge is

predominantly one-directional, the likelihood of a platform for discussion, mutual criticism, exchange and dialogue is small. It becomes a question of who produces the "desired knowledge" (*ibid.*), who is the "owner and guardian" of this desired knowledge (Arrojo 1999: 143) and who makes use of it.[1] What matters at this point is no longer the intrinsic quality – relevancy, efficiency or usefulness – of the models, tools or theories exported by the centre, but rather the authority and power which accompany this process. 'Self-colonization', as Lydia H. Liu terms it (1995: 236), is the state a large part of the world finds itself in today. The result is the widespread and mostly voluntary effort to mime the dominant powers, to mould the indigenous discourses on the model of imported knowledge, with the ultimate goal of being incorporated into the 'modern' world (Phillipson 1993: 65):

> If the Center always provides the teachers and the definition of what is worthy of being taught (from the gospels of Christianity to the gospels of Technology and Science), and the Periphery always provides the learners, then there is a pattern of imperialism [...] a pattern of scientific teams from the Center who go to Periphery nations to collect data (raw material) in the form of deposits, sediments, flora, fauna, archaeological findings, attitudes, opinions, behavioral patterns, and so on for data processing, data analysis, and theory formation (like industrial processing in general). This takes place in the Center universities (factories), in order to send the finished product, a journal, a book (manufactured goods) back for consumption in the center of the Periphery, first having created a demand for it through demonstration effect, training in the Center country, and some degree of low-level participation in the data-collection team. This parallel is not a joke, it is a structure. (Johan Galtung, *The True Worlds. A Transnational Perspective*, quoted in Phillipson 1993: 57)

These days one can hardly carry out research without using central models and theories. These models and theories have attained the aura of 'universality', since through abstraction and generalization they leave the local and particular behind and strive to be value-free, culture-free, context-free and neutral. A good case in point is mathematics. However, just how much mathematics as we know it today is constructed by people from certain cultures, and not from others, how other alternatives were suppressed and gradually came to be forgotten, can be seen in the work

---

[1] This largely unilateral import/ export relationship does not necessarily imply passivity on the part of the periphery. Translation theory, for instance, is not and cannot be exempt from the common fortunes of 'travelling theory' in general (see, e.g. Said 1983; Miller 1996). As happens in almost any other process of transfer and transportation, imported models and theories are transformed, altered or appropriated at and by their destinations. It is important, therefore, "to avoid reductionism by recognizing that what happens in the Periphery is not irrevocably determined by the Centre" (Phillipson 1993:63).

of scholars who deal with what they call 'ethno-mathematics'. Alan J. Bishop refers to studies on different counting systems in the world – some 600 in Papua New Guinea alone, where more than 700 languages are spoken – utilising means other than the decimal system or even numbers (1997: 72). There are also various conceptions of geometry, and not all of them have the "'atomistic' and object-oriented ideas of points, lines, planes and solids" (*ibid.*), features taken for granted in Western mathematics and taught all around the world. Bishop notes that today 'ethno-mathematics' is demonstrating how Western mathematics has contributed to the colonization process under the guise of 'universality'.

Then, what happens to the previous or alternative knowledges – a plural form, by the way, which does not have currency in English – produced about translation in and by the periphery? By the time researchers of periphery-origin have matured in their training, they start regarding traditional ('old') concepts of and thinking about translation and translating found in their own cultures as 'inferior', 'useless', 'simplistic' or 'irrelevant', and put them aside in favour of translation theory in its 'modern' and 'Western' sense. They usually consider the theorising in their own languages and cultures not so much as resources which might feed into their current work but as historical case studies to be placed under the scrutiny of the dominant models. These researchers are 'educated away' from their own culture and society. Even if their point of departure and initial goal were to understand and explain translational – and maybe, therefore, social and cultural – phenomena in their own systems of origin, the more they work *with* central models and tools, the more they are meant to work *for* them. This seems inevitable, because, as I have pointed out above, it runs deep into the accreditation process. Any 'useful', 'publishable', and 'quotable' work, including the present one, should refer to established – read: central – frameworks.

5. Consequences

I would now like to focus briefly on some of the consequences of these asymmetric relations between centre and periphery as reflected in our research on translation. Before I do so, I need to make a brief detour to Maria Tymoczko's *Translation in a Postcolonial Context* (1999b). Tymoczko emphasizes that translation, which is traditionally seen as standing in a metaphoric relation to a source text, also possesses significant metonymic aspects: "for the receiving audience the translation metonymically constructs a source text, a literary tradition, a culture, and a people, by picking parts, aspects, and attributes that will stand for wholes" (1999b: 57). In Tymoczko's view, these metonymic aspects of translation, combined with André Lefevere's notion of translation as 'rewriting', create a major problem in the translation of non-canonical or marginalized literatures (1999: 47). Whereas in a marginalized culture a text constitutes for the original audience a retelling or rewriting of pre-existing material, when that text is translated it is neither a retelling nor a rewriting for the receiving audience. The translator then "is in the paradoxical position of 'telling a new story' to the receptor audience [...] and the more remote the source culture and literature, the more radically new the story will be for the receiving audience" (*ibid.*).

Periphery researchers writing up their research in dominant languages and for an 'international' audience are all 'translators'. They translate their material – mostly from their own culture of origin – into the dominant paradigms and discourses of contemporary translation studies. In order to justify their findings, they need to contextualize the translations they talk about, and the more unknown this context is for the 'international' audience, the 'newer' the stories they tell. Researchers of periphery-origin cannot afford to leave certain historical, literary, social or political information implicit in their work, as they cannot assume such a vast erudition on the part of their audience – even though a similarly vast erudition on central prac- tices and traditions of translation is often expected on their part. Therefore, research on peripheral systems is often full of background information, which would not be necessary to anything like the same extent for research on central systems. In an earlier essay, Tymoczko referred to a similar phenomenon in post-colonial writing as 'frontloading' (1999a: 29). In academic writing, too, I would say, most of the time and energy of periphery researchers necessarily goes to such 'frontloading'.

Paradoxically, in a way similar to interlingual literary translation and post- colonial writing, periphery researchers also have to simplify their material. Tymoczko observes that the greater the distance between an author's or translator's source culture and the receiving culture for which the work in question is intended, the greater will be the impetus to simplify. This is because in attempting to cover the cultural divide the peripheral author/translator will feel the need to be highly selec- tive, picking only certain aspects "to convey and to emphasize, particularly if the intended audience includes as a significant component international or dominant- culture readers" (1999a: 23-4).

Periphery researchers, then, always translate and make their material more ac- cessible to the "international or dominant-culture readers" *within* translation studies. In fact, they actually have to translate their 'raw material' into the dominant lan- guages they are writing in, as in the translation of quotations, concepts, arguments, examples, book titles, etc. Periphery researchers often do not write in their mother tongues, sometimes not even if they do research in their home countries. Both in central and in peripheral institutions the criteria for being accepted into the 'mod- ern' world of translation studies and into academia are very similar. Researchers often need to achieve international recognition first even to be employed back home. This means, in practice, that they have to write in the dominant languages.

The research material of translation studies is necessarily polyglot, but the knowl- edge *about* this material is more and more produced and stored solely in English, French or German (cf. Ahmad 1992: 245-52). Especially the present status of

English as the authoritative *lingua franca* of the academic world creates reader expectations of 'international' or 'universal' theory. Those who carry out their research in 'less common' languages often do not benefit from the means of communication which the discipline itself is focusing on: texts on translation research are not among the priorities of translators who are looking for means to earn their living, and translation scholars themselves hardly translate each other's work. This often leads to the isolation of peripheral theorizing, as in the case, for example, of East European and Russian theories of translation (see, e.g. Jänis 2000; Zlateva 2000; see also *Perspectives* 5:1, 1997).[2]

6.   Non-Western = Peripheral = Postcolonial?

Andrew Chesterman lists the aims of empirical research as follows:[3] (*a*) to provide new material/ 'facts'/ corpora/ case studies, i.e. new data on which existing hypotheses can be tested; (*b*) to apply and test an existing hypothesis, "in order to justify it better or to criticize it"; (*c*) to propose a new idea, conceptual tool or hypothesis which "offers a better way of describing or explaining existing data"; (*d*) to propose a new research methodology or tool, i.e. "a new way of testing [or generating] a hypothesis"; and (*e*) "to propose a new theory, or a better formalization of an existing one" (Chesterman 2000: 11). I would argue that, due to the constraints discussed above and in the *current* situation in translation studies, the periphery researcher is usually expected to deal with the first two of these aims of empirical research. The last three can be less frequently taken up by periphery researchers working *within the dominant paradigms* of translation studies.

This does not at all mean that new conceptual tools, methodologies or theories are not being suggested by the periphery. On the contrary, there is at the present time a great deal happening in the periphery as regards translation theorizing. However, as soon as these works are published under the auspices of international institutions, they tend to be seen as belonging to a 'postcolonial' framework, and to be classified under the heading of 'postcolonial theories of translation', which itself occupies an as yet marginal position within the discipline as a whole.[4] In some cases this is in part due to the research interests of the periphery researchers themselves. After all, when they do write about translation, their work becomes bound up with the asymmetries between their languages and cultures and those of the

---

[2] Although in 'The Future of Translation Theory: A Handful of Theses' (1978) Holmes had already noted the urgency of accessing work on translation theory in the Soviet Union (1988: 102), the two decades since have witnessed slow progress in this respect.

[3] Although empirical research is certainly not the only type of research undertaken by translation scholars, it is the one which is particularly emphasized here because of the discipline's efforts to prove its scholarly status.

[4] Vinay Dharwadker's (1998) article on A.K. Ramanujan's theory and practice of translation is a case in point.

centre. However, this categorization may also be due to a certain expectation that in today's translation studies novelty or subversiveness can only belong to postcolonialism precisely because of its still rather marginal position within the discipline, compared to its – maybe already waning – centrality in other fields of research, such as literary theory.

What exactly qualifies an approach or a piece of research in translation studies as 'postcolonial'? Is political commitment or orientation the most obvious criterion? The references used? Certain keywords? Or are the determining factors the identity of the researcher, such as his/her country of origin or adoption, mother tongue or first language (but *not* the language in which the research is being written), and/or the origin of the material being studied? Defining "what constitutes postcolonial theory's methodology and its 'object of study'" has been a difficult task in general for literary and cultural critics (Mongia 1996: 2). In translation studies, too, the various practices and approaches of the periphery are too quickly subsumed under the term 'postcolonial'. Similarly, what constitutes a 'non-Western' approach in translation? Is it again to do with the identity of the researcher, even if the researcher is mainly using central models on peripheral data? Or is this an umbrella title to be tagged to any topic related to peripheral languages and cultures?

One should be careful in making these distinctions and, most importantly, one should keep in mind that those periphery researchers who could be heard after all – at least, to an extent – are those who write in dominant languages, and preferably, who manage to be published by well-known publishers: as in the case of the present writer in this particular paper in this particular book. Others who write mainly in their own languages and in their home countries are bound to be heard only by their local audience, however important and useful their work might have been for the rest of the world. This point deserves reiteration, since, as Gayatri Spivak observes, the "diasporic [often] stands in for the native informant" (1999: 169):[5]

> [...] Works in often indifferent English translation or works written in English or the European languages in the recently decolonized areas of the globe or written by people of so-called ethnic origin in First World space

---

[5] In her book Spivak's aim is to "track the figure of the Native Informant" through philosophy, literature, history, and culture (1999: ix). However, this tracking first shows up "a colonial subject detaching itself from the Native Informant", and then "a certain postcolonial subject [...] recoding the colonial subject and appropriating the Native Informant's position" (*ibid.*). Spivak notes that the "native informant [is] a figure who, in ethnography, can only provide data, to be interpreted by the knowing subject for reading" (1999: 49). For the purposes of my arguments, I am of course appropriating Spivak's concept of the 'Native Informant'. As she rightly points out, those who are fortunate enough to be writing, doing research, publishing, etc. belong to the centre of their countries of origin and therefore are not 'Native Informants' proper. However, I found the analogy worth pursuing.

are beginning to constitute something called 'Third World literature'. Within this area of tertiary education in literature, the upwardly mobile exmarginal, *justifiably* searching for validation, can help commodify marginality. (Spivak 1999: 170)[6]

In similarly confused fashion, the term 'postcolonial' is being used rather too fuzzily within translation studies today. As Maria Tymoczko rightly points out, there is a misconception of postcoloniality as an ontological category rather than "a complex set of circumstances responding to specific historical conditions associated with the European age of discovery, expansion and imperialism" (2000: 32). Since postcolonial theory is "currently one of the few viable theoretical approaches that addresses directly the geopolitical shifts and problems of power that dominated the twentieth century" and is also "one of the few discourses pertaining to power that has sustained itself since Marxism has fallen out of favour and been widely abandoned in academic circles" (*ibid.*), it seems like the only option left if one wishes to discuss matters of power. However, Tymoczko believes

that the field of translation studies [...] is best served by setting issues of power in their specific spatio-temporal contexts, paying attention to differences as well as similarities. [...] Thus, it is important to distinguish struggles pertaining to power relevant to those who have been colonized *per se* from struggles pertinent to others suffering oppression for other reasons, just as within postcolonial studies it is important to differentiate the specific manifestations of colonialism experienced by the several peoples who have been colonized. In order to do so, however, it will be helpful to have a more articulated theorization of power as it pertains to translation. (2000: 32-3)

Such an "articulated theorization of power" could certainly be instrumental when it comes to examining the power relations found within the discipline itself.

7.   Conclusion

I believe that, while one can and must regard the expansion of translation studies to non-canonical and non-European material as a major step forward, drawing attention to such material is not enough for the establishment of a truly 'international' and 'multilingual' translation studies. Even more important is to learn about the *thinking* of the periphery about translational practices, and not only for the purposes of comparing it to the dominant theories and finding it lacking. Neither is it

---

[6] Spivak ironically notes: "[...] the privileged inhabitant of neo-colonial space is often bestowed a subject-position as geo-political other by the dominant radical. (One is most struck by this when planning or attending international conferences)" (1999: 339).

sufficient to present the experiences of peripheral systems as valuable sources for the solutions of problems encountered within dominant ones, and therefore, as worth their attention.[7]

This does not necessarily mean that we should struggle for a more 'democratic' distribution of scholarly models and influences. Translation studies is one of the disciplines which has at least the potential for more interaction and tolerance between cultures, less ethnocentric views and more open scholarship. Furthermore, since it is still a relatively young discipline, it might as yet have the flexibility before becoming ossified in terms of the sources supplying it with tools, theories and data. If we think it is important to move out of the structure described by Johan Galtung above, periphery researchers have to take some time off from data-collection and concentrate on what is being done and what *has* been done in the peripheral languages and cultures in terms of translation *theory*. If theory continues to be seen as something that will always be supplied by the centre and consumed by the periphery, then the translation theories offered by the centre cannot be truly challenged just by testing them out on data provided by the periphery.

Such a shift of attitudes would require a reconsideration on everybody's part of what 'theory' means and what it is comprised of. Theorizing, if not 'theory', can be found in many different forms and contexts. One can theorize without the "Western forms of abstract logic", avoiding "decisive statements" and not even attempting to produce a monolithic and "wholesale" theory (Christian 1996). Theory is understanding and explanation, and not only "something there and established" (Gillham 2000: 12). Theorizing on translation is not something 'new' to the periphery, where translations have been carried out for centuries, and not without accompanying commentaries and other metatexts. Such theorizing does not claim to explain translation universally, of course. An undertaking of this sort is usually not its concern. Neither

---

[7] For example, Michael Cronin observes: "It is important to stress the relational dynamic of minority languages if only to underline the significance of minority languages to translation theory and practice. This significance is related to three factors. Firstly, languages and political circumstances change. The majority status of a language is determined by political, economic and cultural forces that are rarely static and therefore *all* languages are potentially minority languages. It follows that the historical experience of a minority language can offer useful insights into the translation fate of majority languages should contexts change" (1995: 87-88). Elsewhere he argues: "The issue of translation and minority languages is not a peripheral concern for beleaguered fans of exotic peoples gabbling in incomprehensible tongues but the single, most important issue in translation studies today. The hegemony of English in the fastest-growing area of technological development [telecommunications] means that all other languages become, in this context, *minority languages*. [...] Major languages have much to learn from minority languages. As vocabulary, syntax and cultural memory come under pressure from English, dominant languages are simply experiencing what minority languages have been experiencing for many centuries, and it would be instructive for the former to study the responses of the latter to assimilationist translation pressures. This, in turn, places an onus on translation scholars in minority languages to become more visible in translation studies debates" (1998: 151).

does it necessarily claim coherence or applicability, which could have made it a suitable candidate to be placed in university curricula worldwide, for instance. Yet this does not mean that such theorizing would be devoid of significant insights. What is aimed for would not be an 'all-inclusive theory' but maybe a different understanding of 'theory', a different way of thinking which would not easily assume the position of an overseer.

Let me end by returning to the audience issue. Today, self-positioning and the question of one's intended audience are often presented as major issues in different fields of research. Literary critics have started questioning who it is they write their criticism for. Who is a postcolonial writer writing for? For the colonizer, for the colonized or for an international audience? For whom does a translator translate? And who are we, as translation researchers, doing our research for? Should we prolong the sustained illusion that, in our pursuit of 'pure wisdom and knowledge', we are all offering equal contributions to a common goal, the progress of translation studies as a (scholarly) discipline? Or would we benefit from reflecting more critically on our own working methods, our own relationship to the theories, models, tools and materials we use and develop?

References

Ahmad, Aijaz (1992) *In Theory: Classes, Nations, Literatures*, Bombay: Oxford University Press.

Arrojo, Rosemary (1999) 'Interpretation as Possessive Love: Hélène Cixous, Clarice Lispector and the Ambivalence of Fidelity', in Bassnett and Trivedi (eds), 141-61.

Asad, Talal (1986) 'The Concept of Cultural Translation in British Social Anthropology', in James Clifford and George E. Marcus (eds) *Writing Culture: The Poetics and Politics of Ethnography*, Berkeley/London: University of California Press, 141-64.

Bassnett, Susan (1993) *Comparative Literature: A Critical Introduction*, Oxford & Cambridge Mass.: Blackwell.

----- and Harish Trivedi (eds) (1999) *Post-Colonial Translation: Theory and Practice*. London & New York. Routledge.

Bishop, Alan J. (1990) 'Western Mathematics: The Secret Weapon of Cultural Imperialism', *Race and Class* 32:2. ; reprinted in Bill Ashcroft, Gareth Griffiths and Helen Tiffin (eds.) (1997) *The Post-Colonial Studies Reader*, London & New York: Routledge, 71-6.

Chesterman, Andrew (2000) 'Empirical Research Methods in Translation Studies', *Erikoiskielet ja käännösteoria (VAKKI-symposiumi XX)* 27, 9-22.

Christian, Barbara (1987) 'The Race for Theory', *Cultural Critique* 6; reprinted in Padmini Mongia (ed) (1996) *Contemporary Postcolonial Theory. A Reader*, London & New York: Arnold, 148-57.

Cronin, Michael (1995) 'Altered States: Translation and Minority Languages', *TTR* 8(1): 85-103.

----- (1998) 'The Cracked Looking Glass of Servants: Translation and Minority Languages in a Global Age', *The Translator* 4(2): 145-62.

Devy, Ganesh (1999) 'Translation and Literary History – an Indian View', in Bassnett and Trivedi (eds), 182-8.

Dharwadker, Vinay (1999) 'A.K. Ramanujan's Theory and Practice of Translation', in Bassnett and Trivedi (eds), 114-40.

Gillham, Bill (2000) *Case Study Research Methods*, London & New York: Continuum.

Holmes, James S. (1988) *Translated! Papers on Literary Translation and Translation Studies*, Amsterdam: Rodopi.

Jänis, Marja (2000) Review of Vilén N. Komissarov's Теоретические мето ики обучения перево у (1997), *Across Languages and Cultures* 1(1): 133-6.

Lefevere, André (1998) 'Chinese and Western Thinking on Translation', in Susan Bassnett and André Lefevere (eds) *Constructing Cultures: Essays on Literary Translation*, Clevedon: Multilingual Matters, 12-24.

Liu, Lydia H. (1995) *Translingual Practice. Literature, National Culture, and Translated Modernity – China 1900-1937*, Stanford: Stanford University Press.

Miller, Hillis J. (1996) 'Border Crossings, Translating Theory: Ruth', in Sanford Budick and Wolfgang Iser (eds) *The Translatability of Cultures: Figurations of the Space Between*. Stanford: Stanford University Press, 207-23.

Mongia, Padmini. (1996) 'Introduction', in Padmini Mongia (ed) *Contemporary Postcolonial Theory. A Reader*, London & New York: Arnold, 1-18.

Paloposki, Outi and Riitta Oittinen (2000) 'The Domesticated Foreign', in Andrew Chesterman, Natividad Gallardo San Salvador and Yves Gambier (eds) *Translation in Context: Selected Papers from the EST Congress, Granada 1998*, Amsterdam & Philadelphia: John Benjamins, 373-90.

Perspectives: Studies in Translatology 5(1) (1997) Russian Translation Studies special issue.

Phillips, Estelle M. and D. S. Pugh (1995) *How to Get a PhD: A Handbook for Students and Their Supervisors*, Buckingham & Philadelphia: Open University Press.

Phillipson, Robert (1993) *Linguistic Imperialism*, Oxford: Oxford University Press.

Said, Edward (1983) 'Travelling Theory', in *The World, the Text and the Critic*, Cambridge (Mass.): Harvard University Press, 226-47.

Spivak, Gayatri Chakravorty (1999) *A Critique of Postcolonial Reason: Toward a History of the Vanishing Present*, Cambridge (Mass.) & London: Harvard University Press.

Tymoczko, Maria (1999a) 'Post-Colonial Writing and Literary Translation', in Bassnett and Trivedi (eds), 19-40.

----- (1999b) *Translation in a Postcolonial Context: Early Irish Literature in English Translation*, Manchester: St. Jerome.

----- (2000) 'Translation and Political Engagement. Activism, Social Change and the Role of Translation in Geopolitical Shifts', *The Translator* 6(1): 23-47.

Viswanatha, Vanamala and Sherry Simon (1999) 'Shifting Grounds of Exchange: B.M. Srikantaiah and Kannada Translation', in Bassnett and Trivedi (eds), 162-81.

Zlateva, Palma (2000) 'A Wheel We Have Been Reinventing' [review of Anton Popovič's Проблемы ху ожественного перево о], *The Translator* 6(1): 109-15.

Acknowledgements: This paper, although it started off as an individual self-interrogation, is in its present form the end-result of a collective discussion. I would like to thank Kaisa Koskinen, Alexandra Lianeri, Theo Hermans, Elsie Chan, Morphia Malli, Outi Paloposki, Andrew Chesterman and Kristiina Taivalkoski, who all read the drafts and offered invaluable feedback and insights. The arguments presented here have also benefited from comments provided by the delegates of the 'Research Models in Translation Studies' conference (Manchester, April 2000), including Michael Cronin, José Lambert, Saliha Paker, Gideon Toury and Maria Tymoczko, and by the participants of the Graduate Seminar held at Boğaziçi University, Istanbul, 18 May 2000, including Işin Bengi, Cemal Demircioğlu, Ebru Diriker, Arzu Eker and Şehnaz Tahir.

Notes on Contributors

Derek Boothman lives in Forlì and teaches at the Scuola Superiore di Lingue Moderne per Interpreti e Traduttori of the University of Bologna. He publishes in both Italian and English. His research is centred on Antonio Gramsci's writings in the context of political and cultural theory.

Gordon Brotherston is a Research Professor in the Department of Literature at the University of Essex, a Professor in the Department of Spanish and Portuguese at Indiana University and a Senior Fellow of the Humanities Center at Stanford University. His long-standing research interest lies with the indigenous cultures of the Americas, about which he has published extensively. He is the author of *Latin American Poetry: Origins and Presence* (1975), *Image of the New world* (1979), *Book of the Fourth World* (1992), *Painted Books from Mexico* (1995) and other titles.

Elsie Chan teaches translation at the City University of Hong Kong and is preparing a doctoral dissertation at the University of Warwick. She has also worked as a government translation officer. Her research interests concern comparisons between Western and Chinese translation theories. She has published articles on translation studies in Hong Kong and China, and on Buddhist scriptures in Chinese translation.

Martha Cheung is Professor of Translation and Associate Director of the Centre for Translation at Hong Kong Baptist University. Her translations into English include fiction by Han Shaogong, Liu Sola, Zhu Tianxin, Lai Shêng-ch'uan and the work of Hong Kong poets P.K. Leung, Tsia Yim Pui and Choi Ka Ping. She is the editor of *Hong Kong Collage: Contemporary Stories and Writing* (1998) and, with Jane C.C. Lai, of *An Oxford Anthology of Contemporary Chinese Drama* (1997). She is conducting research on the history of translation in Hong Kong and compiling an anthology, in English translation, of Chinese translation theories from the earliest times to 1911.

Edoardo Crisafulli works as Cultural Officer at the Italian Ministry of Foreign Affairs in Rome. Having studied in Urbino, Birmingham and at University College Dublin, he went on to lecture in Italian at Dublin and subsequently at King Abdul Aziz University (Jeddah) and the University of Manchester before taking up his present post. His PhD dissertation concerned English translations of Dante's *Divine Comedy*, on which he has since published in several journals.

Jean-Marc Gouanvic is a Professor in the Department of French Studies at Concordia University in Montréal, where he teaches on translation theory and the methodology of translation studies. In 1987 he founded the journal *TTR/Études sur* *le texte et ses transformations*, which he edited until 1997. He is the author of *Sociologie de la traduction* (1999). His current research is informed by Pierre Bourdieu's cultural theories and concerns the French translations of modern American writers immediately after the Second World War.

Theo Hermans is Professor of Dutch and Comparative Literature at University College London. In 1985 he edited the collections *The Manipulation of Literature* and *Second Hand*. His most recent book is *Translation in Systems* (1999). His research has been geared mostly to the history and theory of translation.

Jeremy Munday studied and taught at the University of Bradford and now lectures in Spanish Studies at the University of Surrey. He recently published *Introducing Translation Studies: Theories and Applications* (2001). Among his translations is *The Picador Book of Latin American Short Stories* (1998). His research interests include translation theory, systemic functional linguistics, corpus linguistics and literary studies.

Saliha Paker took her BA and PhD in English and Classics at Istanbul University. She has taught and researched in various places, among them London University's School of Oriental and African Studies. An Honorary Research Fellow at the Centre for Byzantine, Ottoman and Modern Greek Studies at the University of Birmingham since 1992, she was appointed Professor of Translation Studies in the Department of Translation and Interpreting at Istanbul's Bogaziçi University in 1995, and continues to teach there. Her latest translation (with Mel Kenne) is Latife Tekin's *Dear Shameless Death* (2001).

Şebnem Susam-Sarajeva has worked as a translator of literary and technical texts, as a research assistant at the University of Bogaziçi, Istanbul, and the University of Helsinki, and as an MA tutor at the University of Middlesex, London. She is currently writing up her doctoral thesis in Comparative Literature at University College London and is also involved with University of Helsinki's MonAKO Multilingual Communications Programme.

Şehnaz Tahir-Gürçağlar teaches translation and interpreting at Boğaziçi University in Istanbul, where she is also writing up her doctoral thesis. Her research interests cover translation and interpreting history, and the relation between popular culture, ideology and translation. She is a free-lance translator and a conference interpreter.

Maria Tymoczko is Professor of Comparative Literature at the University of Massachusetts, Amherst. She has published extensively on medieval literature, as well as on Irish writing in English, including the works of James Joyce. Her translations of early Irish literature appeared in *Two Death Tales from the Ulster Cycle* (1981).

Her most recent full-length critical study is the prize-winning *Translation in a Post-Colonial Context: Early Irish Literature in English Translation* (1999). Her current work focuses on the ideology of translation.

Michaela Wolf, who wrote her MA on translation studies and her PhD on Romance literature, is Assistant Professor in the Department of Translation at the University of Graz. She edited the collection *Übersetzungswissenschaft in Brasilien* (1997) and, with Nadia Grbic, *Text – Kultur – Kommunikation. Translation als Forschungsaufgabe* (1997). Her research focusses on translation history, cultural and postcolonial aspects of translation, and feminist translation.

Index